The Korean Welfare State

INTERNATIONAL POLICY EXCHANGE SERIES

Published in collaboration with the Center for International Policy Exchanges
University of Maryland

Series Editors
Douglas J. Besharov
Neil Gilbert

United in Diversity? Comparing Social Models in Europe and America
Edited by Jens Alber and Neil Gilbert

Child Protection Systems: International Trends and Orientations
Edited by Neil Gilbert, Nigel Parton, and Marit Skivenes

The Korean State and Social Policy: How South Korea Lifted Itself from Poverty and Dictatorship to Affluence and Democracy
Stein Ringen, Huck-ju Kwon, Ilcheong Yi, Taekyoon Kim, and Jooha Lee

The Age of Dualization: The Changing Face of Inequality in Deindustrializing Societies
Edited by Patrick Emmenegger, Silja Häusermann, Bruno Palier, and
Martin Seeleib-Kaiser

Counting the Poor: New Thinking About European Poverty Measures and Lessons for the United States
Edited by Douglas J. Besharov and Kenneth A. Couch

Social Policy and Citizenship: The Changing Landscape
Edited by Adalbert Evers and Anne-Marie Guillemard

Chinese Social Policy in a Time of Transition
Edited by Douglas J. Besharov and Karen Baehler

Reconciling Work and Poverty Reduction: How Successful Are European Welfare States?
Edited by Bea Cantillon and Frank Vandenbroucke

University Adaptation in Difficult Economic Times
Edited by Paola Mattei

Activation or Workfare? Governance and the Neo-Liberal Convergence
Edited by Ivar Lødemel and Amílcar Moreira

Child Welfare Systems and Migrant Children: A Cross-Country Study of Policies and Practice
Edited by Marit Skivenes, Ravinder Barn, Katrin Kriz, and Tarja Pösö

Adjusting to a World in Motion: Trends in Global Migration and Migration Policy
Edited by Douglas J. Besharov and Mark H. Lopez

Caring for a Living: Migrant Women, Aging Citizens, and Italian Families
Francesca Degiuli

Child Welfare Removals by the State: A Cross-Country Analysis of Decision-Making Systems
Edited by Kenneth Burns, Tarja Pösö, and Marit Skivenes

Improving Public Services: International Experiences in Using Evaluation Tools to Measure Program Performance
Edited by Douglas J. Besharov, Karen J. Baehler, and Jacob Alex Klerman

Welfare, Work, and Poverty: Social Assistance in China
Qin Gao

SCHOOL of
PUBLIC POLICY

The Korean Welfare State

Social Investment in an Aging Society

Edited by

KYUNGBAE CHUNG AND NEIL GILBERT

OXFORD
UNIVERSITY PRESS

Oxford University Press is a department of the University of Oxford. It furthers the University's objective of excellence in research, scholarship, and education by publishing worldwide. Oxford is a registered trade mark of Oxford University Press in the UK and certain other countries.

Published in the United States of America by Oxford University Press
198 Madison Avenue, New York, NY 10016, United States of America.

© Oxford University Press 2024

Library of Congress Cataloging-in-Publication Data
Names: Chung, Kyungbae, editor. | Gilbert, Neil, 1940– editor.
Title: The Korean welfare state : social investment in an aging society /
[edited by] Kyungbae Chung and Neil Gilbert.
Description: New York, NY : Oxford University Press, [2024] |
Includes bibliographical references and index.
Identifiers: LCCN 2023013815 (print) | LCCN 2023013816 (ebook) |
ISBN 9780197644928 (hardback) | ISBN 9780197644935 (epub) |
ISBN 9780197644959
Subjects: LCSH: Korea (South)—Social policy. | Public welfare—Korea (South) |
Welfare state—Korea (South)
Classification: LCC HN730.5.A8 K6574 2023 (print) |
LCC HN730.5.A8 (ebook) | DDC 306.095195—dc23/eng/20230502
LC record available at https://lccn.loc.gov/2023013815
LC ebook record available at https://lccn.loc.gov/2023013816

DOI: 10.1093/oso/9780197644928.001.0001

Printed by Integrated Books International, United States of America

Contents

Contributors

Heung-Seek Cho
President
Korea Institute for Health and Social
Affairs

Kyungbae Chung
President
Korean Socio-Economic Society

Neil Gilbert
Milton and Gertrude Chernin Chair in
Social Welfare
University of California, Berkeley

Young-shin Jang
Head of the Policy Research Division
Korea National Council on Social
Welfare

Hyoung-Sun Jeong
Professor
Yonsei University

Sang Chul Park
Endowed Chair Professor
Future Life and Society Research Center
Chonnam National University

Jaeeun Seok
Professor of Social Welfare
Hallym University.

Sang-Mok Suh
Global President
International National Council on
Social Welfare

Kyu Taik Sung
Professor Emeritus
Yonsei University, Department of Social
Welfare
Frances Wu Endowed Chair Professor
Emeritus
University of Southern California

Eugene Yeo
Research Fellow
Korea Institute for Health and Social
Affairs

Introduction

Neil Gilbert and Kyungbae Chung

This book examines the evolution of Korean social welfare policy over the past two decades through the conceptual lens of the "social investment state" and the special challenges posed from this perspective, particularly in a rapidly aging society. Since the 1990s, many of the modern welfare states have experienced a wave of policy reforms seeking to promote labor force participation, human capital, individual responsibility, and economic development while advancing the private delivery of social protection. These reforms were introduced to check the mounting costs of social spending, which, between 1960 and 2009, had climbed from an average of 13% to almost 30% of gross domestic product (GDP) in the developed welfare states of those countries belonging to the Organisation for Economic Cooperation and Development (OECD). The reforms were also triggered by the need to adapt to the competitive demands of markets in the global economy of the 21st century amid growing concerns that modern welfare states were undermining the work ethic.

Starting in the 1990s, many efforts have been made to conceptualize the ways in which contemporary policies have altered the essential character of modern welfare states. These efforts suggest that the policy reforms amount to a paradigm shift from the welfare state to an alternative model variously labeled the *Schumpeterian workfare state* (Jessop, 1994; Torfing, 1997), the *contract state* (Eardley, 1997; Weatherley, 1994), *the enabling state* (Bevir, 2009; Gilbert, 2004; Wallace, 2013), the *postmodern welfare state* (Ferge, 1996), and the *social investment state* (Ferrera, 2009; Giddens, 1998; Peng, 2011). The models designated by these different labels convey a similar understanding of an essential change taking place: specifically, that the welfare state which served as an institutional counterforce to capitalism in the 20th century was being transformed to serve as an institutional support of capitalism aimed at boosting productivity in the 21st century. This is manifest not only in the work-oriented policy reforms designed to activate the unemployed

Neil Gilbert and Kyungbae Chung, *Introduction* In: *The Korean Welfare State*. Edited by: Kyungbae Chung and Neil Gilbert, Oxford University Press. © Oxford University Press 2024. DOI: 10.1093/oso/9780197644928.003.0001 and welfare recipients, but in the so-called *family-friendly policies* such as public child care and parental leave, which some people suggest are more aptly described as "market friendly." According to Jane Lewis (2006), family policy in the European Union "has been explicitly linked to the promotion of women's employment in order to further the economic growth and competition agenda."

The social investment framework introduced by Anthony Giddens in 1998 is among the prevailing analytic perspectives applied in examining contemporary policy reforms in modern welfare states (Cantillon, 2014; Cronert and Palme, 2019; Jenson and St-Martin, 2003; Midgley, 1999; Peng, 2011; Stoesz, 2018). This framework, as Ito Peng (2011) notes, "has been adopted by countries not only in the English speaking world, but also in East Asia, including Japan and South Korea." She argues that the primary motivation for social investment in Korea was driven by concerns over its low fertility rates and population aging, which are reflected in policies aimed at human capital activation and mobilization.

The Korean welfare state developed later than most of the other welfare states in the OECD countries. Since the turn of the 21st century, the Korean welfare state, along with its economy, rapidly matured, increasing both the scope of social welfare coverage and the fiscal capacity to pay for these benefits. In 2000, Korea's GDP per capita of US$18,082 (controlling for purchasing power) was about two-thirds that of Japan. By 2018, the Korean GDP per capita had more than doubled to US$40,111, about 94% that of the Japan. This remarkable surge of economic growth was accompanied by the significant expansion of the Korean welfare state, initiated under President Kim Dae-jung's administration, which ushered in a decade of progressive government.

Elected in December 1997, President Kim Dae-jung characterized his position on social welfare policy as "productive welfare." According to this approach, the welfare state "strives to build a society that improves the quality of life for all people, including the socially estranged, by encouraging the active economic participation of all people in the nation and by assuring a fair distribution of wealth" (Office of the President, 2000, p. 21). To achieve these ends, three main components of productive welfare include (1) equality of opportunity to participate in production, (2) financial transfers that would provide those temporarily excluded from the market with the necessary relief to enable rapid reemployment and would allow those permanently excluded from the market to maintain a minimum standard of living, and

(3) measures that encourage self-support through suitable education and training. The productive welfare agenda was clearly framed by the language and objectives of the social investment state (Peng, 2011).

Under the banner of "productive welfare," Kim Dae-jung's administration reformed public assistance policy and firmly established the Korean welfare state's four major pillars of social protection. With these developments, the Korean welfare state instituted a universal system of social security only four decades after it initially began, with the Government Employees Pension of 1960. Although Korea's social security net is still seen as lacking inclusiveness and offering modest benefits, every citizen who makes the required contribution is covered, at least formally, by social insurances. While recognizing the need to provide social supports for people unable to work (mainly disabled and elderly people), the main thrust of productive welfare emphasized work-oriented policies intended to increase productivity and self-sufficiency, following the tenets of the social investment state (Mishra et al., 2004).

After the introduction of productive welfare policies, progressive and conservative administrations continued to shape the Korean welfare state. The progressive government of President Roh Moo-hyun, for example, introduced the Basic Old-Age Pension and the earned income tax credit (EITC) to supplement the wages of working low-income families, the type of work incentive policy that typified the social investment approach. From 2008 to 2017, Roh's administration was followed by the election of Lee Myung-bak and Park Geun-hye, two conservative-leaning presidents who made a limited impact on expanding the scope and functions of the Korean welfare state.

The 2017 election of President Moon Jae-in promised to usher in a new progressive era of welfare state development. In September 2018, President Moon presented his ambitious model of an *innovative inclusive state* (IIS), reflecting a vision of the state that promotes innovative economic development and socioeconomic inclusion. A 2019 report of the National Research Council for Economics, Humanities and Social Sciences identifies five key features of the IIS: educational policy for creative learning to strengthen national capacity; industrial policy promoting innovative, inclusive growth; employment policy innovations; and social dialogue—further demonstrating the social investment approach.

The Moon administration's ambitions for the advancement of the IIS came at a time when the country was facing the unprecedented challenges of a rapidly aging society. The Korean welfare state has been maturing over the recent decades, promising pensions for the elderly, long-term care for disabled people, income subsidies for low-income workers, training for the unemployed, and high-quality early education for children. At the same time, the Korean population has been rapidly aging due to a precipitous decline in the fertility rate and a steep rise in life expectancy. With the fertility rate plummeting from 6.5 births in the 1950s to .95 births per woman in 2018, Korea stands out as having one of the lowest levels of fertility in the advanced industrial democracies that make up the membership of the OECD. UN projections foresee the Korean fertility rate remaining far below the replacement rate of 2.1 up to the 22nd century.

While the fertility rate is falling, life expectancy is on the rise. Korea's life expectancy of 83 years (80 for men and 86 for women) is considerably higher than the worldwide average: it is the 9th highest in the world and expected to keep rising. The UN Population Division estimates that life expectancy in Korea will climb to 95 years by the turn of the 22nd century. Increasing longevity joined with declining fertility rates are responsible for the demographic transition to aging societies throughout the world. Over the next 35 years, the number people age 65 years and older as a proportion of the working-age population (15–64 years of age) is expected to almost double from 13% to 25% worldwide. And Korea is projected to have one of the largest increases in the dependency ratio between 2000 and 2050, by which time the Korean dependency ratio will reach around .9: that is, there will be close to one person 65 and older for each person in the working age (15–64) population. (Estimates on this vary. A recent OECD report places the ratio at around .7 in 2050 [OECD, 2018]).

With fewer children being born as parents are living longer, the demographic transition to an aging society generates an increasing challenge to the state's capacity to fund the rising fiscal obligations of the Korean welfare state. As the proportion of the working population diminishes, there are fewer people contributing to the pay-as-you-go defined benefit pension scheme and more retired elderly people collecting their pensions. Although the Korean National Pension Service has grown to be the world's third largest pension fund with US$564 billion in assets, projections indicate it will be depleted by 2057. The demographic transition also poses an immense social pressure on the family's traditional duties for the care of its members because there will be fewer children available to exercise familial responsibility for the personal care of elderly parents and grandparents. The increasing needs of the elderly present a substantial challenge to the welfare state's orientation toward social investment policies to advance economic development.

In examining the modern context and development of the Korean welfare state, this volume is divided into three parts that focus on the sociopolitical evolution, the core policies of the Korean welfare state, and the contemporary policy challenges of Korea's rapidly aging society.

Part I traces the sociopolitical evolution of the Korean welfare state over the past three decades. Chapter 1 examines the Korean welfare state's growth in the post-democratic era from 1987 to 1997, the expansion and consolidation of the four pillars of social insurances and public assistance programs under the progressive governments of Kim Dae-jung and Roh Moo-hyun, followed by two conservative administrations and the current administration of President Moon promoting the innovative inclusive welfare state. Chapter 2 investigates the emergence of innovative inclusive welfare state, the interrelationships between income-driven growth, inclusive growth, innovation growth, and inclusive welfare, followed by an analysis of the social welfare policy measures needed to achieve inclusive welfare. Chapter 3 points the way toward a future model for the Korean social investment framework, one that integrates thinking about social welfare policy and economic development. The model of *welfarenomics* seeks to advance the social investment perspective by (1) building a foundation for "workfare" through developing customized job programs for welfare beneficiaries, (2) utilizing various welfare programs as means for social innovation, and (3) applying management concepts to improve the operation of welfare programs.

Part II surveys the core policies of the Korean welfare state. Chapter 4 analyzes the foundational programs of Korea's income security system, which encompasses the old age pension, the basic pension, unemployment insurance, worker's injury insurance, and the national basic livelihood benefit. The analysis examines the basic characteristics (funding, eligibility, coverage, and adequacy) of these programs, along with issues and directions for reform. Chapter 5 focuses on the structure and operation of Korea's National Health Insurance, detailing the benefits package, public and private delivery of services, financing, and future challenges.

Part III explores several key policy challenges encountered by the Korean approach to social investment as it seeks to maintain social protection in a rapidly aging society. Chapter 6 assesses the scope and quality of the long-term care system and discusses the challenges of finance, eligibility determination, and coordination between health and long-term care services.

Chapter 7 addresses the introduction of community care services in 2018, which offer a major alternative to the costly provision of long-term care. The 2018 masterplan for the establishment of community care is analyzed along with the structure and function of the three pilot projects designed to provide a roadmap to universal provision. Addressing the traditional ways for dealing with elder care, Chapter 8 examines the extent to which the value of filial piety conveys family responsibility for elder care and how it has been modified in modern times. Chapter 9 reframes the conventional view of aging by advancing the concept of confident aging, which argues for policies that encourage a longer working life for the elderly. The volume concludes with a postscript that reviews the contemporary Korean discourse that goes beyond the social investment state to the political interests in a universal basic income policy.

References

Bevir, M. (2009). *Enabling state*. SAGE Publications Ltd. https://doi.org/10.4135/978144 6214817

Cronert, A., and Palme, J. (2019). Social investment at the cross-roads: The third way or the enlightenment path forward? In B. Cantillon, T. Goedeme, and J. Hills (Eds.), *Decent incomes for all* (pp. 201–222). Oxford University Press.

Cantillon, B. (2014). Beyond social investment: Which concepts and values for social policy in Europe? In B. Cantillion and F. Vandenbroucke (Eds.), *Reconciling work and poverty reduction* (pp. 2666–2318). Oxford University Press.

Eardley, T. (1997). New relations of welfare in the contracting state: The marketisation of services for the unemployed in Australia. Social Policy Research Center (SPRC) Discussion Paper 79. University of New South Wales.

Ferge, Z. (1996), The change of the welfare paradigm: The individualisation of the social. Paper presented at the Annual Conference of the British Social Policy Association, Sheffield, July 16–18.

Ferrera, M. (2009). From welfare state to the social investment state. *Rivista Internazionale di Scienze Soc, 117*(3/4), 513–528.

Giddens, A. (1998). *The third way: The renewal of social democracy*. Polity Press.

Gilbert, N. (2004). *Transformation of the welfare state*. Oxford University Press.

Jenson, J., and Saint-Martin, D. (2003, Winter). New routes to social cohesion? Citizenship and the social investment state. *Canadian Journal of Sociology, 28*(1), 77–99.

Jessop, B. (1994). From Keynesian welfare to the Schumpeterian workfare state. In R. Burrows and B. Loader (Eds.), *Towards a post-Fordist welfare state?* (pp. 13–38). Routledge.

Lewis, J. (2006). Men, women, work, care and policies. *European Journal of Social Policy, 16*(4), 387–392.

Midgley, J. (1999). *Social development: The developmental perspective in social welfare*. Sage.

Mishra, R., Khunle, S., Gilbert, N., and Chung, K. (Eds.). (2004). *Modernizing the Korean welfare state: The productive welfare model.* Transaction Publishers.

Office of the President, Republic of Korea. (2000). *DJ Welfarism: A new paradigm for productive welfare.* Tae Sul Dang.

Peng, I. (2011). Social investment policies in Canada, Australia, Japan, and South Korea. *International Journal of Child Care and Education Policy, 5*(1), 41–53.

Stoesz, D. (2018). *The investment state: Charting the future of social policy.* Oxford University Press.

Torfing, J. (1997). From the Keynesian welfare state to a Schumpeterian workfare regime: The offensive neo-statist case of Denmark. Paper presented at the 9th International Conference on Socio-Economics, Montreal, Canada July 5–7.

Wallace, J. (2013). *The Rise of the Enabling State.* Carnegie UK Trust: London. https://d1s su070pg2v9i.cloudfront.net/pex/pex_carnegie2021/2013/11/09195504/pub14550114 991.pdf

Weatherley, R. (1994). From entitlement to contract: Reshaping the welfare state in Australia, *Journal of Sociology and Social Welfare, 3*(13), 153–173.

PART I
EVOLUTION OF KOREAN SOCIAL POLICY

1

Development Trajectory and Future Directions of the Korean Welfare State

Eugene Yeo

Introduction

Since the dawn of industrialization, social welfare has been touted as both a "problem" and a "solution." The welfare state is a European invention. Early industrialized states in Western Europe sought to address the collapse of their communities and the impoverishment of the masses by introducing poor laws, mutual aid, and friendly societies. Since those early days, the welfare state has evolved along a trajectory that led it to be both celebrated as an excellent mechanism for countering the inherent volatility of the market economy and thereby enabling stable reproduction on the one hand, and criticized as a disruptor of the self-regulatory capabilities of the market and an inhibitor of economic growth that encourages wasteful spending and discourages people's willingness to work. What is certain today, however, is that no advanced market economy can survive on its own without some level of welfare. South Korea, where the market economy has developed and expanded rapidly, is no exception in this regard.

Social welfare is an especially complex and serious challenge in Korea. In the early years of Korea's industrialization, the country managed to survive with virtually no system of public welfare under a series of authoritarian regimes. European welfare 'states' have defined themselves as 'civil servants' dedicated to shielding their citizens from the volatility of the market—a controversial self-definition, indeed, and one that we will touch on here. By contrast, the Korean 'state' has appointed itself as a 'leader' of economic development, having singlehandedly undertaken massive development projects while supporting the growth of large conglomerates to promote such projects. This growth-centered developmentalism had its validity when abject poverty pervaded Korean society. Throughout the

Eugene Yeo, *Development Trajectory and Future Directions of the Korean Welfare State* In: *The Korean Welfare State*. Edited by: Kyungbae Chung and Neil Gilbert, Oxford University Press. © Oxford University Press 2024.
DOI: 10.1093/oso/9780197644928.003.0002

country's decades of high industrial growth, both policymakers and the general public accepted the authoritarian approach to development that advocated the "trickle-down" effect. To the Western welfare states that struggled with stagflation in the 1980s, leading them to near crises of legitimacy, Korea was the most mysterious and threatening of the so-called four dragons of East Asia. However, as the Korean state and the market enlarged themselves during this period, community and family structures began to crumble.

Watershed moments in the onward march of this development-centered order came in the forms of the Democratization Movement of 1987 and the Asian Financial Crisis of 1997. These two major events, occurring a decade apart, served as decisive catalysts for the radical growth of democracy and welfare in Korea. Democratization gave people the freedom to express their growing and increasingly loud demands for the empowerment of civil society and welfare policy. The Asian Financial Crisis, on the other hand, exposed the depths of long-accumulated contradictions in the state-led developmental economy at both the market and social levels. The two consecutive progressive administrations that governed Korea in the aftermath of the financial crisis did much to ensure the expansion and qualitative improvement of welfare benefits and services in Korea. However, whereas the West had 80 to 150 years to address the contradictions of the market economy and build and rebuild welfare states in the light of the economic, social, cultural, and demographic features of their given societies, Korea's achievement of the same in the span of only three decades naturally engendered significant complications. The welfare state was introduced in Korea without in-depth considerations of the premodern, industrial, and postmodern contradictions characterizing Korean society. Most regrettably, it was introduced in the absence of philosophical commitment on the part of policymakers to the necessity of social welfare as the founding pillar of the welfare state as well as a lack of understanding among the public. Because they had not meticulously considered the form and structure of the welfare state, Korean policymakers introduced welfare programs rather haphazardly and reactively, as hurried responses to problems. As a result, some programs grew disproportionately large, while other more necessary ones shrank, leading to major holes in some areas and smaller leaks in others.

In this chapter, I attempt to summarize the trajectory and achievements of the Korean welfare state since the days of democratization and the Asian Financial Crisis. I then discuss the path-dependent nature and limitations of such evolution, with a view to finding policy implications for the future growth of the Korean welfare state.

Trajectory of the Korean Welfare State's Growth

Expansion in the Early Post-Democratization Period (1987–1997)

Roh Tae-woo, elected as Korea's president through the first direct election held following the Democratization Movement of 1987, recognized the need to switch from repression to persuasion in dealing with the public. Whether as a result of directly mobilizing power resources or as part of a new political strategy that favored "the carrot over the stick," a great number of welfare programs were introduced from 1987 to 1997.

As for social security, the National Pension (NP) was introduced first, requiring employers with at least 10 full-time workers to subscribe to the pension insurance program beginning in 1988. Starting in 1992, the scope of the NP and Workers' Compensation Insurance (WCI) was expanded to include all employers with five or more full-time workers. The National Health Insurance (NHI), first introduced in 1977 as a requirement for businesses employing at least 500 workers each, saw the threshold number of employees drop radically over the following decade, declining to 300 in 1979, 100 in 1980, 16 in 1982, and finally to 5 in 1988. In addition, separate public health insurance schemes were introduced for rural communities in 1988 and urban communities in July 1989. Health insurance thus became the first of the social insurance programs to be provided to all citizens of Korea (National Law Information Center [NLIC], accessed on November 1, 2018). Particularly important to note with respect to the rise of public aid and the social service distribution system in Korea during this period is that the introduction of agents specialized in social service in 1988 firmly established welfare as an essential part of Korean policymaking and the country's social makeup (Kang, 2014, pp. 289–290). A series of welfare statutes were also introduced during this decade, including the Gender Equality in Employment Act (1987), Maternal Welfare Act (1989), Act on Welfare of Persons with Disabilities (1989), Act on Promotion of Employment for Persons with Disabilities (1989), Child Care Act (1991), and Act on Promotion of Employment for the Aged (1991). In addition, the Minimum Wage Act was enacted in December

1986, leading to the implementation of a minimum wage in 1988, and public housing for the poor was introduced in 1989.

Welfare policy grew so rapidly during this decade that the period is also referred to as one of "welfare explosion" (Nam, 2018). As Table 1.1 illustrates, the share of the health and welfare budget soared from less than 3% prior to 1987 to more than 4% in 1990, showing an increase of 55.8% compared to 1985.

However, under President Kim Young-sam's government, which is remembered as the first "civilian" (non-authoritarian and non-military) government in Korea, welfare spending remained stagnant and even dropped at some points. The proportion of the government budget allotted to health and welfare spending was 4.19% in 1990, but it dropped to 3.82% in 1995. The Kim administration then unveiled the Five-Year Plan for a New Economy, joining the global trend toward reducing state intervention and boosting the market. The plan reflected a shift toward non-interventionism in the Korean state's approach to welfare. On March 23, 1995, the Kim administration released the "President's Welfare Initiative for Bringing Quality of Life Up to the World Standard" and launched the National Welfare Planning

Table 1.1 Annual health and welfare budgets
(Units: 100 million Korean won, %, %p)

Year	Health and welfare budget (A)	Government budget (B)	A/B (%)	Change over five years (%p)	Percent change over five years (%)
1961	14	571	2.45	—	—
1965	31	946	3.27	0.8[1]	33.5[1]
1970	85	4,462	1.90	−1.4	−41.9
1975	426	15,863	2.68	0.8	41.1
1980	1,769	64,785	2.73	0.0	1.9
1985	3,365	125,323	2.69	0.0	−1.5
1990	11,518	274,557	4.19	1.5	55.8
1995	19,838	518,811	3.82	−0.4	−8.8
2000	53,100	864,740	6.14	2.3	60.7
2005	89,067	1,352,156	6.58	0.4	7.2
2010	310,195	2,928,000	10.6	4.0	61.1

Note: Compared to 4 years prior.

Source: Seven Decades of the Health and Welfare History Compilation Committee (2015a, p. 101, table 4-1). (Figures in the last two columns were calculated by the author.)

Group. This move demonstrated the administration's pride in having achieved an economic growth rate of 8.3% the previous year, the need to prepare for the upcoming general elections in 1996, and its decision to increase welfare spending so that Korea could join the Organisation for Economic Cooperation and Development (OECD). Throughout its 5 years, the Kim administration's health and welfare budget never exceeded that of its predecessor (Kim and Seong, 2000). Major statutes that were enacted during the civilian government's years included the Employment Insurance Act (1993; effective until July 1995) and Rural Pension Act (effective until July 1995). A number of other statutes pertaining to social services were also enacted during this period. While the effects of these statutes were nominal rather than substantial under Kim Young-sam's presidency, they nonetheless paved the ground for systematizing a wide range of welfare programs that had begun to take root in Korea at the time. Examples include the Framework Act on Social Security (1995), Framework Act on Women's Development (1995), Juveniles Framework Act (1995), Mother and Child Health Act (1995), Mental Health Act (1995), Act on the Punishment of Sexual Violence and Protection of Victims (1994), Juvenile Protection Act (1997), Community Welfare Fundraising Act (1997), Act on the Prevention of Domestic Violence and the Protection of Victims (1997), and Act on Enhancement of Convenience for the Disabled and the Elderly (1997) (NLIC, 2018).

Expansion of Welfare in the Post-Asian Financial Crisis Period

Universal Social Insurances and Basic Social Security Net

The Asian Financial Crisis quickly spread to Korea in 1997, and the country was put on a moratorium as a result of the rapid depletion of its foreign reserves. Prior to this crisis, the only year in which the Korean economy had recorded a negative growth rate was 1980 (−1.7%), in the aftermath of the oil crisis of 1979. The Asian Financial Crisis hit the Korean economy so hard that it recorded an unprecedented negative growth rate of −5.5% in 1998 (Statistics Korea, 2015, p. 65).

The social and economic repercussions of the Asian Financial Crisis were on a scale incomparable to that of the oil crisis that Korea suffered in 1980. The unemployment rate rose to 7.0% in 1998 and peaked at 8.8% in February the following year. The poverty rate, which had ranged between 6% and 8%, rose to 10.9% in 1998 and 11.4% in 1999.

The Asian Financial Crisis led to groundbreaking reforms in Korean politics as well. Although the democratization movement of the 1980s had succeeded in toppling the military authoritarian regime and ushered in direct elections for the presidency, the conservative (military-affiliated) party continued to rule Korea until 1997. The historic election of Kim Dae-jung, a long-time champion of progressive ideas and democratization, as president in December 1997 finally ushered in a decade of progressive government. The destructive effects of the economic crisis and the consecutive elections of two progressive governments worked together to revolutionize and expand the welfare system over the ensuing decade.

It was during this decade that a universal and integrated (at least formally) social security net was finally established. Leading this change was the integration of the public health insurance schemes in 1998. The public health insurance system had thus far been divided between the national system providing medical coverage for workplace-based policyholders and local medical insurance cooperatives providing coverage for other types of policyholders. The decentralized and cooperation-based vision of public health insurance clashed with the centralized vision from the very beginning, with the former prevailing up until the new administration. Under the decentralized system, however, the problems of inequality and fiscal imbalance were unavoidable. Starting the early 1990s, in particular, local medical insurance cooperatives began experiencing serious financial difficulties, with 65 urban cooperatives declaring deficits. Under the newly elected Kim Dae-jung administration, the integration of public health insurance schemes was carried out in three phases. Phase 1, which began in October 1998, integrated the finances of local cooperatives and brought local cooperatives and the pension schemes for public/private school staff under the control of the National Medical Insurance Corporation, a public enterprise. Phase 2 was initiated in July 2000, with the merging of workplace-based cooperatives with the National Medical Insurance Corporation to establish the National Health Insurance Service (NHIS). Phase 3 was carried out starting January 2002, when the finances of all disparate insurance schemes were centralized to provide a single system of universal healthcare (Six Decades of the Korean Economic History Compilation Committee, 2011, p. 143).

The National Pension Act (NPA), amended on December 31, 1998, and effective starting the following day, brought NP to all Korean citizens, including self-employed people, thereby becoming the first social insurance program to become universal. As part of efforts to reinforce the pension's ability to secure people's postretirement income, policymakers reduced the minimum period of time required for eligibility to claim benefits and introduced installment-based benefit payouts. They simultaneously reformed the pension system to ensure its fiscal sustainability by lowering the pension income to 60% of lifetime income and raising the eligible age, phase by phase, to 65. The raising of the eligible age was an expected change, because the NP was introduced on an accumulative basis (with comparatively low contribution rates), yet with promises of high levels of defined benefits. In justifying the rationality of their reform, policymakers pointed out that it was necessary to make the benefits universal and ensure long-term fiscal sustainability. Given its accumulative basis, the NP struck the public as "forced savings" and encountered strong objection from low-income groups, including small businesses (with fewer than five workers), temporary and day laborers, and self-employed earners. Nevertheless, the three phases of reform ushered in an age of universal public pension within a relatively short span of time (Nam, 2018; (Six Decades of the Korean Economic History Compilation Committee, 2011, pp. 143–144).

Under the amended Enforcement Decree, the Employment Insurance, first introduced in 1995, was expanded as of October 1, 1998, to include all employees, even those of small businesses employing fewer than five workers. This was in response to abrupt increases in the number of businesses shutting down and going bankrupt amid the Asian Financial Crisis. The WCI, which was the first social insurance ever introduced in Korea, was also expanded to include all employees, barring workers of certain types of businesses (such as small rural businesses with fewer than five workers each) as of July 1, 2000, after the amendment of the Enforcement Decree on June 27 the same year (NLIC, 2018). With these measures, the social security net in Korea, which first began to take shape with the Government Employees Pension of 1960 and WCI of 1963, became universal after only four decades. Although Korea's social security net is still criticized for lack of inclusiveness and a "good waist," every citizen in Korea is covered, at least formally, by social insurances.

The livelihood security system, which had been providing relief for the poor in the mold of the poor law up until this point, was also finally reformed to create the National Basic Livelihood Security Program (NBLSP), complete with the form and substance of a modern public assistance system. The dismissal, by the Constitutional Court in 1997, of a petition raised in 1994 for minimum livelihood support from the state effectively absolved the Korean state of the responsibility to provide for the minimum living conditions of its citizens. The Asian Financial Crisis and the International Monetary Fund (IMF)'s recommendation to provide a "denser social safety net" served to re-shape public opinion. Nongovernmental organizations (NGOs), including democratic and labor groups, therefore succeeded in politicizing the overhaul of the livelihood security system. President Kim Dae-jung's so-called *Ulsan remark*, which he made on July 23, 1998, set the enactment of the NBLSP Act on an accelerated track (Yeo, 2004, pp. 140–141). After the Act was initiated on September 7, 1999, the NBLSP finally took effect, after some preparation, on October 1, 2000. Its predecessor was a system of categorical public assistance that divided between homebound recipients lacking the ability to work, on the one hand, and self-help recipients capable of working, on the other, based on demographic criteria. The old system gave the former in-kind and some cash benefits while giving the latter only in-kind benefits, such as opportunities to work and receive training. The new NBLSP, on the other hand, is a general public assistance system that defines recipients not according to whether they are able to work, but according to whether they have sufficient support in the form of family members or personal wealth. The new program provides various types of cash and in-kind benefits, including livelihood, medical assistance, and housing benefits. By adopting an income supplementation approach that supports recipients with cash or in-kind benefits that allowed them to meet the minimum cost of living ("necessary to maintain a healthy and culturally informed life"), the NBLSP also institutionally espouses the national minimum principle, which is a major pillar of the welfare state.

Expansion of Semi-Universal and Near-Poverty Benefits and Social Services

The Kim Dae-jung government finalized the form of the welfare state in Korea by universalizing the four major social insurances and refining the public assistance program, firmly placing "solidarity" at the core of the welfare state ideal. The Roh Moo-hyun government, the progressive heir to the Kim administration, was bent on consolidating the welfare state and overcoming new challenges that characterized the birth of that state, such as polarization, low birth rate, rapid population aging, and the increase in working poverty. In the meantime, concerns regarding fiscal soundness and the reigning ideology of "welfare for growth" still shaped and limited the evolution of welfare in Korea.

The Roh administration did not do much by way of expanding and universalizing the social security net. Rather, the administration undertook reforms in the interest of fiscal sustainability, culminating in the second attempt to reduce pension benefits in continuity with the pension reform of 1998. The income replacement rate of the NP thus dropped by 0.5 percentage points every year from 2009, from 50% promised for contributions over 40 years starting in 2008 (Nam, 2018). The Roh administration stoked controversy further by promoting the industrialization of medicine and introducing bill-reimbursing medical insurances that amounted to privatization of healthcare. The Roh administration also sought to enhance the efficiency of the collection of social insurance premiums by centralizing the collection of all four social insurances. The Korea Workers' Compensation and Welfare Service (KWCWS) thus started collecting the premiums for both the Employment Insurance and the WCI in January 2005.

Yet the Roh administration also brought about a significant expansion of welfare in Korea by introducing diverse cash benefits to narrow the gap between social insurances and the NBLSP and actively diversifying and increasing social services (childcare, Long-Term Care Insurance for Seniors, etc.) to counter the new societal risks arising in the face of the low birth rate and population aging.

First, the contributions-based NP, low levels of pension income, breadth of blind spots of the pension system, and failure of the NBLSP to protect people with family members able (but often unwilling) to work and support them were worsening the problem of poverty among the elderly population. In view of this, the Basic Old-Age Pension Act was enacted on April 25, 2007, with benefits first paid out as of January 2008. The new pension was designed to pay 5% of the average income of National Pensioners (i.e., the A-value in the NP benefit calculation formula) to seniors with incomes recognized to be in the bottom 70% (Seven Decades of the Korean Health and Welfare History Compilation Committee, 2015b, p. 238).

In addition to introducing the Basic Old-Age Pension to counter rising poverty among the elderly population, the Roh administration introduced the earned income tax credit (EITC) as part of the newly amended Restriction of Special Taxation Act (effective as of January 2007) to provide a kind of wage support for working low-income families. While the EITC was first launched by statute on December 30, 2006, payout of benefits did not start until 2009, based on reported income earned in 2008. The eligibility criteria were rather stringent at first, requiring (1) an annual household income of less than 17 million Korean won, (2) the presence of at least one child under the age of 18, (3) non-ownership of home or ownership of a home valued at 50 million won or less, and (4) possession of combined assets of less than 100 million won ((Six Decades of the Korean Economic History Compilation Committee, 2011, p. 147).

As Figure 1.1 shows, the plummeting birth rate fueled the perceived demographic crisis during Roh's presidency. As the total fertility rate dropped further from 1.17 per woman in 2002 to 1.08 in 2005, pessimistic forecasts of Korea's future began to float around, pointing to such issues as long-term labor shortages, contraction of the domestic market, decline in the potential growth rate, and an eventual fiscal crisis driven by the abrupt rise in the demand for welfare spending for seniors. The Roh government thus began devising master plans to counter these potential problems, leading to the establishment of the so-called *Bud Plan* (First Mid- to Long-Term Childcare Master Plan, 2006–2010). The first and foremost policy response to the plummeting birth rate was to strengthen childcare services. The plan declared that all infants and toddlers, not just those of low-income households, had the right to childcare services, thereby heralding the age of universal childcare. In addition, income-differentiated childcare allowances

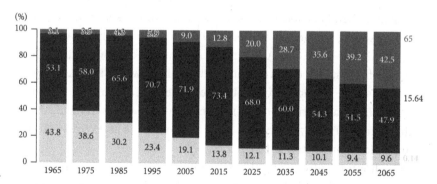

Figure 1.1 Age makeup of Korea's demographic composition, 1965 to 2065 (median).

Source: Statistics Korea (2016, p. 9, figure 7).

and basic subsidies were introduced to assist even middle-class families during this time (Kim, 2017, pp. 175–177).

Rapid population aging also led to increased demand for societal involvement in elderly care. The increase in life expectancy, along with the low birth rate, was expected to dramatically increase the proportion of seniors in the national population and raise the elderly dependency ratio (ratio of the number of seniors to every 100 working-age people). Whereas the working-age population was projected to reach a peak of 37.63 million in 2016 and decline afterward, the elderly population was projected to increase rapidly to 28.7% of the total population in 2035 and further to 42.5% by 2065. The elderly dependency ratio was thus predicted to skyrocket from 17.5 in 2015 to 50 by 2036 and 88.6 by 2065 (Statistical Office, 2016). Such a dramatic transformation of Korea's demographic composition would not only increase the financial burden of elderly care, but also make the provision of physical and mental care for seniors a serious social challenge. As Roh had won the presidency in part thanks to his campaign pledge to introduce long-term care insurance for seniors, the administration under him assembled the Public Long-Term Care Insurance Steering Group in March 2003. One year later, the Public Senior Care Insurance Executive Committee and its working-level group were created as part of the Ministry of Health and Welfare to develop an execution model. After three trial phases, the Long-Term Care Insurance (LTCI) for seniors was finally introduced on July 1, 2008 (Seven Decades of the Korean Health and Welfare History Compilation Committee, 2015b, p. 252).

Although the Roh administration sought to expand coverage provided by the NBLSP by reducing the measurement period of the minimum cost of living and relaxing the criteria for supporting family members and asset-income conversion, the NBLSP remained largely intact. To provide relief for people in need who had been turned away by the stringent family support and asset requirements of the NBLSP, the Emergency Welfare Relief Program was introduced in 2006. Medical benefits were also introduced for near-poverty households.

The Roh administration also sought to devolve social services to local governments in 2005 as part of its efforts to introduce more balanced regional development and steered the creation of the Community Living Support Service System in 2007 to improve the distribution of public benefits and services. Finally, it also pushed for increasing disability allowances, introducing mobility support for people with disabilities, and enacting statutes prohibiting discrimination against and providing special education for people with disabilities in 2007 (Nam, 2018).

Stagnation of Welfare Under the Conservative Administrations

Lee Myung-bak and Park Geun-hye were two conservative-leaning presidents who were consecutively elected after Roh left office. Although these two conservative administrations started with somewhat different approaches to welfare, they both eventually came to neglect welfare in the end. Lee Myung-bak placed economic growth as the foremost goal of his agenda when he was running for the presidency. It was therefore unsurprising that his election would lead to a contraction of welfare spending. Park Geun-hye, on the other hand, set out by espousing a much more active welfare policy, so much so that progressives lamented that Park's party had hijacked the welfare frame. The Park administration started by pushing for the overhaul of the Framework Act on Social Security and promising to make old-age pension universal.

Nevertheless, the two consecutive governments together introduced only a handful of new welfare measures. One was the Durunuri Program, which sought to support underpaid workers in small businesses who were not included in the scope of the social security net. Although the Kim administration sought to make the four major social insurances universal, a significant number of working people had in fact been left out of the coverage provided by the system. After a trial phase in the first half of 2012, the Durunuri Program was launched, in July 2012, to subsidize the NP and Employment Insurance premiums of eligible workers working at small businesses employing fewer than 10 workers. The program specifically funded half of the matching premiums to be paid by both employers and employees (Seven Decades of Korean Health and Welfare History Compilation Committee, 2015b, pp. 412–13).

While efforts to expand childcare services started under the Roh administration, the Lee administration introduced the universal daycare program known as the Nuri Program for toddlers aged 5 and younger, as well as free childcare support for all children aged 2 and younger. Later, the Park administration expanded the free childcare support for children aged 3 and 4. Of the OECD member states, Korea is the only country that provides universal and unconditional childcare support for young children irrespective of parents' income and working status (Kim, 2017, p. 177). The Lee administration also introduced the home care allowance in 2009, for families raising infants and toddlers without the help of daycare facilities. While the allowance initially targeted low-income and near-poverty families only, it was expanded to benefit all families with young children in 2013. These free childcare and home care allowance programs grew rapidly, driven by the government's need to counter and stem the plummeting birth rate and also to appeal to young people and parents as constituents. The rapid growth of childcare support, however, sparked controversies over the public nature and quality of the childcare services provided. Moreover, it also led to the escalation of conflicts between kindergartens and daycare centers and between the central government (Ministry of Education [MoE]) and regional educational offices over the allocation of fiscal resources.

The NBLSP also underwent radical changes. Since its introduction, there were demands that the programs' benefits be customized to individual recipients' needs. The Park administration restructured the program in July 2015, to tailor all its benefits to individuals' needs. Whereas the Ministry of Health and Welfare (MoHW) had single-handedly decided and paid out all benefits of the program until that point, the tasks under the program were now divided among multiple departments, including the MoHW (living, medical, funerary, childbirth, and self-help benefits); Ministry of Land, Infrastructure, and Transport (MoLIT, housing benefits); and MoE (education benefits). Furthermore, while the old program had defined and applied the minimum cost of living as the baseline for determining eligibility and the amounts of benefits to be provided, the reformed program introduced a number of different metrics to be defined and applied for different benefits. The reform introduced flexibility in the operation of the program. However, it has been criticized for rendering the minimum cost of living as meaningless as the poverty line and for its decentralized approach blocking the consistent and integrated evolution of the program.

Park, who won the presidency in part thanks to her campaign pledge to provide 200,000 won a month as a basic pension benefit for each and every eligible senior, assembled the National Pension Commission shortly after her election to initiate discussions on making the basic pension universal. However, the results, decided in July 2013 and made effective as of July 2014, did not live up to the promise of the universal old-age pension plan that was initially touted. It was in effect identical to the existing old-age pension, paying the average income of 70% of seniors receiving NP benefits or 10%

of the A-value (Seven Decades of the Korean Health and Welfare History Compilation Committee, 2015b, p. 239). Except for the change of name, a slight increase in the amount of pension benefits, and adjustments made to the basic pension benefits for pensioners already receiving NP support, the newly introduced basic pension was not markedly different from the existing old-age pension.

On the other hand, pursuant to the Disability Pension Act, which was enacted on April 21, 2010, recipients of NBLSP and near-poverty individuals with severe disabilities started receiving disability pension benefits as of July 1 of the same year. The new pension, however, became a source of much controversy because it did nothing more than pay slightly more for severely disabled individuals who were already eligible for the disability allowances along with people with relatively mild forms of disabilities.

Discussion

The process through which the welfare state grew and expanded in Korea in the aftermath of democratization and the Asian Financial Crisis can be summarized as follows.

First, it is important to remember that the development-oriented state in Korea prioritized economic growth above all else and heavy-handedly directed economic development under authoritarian regimes for decades. Therefore, democratization, the Asian Financial Crisis, and the subsequent expansion of welfare were not enough to put a stop to state-driven developmentalism. The Kim Young-sam administration took a step back from direct and state-led authoritarian development, but it still prioritized economic growth as the guiding principle of all policy objectives. Under Kim's presidency, statism survived alongside a newfound focus on the market. This new policy focus ultimately led to the growth of a particular brand of market economy, one led and shaped largely by multinational conglomerates, at the center of economic policymaking. The equal emphasis on growth and the market served to prevent the Kim administration from pursuing its other policy goals (i.e., social equity and balanced development). Instead, it reinforced the policy preference for a less-expensive and low-welfare state in Korea. Remember that the share of social welfare in overall government spending dwindled during the Kim Young-sam years.

The two progressive governments that were elected after the Asian Financial Crisis were unsurprisingly more pro-welfare than their predecessors or conservative successors. The Kim Dae-jung administration's slogan of "productive welfare," however, did not manifest in any significant departure from the economy-focused thinking that still drove much of policymaking and the residual and selective approach to welfare. It wasn't until the Roh administration that welfare was spotlighted. The Roh administration was the first, and remains the only, government in Korean history to have championed welfare as its first and foremost objective. The Roh administration oversaw the transformation of Korea's welfare system, introducing the Basic Old-Age Pension, EITC, LTCI, childcare services, mobility support services for people with disabilities, the Emergency Welfare Relief Program, and the Community Living Support Service System. While the Kim Dae-jung administration aligned itself with neoliberalism and maintained a residual and selective approach to welfare, the Roh administration pursued a more sophisticated, active, and universal approach. Upon closer examination, however, one would find that even the sweeping transformation of welfare under the Roh administration failed to set the welfare system apart from the pro-market perspective, which resembled the social investment state. The EITC, privatization of childcare and convalescent hospitals, and industrialization of nursing and care services are evidence to this. The privatization of medicine and health services, the second drop in the income replacement rate of the NP benefits (2007), increased tax breaks for private pension plans, and the introduction of retirement pension programs (2005) attest to the fact that even Roh's "participatory government" adhered faithfully to the market- and growth-centered view of its predecessors. Despite its status as the most pro-welfare of all governments in Korean history, the Roh administration's welfare strategy seemed rather vague and even ambivalent.

Second, notwithstanding the rapid expansion of the social security net, the income security system still has large holes, and the support it offers is insufficient to satisfy the needs of any beneficiary. The discontinuity of market income beyond retirement is a universal and grave risk faced by the majority of the population. Now in the era of rapid aging and increased life expectancy of the Korean population, the considerable coverage gap in the old-age income security system is by far the most serious problem with the welfare structure in Korea today. Other social insurances, however, also have gaping holes. As Figure 1.1, irregular workers and struggling small business workers are especially likely to be excluded from the social security net. Only 69.6%

of people working at small businesses employing fewer than five workers have employment insurance, and that figure drops to 68.7% among irregular workers. Although retirement pensions can provide at least some supplement to the already low NP income, only 16.5% of small business workers and 21.8% of irregular workers are able to participate in retirement pension schemes.

Most importantly, owing to the top-down manner in which the social security net has been expanded, all in the absence of minimum guaranteed income, the social security net excludes large numbers of the country's most vulnerable people, including small business owners and workers, self-employed people, and irregular workers. Even those who participate in social insurance plans receive income that falls short of the minimum cost of living. People who work in highly specialized trades with stable and high levels of income and employees of large corporations and public enterprises who enjoy high job security and at least middle levels of income can earn enough during their period of employment to prepare for old age. They are also likely to have multiple other sources of old-age income aside from public pension schemes, such as private retirement plans. Small business owners and workers, irregular workers, and self-employed people, on the other hand, are not only deprived of stable and sufficient income during their careers and corporate benefits such as retirement pensions post-retirement, but they are also excluded from public social insurances. The security of welfare as social income, in other words, is something that only some lucky people can enjoy and in itself serves as a marker of the polarization and fragmentation of the Korean labor market. Although the Korean government has introduced additional programs, such as the Durunuri Program, to address the holes in the social security net, these social insurance subsidies are unlikely to serve the cause of tightening the social security net as a whole.

Third, the range and quantity of social services have grown exponentially over the past two decades, whether under progressive governments or conservative ones. Such rapid expansion of social services largely reflects the need for policy intervention to address the demographic changes that have been accelerated by the plummeting birth rate and population aging, collapse of the traditional family-based division of labor, and the growing demand for the socialization of care. Although the universalization of social services has taken place in Korea at a rate unprecedented anywhere else in the world,[1] such speed was achieved in large part at the price of compromising on the quality and public nature of the services provided. This has caused the proliferation of underqualified and small service providers, which has become a major problem. "Universal but non-public" social services came about as a result of the state indiscriminately fostering care services provided by the private sector rather than increasing the number of public channels of such services that can better ensure quality. The current phenomenon, on the other hand, also reflects the "tacit covenant" between the state and the market that has existed since Korea's liberation from Japanese occupation: namely, the practice of the state starting and financing services and the market operating those services on the state's behalf. This phenomenon, of course, is attributed to the underlying purpose for which past administrations expanded social services—that is, to create new industries and jobs. Whether intended or not, a certain form of clientelism has thus arisen among the government, social service providers, and social service workers. This clientelism is supply-centered and for-profit and therefore fosters the multiplication of poor-paying jobs and undermines the quality of care services. Whereas the supply side of social services is well organized and wields a significant influence over the policymaking process, the demand side remains unorganized and maintains stakeholder status only for a short period of time. Going forward, the absence of a mechanism to ensure the adequate representation of service users in the policymaking process will make it even more difficult to ensure that social services cater to public values.

Conclusion

The welfare state in South Korea has made truly remarkable progress over the past three decades, and it is no longer possible for Koreans to imagine a life outside the welfare regime. Few citizens would be able to maintain the security of their lives without public childcare services and education for their children, basic pension and long-term care services for the elderly, disability services, and universal healthcare system serving all citizens. It is also true, however, that market uncertainty has deteriorated over the past decades, threatening Koreans' security and future. The polarization of industries and the labor market and the sweeping march of the Fourth Industrial Revolution are accelerating and aggravating inequality and polarization. As a result, citizens have come to pursue their own welfare, leading them to engage in a fierce zero-sum game of ensuring their security at the expense of others. The obsession with investment in education for one's own children, the rising popularity of tedious but stable jobs over in-novative risk-taking ones, and the growing tendency to equate welfare with wealth are only some signs of this trend. Despite the impressive growth of welfare in Korea so far, we still need a stronger social security net and, just as importantly, better society-wide understanding of what the welfare state truly is.

We are at a crossroads where we need to decide, first and foremost, to move beyond the developmentalist legacy of the state and strike a better balance between the economic and the social. The old habits of the Korean mind, consisting of growth-centrism, competition for an edge in education, and selfish familyism, still hold sway in the minds of Korean policymakers and citizens alike. The fiercer market competition becomes, the more accepting Korean society becomes of selfish familyism/clannism and self-destructive investment in anything to get ahead of others, most notably education. Engrossment in the market ideology and private investment culminates in inefficient and surplus investment in pursuit of social values and inequality in the labor market. This in turn reinforces the desire to reap returns on pri-vate investment, which has the effect of strengthening resistance against tax increases. In the meantime, excessive investment in the education and future of their children leads people to neglect the need to prepare adequately for old age and ultimately contributes to elderly poverty (Yeo, 2014). In a so-ciety like Korea's, where economic concerns dominate over social issues, it is unlikely that a universal welfare state backed by strong solidarity among cit-izens will emerge. Policymakers must therefore develop and practice educa-tion, for youth and citizens alike, that focuses on social as much as economic issues, notwithstanding the painstaking and time-consuming labor such an endeavor would entail.

Second, filling in the holes of the social security net is a task the state cannot afford to neglect. To solve this problem requires thorough, re-fined, and purpose-oriented analyses of the current situation in Korea. Policymakers need to better understand, and come up with better responses to, the particularities of the Korean labor market amid the global trends of postindustrialization and the Fourth Industrial Revolution. Characterizing the Korean labor market today are the high proportions of irregular and un-paid workers and the low participation of women. The rapid and top-down expansion of the social security net furthermore has not helped the pursuit of a universal income security system. A welfare state that does not protect the most vulnerable groups—underpaid irregular workers, small self-employed businesses, non-working women, etc.—is a failed welfare state. A social security net that is designed to prioritize fiscal stability above all else is unlikely to guarantee minimum income for the poor. Western welfare states have begun to recognize the impossibility of ensuring security and minimum income for citizens using only public insurance plans and have thus started introducing various supplementary measures. The bifurcation of the labor market and belated start and hurried adjustment of the welfare system has further exacerbated the same problem in Korea. A more innovative approach to income security is needed.

Finally, it may be a little too late to start, but policymakers must make efforts to ensure that social services cater to public values and ideals. The sense of crisis caused by the plummeting birth rate and rapid population aging, the need to increase employment among women, the demand to create new industries and jobs, and the proliferation of discourses on the state's role in social services and social investment all generated the momentum that drove the relatively rapid universalization of social services in Korea. In the process, though, the public function and quality of social services were nearly lost. The path-dependent legacy of Korea's developmentalism and the pro-market approach to policy services have left the provision of social services almost exclusively to the private sector, leading to mixed results. Social services, undoubtedly, are where welfare mixes are most often attempted in many welfare states worldwide. In numerous countries around the world, the finance and operation of social services are functions of a mix of the state, private sector, and third sector. Nevertheless, that social services are meant to serve public good above all else is a widely accepted core value of advanced welfare states. Although the quick universalization of social services is significant as a policy response to low birth rates and population aging, the failure of social services to serve the common good is bound to raise skepticism over the legitimacy of massive government spending on welfare. The Korean case shows that universalization does not necessarily promote the common good and that universalism and universalization are separate matters. We also need to revisit the tendency to equate universal services with free services. Early proponents of social service expansion called for a balance of cash benefits and social services. Now that the elderly poverty rate easily exceeds 40% in Korea, however, we may need to "rebalance."

Note

1. According to Bettio and Plantenga (2004), a study conducted at a time when the social service regime started a phase of explosive growth in Korea, the quality of child and elderly care services remained mostly poor in southern European states; was at a middle level in Austria, Germany, and other continental European states; and was also mostly at a middle level in northern Europe, except for some in-kind benefits, such as paid leaves.

References

Bettio, F., and Plantenga, J. (2004). Comparing care regimes in Europe. *Feminist Economics* *10*(1), 85–113.

Kang, H. (2014). Particularities of the welfare distribution system. In Y. Yeo et al. (Eds.), *Developing a Korean welfare model: Korean particularities and welfare state* (pp. 285–324). KIHASA.

Kim, S. (2017). Restructuring family support policy. In Y. Yeo et al. (Eds.), *Developing a Korean welfare model: Changing the welfare environment and alternatives* (pp. 169–216). KIHASA.

Kim, T., and Seong, G. (2000). *Theories of the welfare state,* Nanam.

Korea Economy 60 Year History Compilation Committee. (2011). *The 60-Year History of the Korean Economy: Social Welfare·Health.*

Nam, C. (2018). *Backgrounds and characteristic features of welfare systems at different turns of contemporary Korean history.* Unpublished manuscript.

National Law Information Center (NLIC). (2018). http://www.law.go.kr

Seven Decades of the Korean Health and Welfare History Compilation Committee. (2015). *Seven decades of health and welfare: From an age of poverty to a welfare society.* MoHW.

Six decades of the Korean economic history compilation committee. (2011). *Six decades of Korean economic history: Welfare and health.*

Statistical Office. (2016). *Future population projections: 2015–2065.*

Statistics Korea. (2015). *A statistical glance at the changes in Korean society in the seven decades following liberation.*

Yeo, E. (2004). Value-oriented issues and institutional reflections in the formation of the national basic livelihood security program. In Y. Yeo et al. (Eds.), *The value basis and institutional reflections of public assistance: Focusing on the formation of the National Basic Livelihood Security Program* (pp. 134–185). KIHASA.

Yeo, E. (2014). Conclusion: Korean particularities and the search for a Korean welfare state. In Y. Yeo et al. (Eds.), *Developing a Korean welfare model: Korean particularities and welfare state* (pp. 423–432). KIHASA.

Yeo, E. (2016). Efforts of the welfare state—Part II: Typology of welfare spending. In Y. Yeo et al. (Eds.), *Developing a Korean welfare model: Placing the current Korean welfare state in the comparative context of welfare regimes* (pp. 303–354). KIHASA.

2

The Inclusive Welfare State in Korea

Heung-Seek Cho

Introduction

The Candlelight rallies, which started in October 2016, aimed to re-establish the Republic of Korea as a properly functioning country. The will of the people was to remove a deep-rooted corruption through political impeachment, reduce social polarization and guarantee a fairer economy, resolve opportunity inequality, and establish peace on the Korean Peninsula.

According to the wishes of the electorate, President Moon Jae-in declared his willingness to oversee an administration that worked with the people through the slogan of "equality of opportunity, the fairness of procedures, and justness of result." The administration's 5-year plan for state affairs, issued by President Moon in July 2017, contained various policy measures to improve quality of life for the Korean people over that time. In early September 2018, President Moon presented the big picture of a social policy in balance with economic policy by declaring the new government's national model to be one of an *innovative inclusive state* (IIS).

This chapter investigates the background of the emergence of the IIS and the interrelationships between concepts and terms such as income-driven growth, inclusive growth, innovation growth, and inclusive welfare. Finally, I examine the challenges faced by the Moon Jae-in administration's social welfare policy.

Background of the Inclusive Welfare State

Changes in the Economic and Social Systems

The year 2019 marked the 100th anniversary of the establishment of the provisional government of the Republic of Korea through the declaration of the

Heung-Seek Cho, *The Inclusive Welfare State in Korea* In: *The Korean Welfare State*. Edited by: Kyungbae Chung and Neil Gilbert, Oxford University Press. © Oxford University Press 2024. DOI: 10.1093/oso/9780197644928.003.0003

Democratic Republic that ended the dynastic politics of 4,252 years. Korea was colonized by Japan for 35 years, from 1910 to 1945, and the two Koreas were divided by foreign powers. On December 12, 1948, the United Nations recognized South Korea as the sole legal government of Korea. The administration of Korea's first president, Rhee Syngman, was followed by the second republic period under President Yun Bo-seon and Prime Minister Chang Myon, after which Major General Park Chung-hee organized and carried out the May 16, 1961 military coup. Since the establishment of the military government in 1963, by Park Chung-hee, Park's administration pursued economic growth-oriented policies, such as the export economy and the *chaebol*-centered economy, and contributed to Korea's economic growth. The gross domestic product (GDP) increased by more than 31,000 times in 2014, and gross national income (GNI) per capita increased 420 times from US$67 in 1953 to US$28,000 in 2014. As the economy stabilized, consumer price inflation decreased significantly from 167.5% in 1950, to 28.7% in 1980, and further to 1.3% in 2014, resulting in a significant improvement in people's lives (Statistics Korea, 2015). By 2018, Korea had achieved unprecedented economic growth with its GDP per capita reaching the level of US$30,000 (see Figure 2.1).

The Korean model of economic development involved centralization. mobilization of financial and human resources under government control, and, finally, the accumulation of industrial capital. The government had played a role in establishing and executing the economic development strategy, and the market had played a key role in economic development under the protection of the government. Finance and labor were the tools for economic growth, especially under government control of labor, and the people built a system to provide funds and human resources through forced savings.[1]

The Park Chung-hee military administration initiated its first 5-year economic development plan in 1964. Unlike previous administrations, the economic policies of export-oriented and heavy chemical industries were adopted as growth strategies. From the 1960s to the late 1970s, the characteristics of economic policies pursued by the Park Chung-hee regime were as follows: (1) economic growth is important; (2) growth is led by the government; (3) foreign investment is inevitable; (4) growth happens through exports; and (5) a policy of low wages and rising prices.

---

[1] The main contents of the following section are summarized based on the National Economic Advisory Council (2005), *Changes in Korean economic development model and new prospects.*

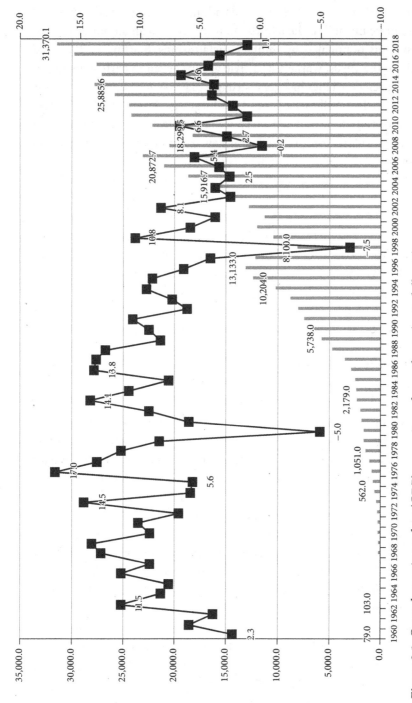

Figure 2.1 Gross domestic product (GDP) per capita and growth rate (unit: dollar, %)

Note: Blue line: Gross domestic product per capita (nominal, in dollars). Red line: Gross domestic income.

Source: Bank of Korea, *Bank of Korea Economic Statistics System*, each year.

In December 1979, the Chun Doo-hwan administration took power through a military coup. Although this administration overcame political and economic turmoil in the late 1970s, it still created an authoritarian political systems dominated by military dictatorships. Starting in 1987 and throughout the 1990s, workers and civic groups began to participate in political and social activities in a great struggle that was accompanied by many changes in society. Following Chun Doo-hwan's government, the Roh Tae-woo administration introduced social welfare policies such as a revision of Labor Law 3, enforcement of the Labor Law, a minimum wage system, and the implementation of the national pension system at the end of the 1980s.

The Kim Young-sam administration, in the 1990s, was the first civilian government to emerge after a long military dictatorship. Kim's administration emphasized three major reforms (1) anti-corruption, (2) revitalization of the economy, and (3) the establishment of national discipline with the creation of a "New Korea." One of the main features of the 1990s was the activation of a civil movement, which began to address various social problems through organizations such as the Citizens' Coalition for Economic Justice Practice in 1989, the Union for Environmental Movement in 1993, and the Democratic Society and Citizen Solidarity for Participatory Democracy in 1994.

The 1997–1998 economic crisis was a turning point that greatly changed Korean society. In response to this crisis, the economic models of the United Kingdom and the United States were introduced, which involved interventions in the market economy in the form of regular restructuring, layoffs, and expansion of irregular jobs and irregular workers. In addition, measures for reforming the social safety net were implemented to mitigate social unrest, but these measures emphasized aspects of residual and selective welfare. Although the social welfare reforms involved expansions of the national pension system and employment and industrial accident insurance and the introduction of the National Basic Livelihood Security System and basic old-age pension system, these measures were limited by eligibility criteria and low benefit levels. These limitations remain to this day, posing a continuing problem in that the government is unable to respond appropriately to periodic crises.

Since the turn of the century, the strategy of economic development in the form of a developmental state has adopted the neoliberal model, which has led to a number of serious economic and social problems such as the expansion of the irregular economy, income inequality and deepening of

polarization, deterioration of quality of life, low fertility, and an aging population (Sung, 2018).

Examining the problem of irregular workers (see Figure 2.2), we can see
that the number of irregular workers in Korea started to increase sharply
since the 1997 economic crisis, with the greatest increase among those age 50
and older. This increase in older irregular works is because of the increasing
number of middle-aged and elderly workers who are leaving the labor
market early; early retirement has become a commonplace. Increasing numbers of irregular workers lead to a problematic wage gap between full-time
and irregular workers.

In fact, the ratio of workers' wages in small to medium enterprises
compared to those in large industrial organizations dropped steadily from
73.5% in 1993 to 52.5% in 2014 and remained at 54.5% in 2016. However,
considering the *chaebol*-centered[2] economic structure in Korea and the
slowdown in growth and the decline in potential growth rate, the problem
of the dual structure of the labor market is expected to be difficult to resolve
anytime soon.

Moreover, there are serious problems in relation to market income inequality. As shown in Figure 2.3, the Gini coefficient for Korean market income has increased from .330 in 2006 to .353 in 2016. There was, however,
a slight decrease in the Gini coefficient for disposal income over this period.
Relative poverty (50% of median income) also rose by 2.9 percentage points,
from 16.6% in 2006 to 19.5% in 2016, indicating that market income distribution and poverty are still important social issues. In fact, the Korean poverty
rate of 14.4% is 3% higher than the Organisation for Economic Cooperation
and Development (OECD) average of 11.4%, and is about twice as high as
that of developed countries in Northern Europe.

In addition, as shown in Figure 2.4, Korea's absolute poverty rate based
on market income has been on the rise, although both slight increases and
decreases are seen depending on the period surveyed. The absolute poverty
rate based on market income (poverty rate 3) was 7.8% in 2003 and 10.9%
in 2009; it started to fall after 2009 and then rose again after 2012. In 2016,
it recorded a high of 10.8%. The absolute poverty rate (poverty rate 4) based

---

[2] A chaebol refers to a blood-related enterprise in which management with large capital consists
mainly of relatives such as family members and relatives. In Korea, pan-Samsung, pan-Hyundai, pan-
SK, pan-LG, and pan-Lotte are representative. However, in addition to such a large conglomerate that
anyone can recognize just by hearing its name, there are many companies across the country that
have chaebol characteristics on a smaller scale.

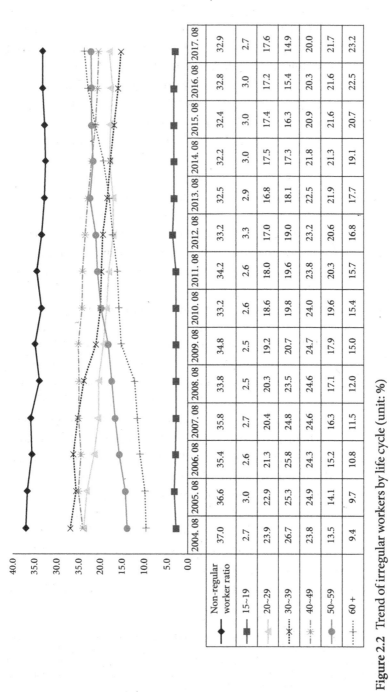

	2004. 08	2005. 08	2006. 08	2007. 08	2008. 08	2009. 08	2010. 08	2011. 08	2012. 08	2013. 08	2014. 08	2015. 08	2016. 08	2017. 08
Non-regular worker ratio	37.0	36.6	35.4	35.8	33.8	34.8	33.2	34.2	33.2	32.5	32.2	32.4	32.8	32.9
15~19	2.7	3.0	2.6	2.7	2.5	2.5	2.6	2.6	3.3	2.9	3.0	3.0	3.0	2.7
20~29	23.9	22.9	21.3	20.4	20.3	19.2	18.6	18.0	17.0	16.8	17.5	17.4	17.2	17.6
30~39	26.7	25.3	25.8	24.8	23.5	20.7	19.8	19.6	19.0	18.1	17.3	16.3	15.4	14.9
40~49	23.8	24.9	24.3	24.6	24.6	24.7	24.0	23.8	23.2	22.5	21.8	20.9	20.3	20.0
50~59	13.5	14.1	15.2	16.3	17.1	17.9	19.6	20.3	20.6	21.9	21.3	21.6	21.6	21.7
60 +	9.4	9.7	10.8	11.5	12.0	15.0	15.4	15.7	16.8	17.7	19.1	20.7	22.5	23.2

Figure 2.2 Trend of irregular workers by life cycle (unit: %)

Source: Statistics Korea, KOSIS (accessed on September 1, 2018); as cited in Kim Tae-wan et al. (2019), *Vision and strategy of inclusive growth*, p. 12.

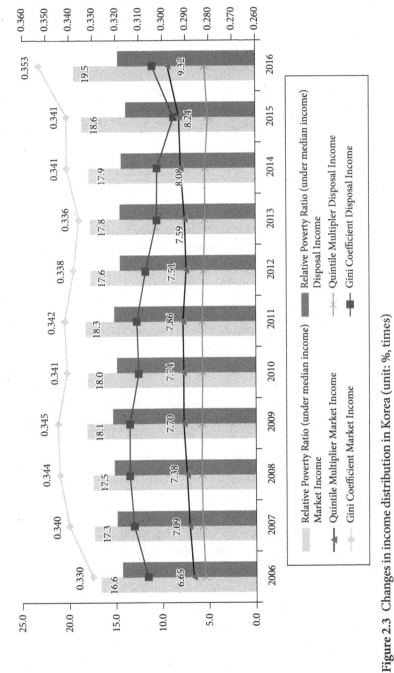

Figure 2.3 Changes in income distribution in Korea (unit: %, times)

Source: Statistics Korea, KOSIS (accessed on September 1, 2018); as cited in Kim Tae-wan et al. (2019), *Vision and strategy of inclusive growth*, p. 12.

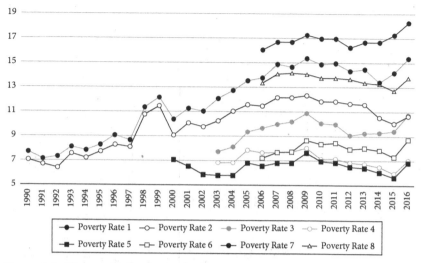

Figure 2.4 Changes in absolute and relative poverty rates

Note: Poverty rate 1: Median income 50%, the poverty rate based on market income (urban households). Poverty rate 2: median income 50%, the poverty rate based on disposable income (urban households). Poverty rate 3: absolute poverty rate (whole household), market income. Poverty rate 4: absolute poverty rate (all households), disposable income. Poverty rate 5: absolute poverty rate (urban households, disposable income based on two or more persons). Poverty rate 6: absolute poverty rate (including one city household, based on disposable income). Poverty rate 7: middle income 50%, the relative poverty rate (total household-market income). Poverty rate 8: middle income 50%, the relative poverty rate (all households-disposable income).

Source: Korea Institute for Health and Social Affairs (2017). *Annual Report on Poverty in 2017.*

on disposable income, as measured by taxes and transfer income (including welfare benefits), rose from 6.9% in 2003 to 8.1% in 2009 and then declined to 7% in 2016.

Although poverty remains a major issue in Korea, the country's overall wealth is relatively high. In 2018, the per capita GNI of Korea was US$31,349. As such, it has grown to become the seventh country to join *30-50 club* (countries with a greater than US$30,000 GNI per capita and more than 50 million people) by exceeding US$30,000. The 30-50 club includes the United States, France, Italy, the United Kingdom, and Germany. After Japan, Korea became the second Asian country to join the club. However, after the economic crisis of 1997–1998, the standard of living has not improved much for many Korean citizens, as reflected in the rates of poverty, the widening the gap between generations, and the growing gap between large and small enterprises, along with the increasing costs of private education, housing, and medical care.

At the same time, Korea recently experienced an aging of its population similar to that in other developed countries. The number of households with one or two people has started to increase since 2010, and the proportion of one-person households in 2016 reached 27.9%. As illustrated in Table 2.1 the population growth rate is steadily declining from 0.37% in 2018 to a projected negative rate of –0.32% in 2040. In particular, the share of the youth population between 0 and 14 years of age decreased from 34.0% in 1980 to less than 20% in 2005 and 12.9% in 2018. At the same time, the proportion of elderly age 65 and older increased from 3.8% in 1980 to more than 7% in 2000 and to 14.3% in 2018; it is expected to grow to more than 20% in 2025 and beyond.

The old-age dependency ratio increased from 6.1% in 1980 to 21.8% in 2020. The share of old-age dependency ratio in the total dependency ratio increased from 20.0% in 1995 to 55.3% in 2020 and is expected to reach more than 75% in 2040. While the proportion of the economically active population (those in the 16–64 age group) grew from 62.2% in 1980 to 73.4% in 2015, it then declined to 71.7% by 2020 and is expected to decline to 56.4% by 2040.

Changes in the Welfare System: The Limits of Social Policy

The foundation of the welfare system in Korea was established by the Park Chung-hee administration. In the 1960s, the welfare system based on the era of industrialization involved a minimalist approach to social policy, one designed to provide the minimum social welfare provisions required for growth. A fundamental change to this approach has not been made until recently.

The characteristics of the welfare system for 36 years, from 1961 to 1997, were as follows. First, the developmental paradigm focused on the development of the private insurance market. Second, investment in the education system was nationalized and education marketized. Third, oppressive and controlled labor policies were established to produce economic growth. Fourth, patriarchy and restricted women's policies were seen as a means of national development. And fifth, post-regulation policies focused on pollution prevention.

Under the progressive Kim Dae-jung and Roh Moo-hyun administrations from 1998 to 2007, the welfare system expanded, incorporating a mixture of the developmental state, neoliberalism, and the progressive reform of conservative

Table 2.1 Proportion of population and support expenditures (unit: %)

	1980	1985	1990	1995	2000	2005	2010	2015	2018	2020	2025	2030	2035	2040
Population growth rate (%)	1.57	0.00	0.00	1.01	0.84	0.21	0.5	0.53	0.37	0.31	0.2	0.07	-012	-0.32
Youth (0–14) portion (%)	34.0	30.2	25.6	23.4	21.1	19.1	16.1	13.8	12.9	12.6	12.1	11.5	11.3	10.8
Production possibility (15–64) portion (%)	62.2	65.6	69.3	70.7	71.7	71.9	73.1	73.4	72.8	71.7	68.0	64.0	60.0	56.4
Aged (+65) portion (%)	3.8	4.3	5.1	5.9	7.2	9.0	10.8	12.8	14.3	15.6	20.0	24.5	28.7	32.8
Total dependency ratio	00.7	52.5	44.3	41.4	39.5	39.1	36.9	36.3	37.4	39.4	47.1	56.2	66.8	77.4
Youth dependency ratio	54.6	46	36.9	33	29.4	26.6	22	18.8	17.8	17.6	17.7	18	18.9	19.2
J ld aged dependency ratio	6.1	6.5	7.4	8.3	10.1	12.5	14.8	17.5	1-19.6	21.8	29.4	38.2	47.9	58.2
Old aged dependency ratio I total dependency ratio	10.0	12.4	16.7	20.0	25.6	32.0	40.1	48.2	52.4	55.3	62.4	68.0	71.7	75.2
Aging index	11.2	14.2	20	25.2	34.3	46.9	67.3	93	1105	1237	1656	2121	2537	3032

Source: Statistics Korea (KOSIS), major population indicators (sex ratio, population growth rate, demographic structure, support costs, etc.); as cited in Kim Tae-wan et al. (2019), *Vision and strategy of inclusive growth*, p. 14.

welfare policy. This mixture involved the democratization of education; neoliberal labor policies, such as flexibility of the labor market; measures to improve gender equality; and some progress toward preventive environmental policy.

From 2008 to 2017, the characteristics of the welfare system underwent further change in response to the conservative administrations of Lee Myung-bak and Park Gyun-hye, which generally emphasized a neoliberal approach. This approach included policies oriented toward selective eligibility, educational choice and competition, weakening of labor's bargaining power, gender policy aimed at solving low fertility and low economic growth rather than realizing gender equality, and decreasing emphasis on environmental protection policies.

In sum, while the per capita GDP rose dramatically over these decades, the development of social policies for improving the quality of life, such as welfare, education, labor, gender equality, culture, and environment protection, lags behind. This imbalance between economic progress and social well-being is getting worse. Since the decline of export-led growth has weakened, the social safety net remains insufficient even after the 1990s, and the middle class is building a private safety net through private insurance.

Recognizing the importance of social policy, the Kim Dae-jung and Roh Moo-hyun administrations can be credited with a number of achievements such as the establishment of the National Basic Livelihood Security Act, the expansion of childcare services, and the implementation of gender equality policies. However, the minimum social policy strategy is still in play, especially in regard to the labor market, the gender gap, and the relatively low level of public welfare expenditure in light of economic capacity. For example, OECD data in Figure 2.5 show that the ratio of social expenditure (excluding education) to GDP in Korea has increased substantially since 1990, reaching almost 10% of GDP in 2015. Having started much earlier, the European welfare states achieved this level of social expenditure (excluding education) in the 1960s and 1970s. However, as previously noted, by 2018, Korea was the seventh large country to achieve a per capita GNI of more than US$30,000. When educational spending is included, the total Korean social expenditure amounts to 15% of GDP, which is still well below the OECD average of 25.4% including education.

This relatively low level of social expenditure cannot meet the increasing demand to mitigate structural problems such as social polarization, youth unemployment, the gap between large and small enterprises, and, particularly, the rapidly declining birth rate and increasingly aging society. Korea is experiencing a demographic squeeze as the number of deaths is higher than that of births.

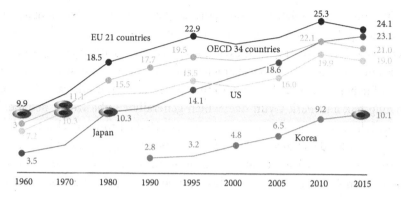

Figure 2.5 Social expenditure ratio to gross domestic product (GDP) (1960–2015): Excluding education expenditures

Source: OECD (2014), "Social Expenditure Update: Social spending is falling in some countries, but many others remain at historically high levels"; OECD (2017), *Social Expenditure Database*; Presidential Directive Policy Planning Committee/Ministry of Relations (2018), as cited in *Moon Jae-in government "inclusive state" vision and strategy*, p. 8.

As such, the Republic of Korea is becoming an "insecure" nation with a low quality of life, even in the age of US$30,000 per capita GNI. For example, according to the OECD's 2017 Better Life Index, of the 38 countries surveyed, the five top-ranking countries were Norway, Denmark, Australia, Sweden, and Canada; Korea's rank slide from 25th in 2014 to 29th out of the 38 countries in 2017. Among the 11 areas of life that were evaluated, Korea placed among the top 10 countries on residential, education, and citizen participation, but 38th on community and 36th on environment. And while Korea's GNI exceeds US$30,000 per person, it was ranked 35th on the balance of work and life, suggesting a need to shift to a policy that can embrace people and pursue happiness in an overcompetitive society. To move in this direction requires a stronger and more inclusive welfare system.

Moon Jae-in Administration's Inclusive Welfare State

The Emergence of Inclusive Growth

The Republic of Korea has solved the problem of absolute poverty through economic growth, which has lifted considerably the general standard of living. However, despite the rapid growth of the economy, the social welfare and social security system was not fully equipped to deal with the 1997 economic crisis. The experience of this crisis taught the government that the development of an economic growth center alone cannot guarantee the well-being of the people and can result in increasing inequality. In spite of its high economic growth, Korea experienced so-called Bhagwati-named *immiserizing growth*, in which initial increases in social welfare due to economic growth are offset by adverse changes in international demand.

The problems of distribution caused by low growth and unemployment call for a transition from a traditional growth-oriented economic development model to a new growth model that mitigates inequality and facilitates more widespread distribution. As an alternative, international organizations have come up with the concept of *inclusive growth*. The International Monetary Fund (IMF) (2007) defined inclusive growth as the maximal distribution of a broad share of the benefits and opportunities of economic growth. The World Bank (2009) sees it as growth that engages in distribution. The European Union (2010) recommends growth that promotes social integration and regional integration by equally distributing life opportunities to EU members at all levels and in all regions through employment expansion, capacity building, job training, social security, and poverty eradication. The OECD (2014) also emphasized the idea of a growth process that creates opportunities for all income brackets and equally distributes the fruits of prosperity to all members.

While there is no universally accepted definition, the narrow definition of inclusive growth usually focuses on its distributional aspect, in which growth can be considered inclusive if it helps to improve equality. More broadly, however, growth is considered inclusive if it is high, sustained, and extensive across sectors in per capita terms while it also (1) reduces poverty (includes the poor in the group with socially acceptable levels of income), (2) reduces inequality (includes the poor in prosperity sharing), (3) creates jobs (includes people in the productive part of society), (4) reduces the gender gap (includes both women and men in the economy), (5) improves governance (includes everyone in the wealth distribution, not just a few at the top), and (6) responds to climate change (includes future generations in prosperity sharing). Clearly, a common thread through these inputs is that they seek to promote inclusion (Loungani, 2017; Loungani and Ostry, 2017).

Inclusive growth policy encompasses issues that may otherwise seem dispersed. It highlights the interconnections and complementarities between several policy areas that need to foster inclusive growth. Therefore, the goals of an inclusive growth policy involve income distribution that reduces poverty and inequality; an emphasis on education as investment in human capital; an emphasis on economic innovation by creating technology for increasing value and productivity; a prohibition on discrimination, the creation of jobs, and wide participation in labor markets; and an emphasis on a progressive tax system for the expansion of social security. But what should not be overlooked here is that "inclusive" implies fairness, closeness, and mutual respect.

Understanding of Inclusive Welfare

Accepting the inclusive growth policy implied by the OECD, Moon Jae-in emphasized that inclusive growth includes income-led growth, innovation growth, and a fair economy. Here, "inclusive growth" refers to "growth that can evenly distribute the share of growth without excluding any people for the purpose of national development," which is one of the growth discourses.

Income-led growth is a consumer-centered growth model for workers and ordinary citizens. *Innovation growth* is a supplier-centered growth model for companies and service organizations and is a discourse on how the economy will grow in the future. In contrast, the *fair economy* is a necessary factor for establishing economic democratization. The fair economy involves economic policies that promote the environment for growth through sound market competition while improving the equitable allocation of the market's benefits. The fair economy is a prerequisite for inclusive growth.

On the other hand, *inclusive welfare* is defined as "welfare for individuals to make their daily lives happier by eliminating the gaps in the welfare system and strengthening the protection against social risks." Inclusive welfare entails promoting welfare policies that support equal opportunity, solving labor market discrimination problems, building human and social capital through education, creating balanced jobs in the public and private sectors, and establishing a progressive tax system for social security expansion (see Cho Heung-Seek, 2018).

In this sense, inclusive welfare is a concept closely linked to inclusive growth; that is, inclusive welfare is achieved through inclusive growth at the same time that inclusive welfare can further stimulate inclusive growth. The golden quadrangle model of inclusive growth and inclusive welfare is illustrated in Figure 2.6.

The concept of the IIS sets education as a new main goal, one which involves an investment in human capital that builds competence and empowerment. In addition, it emphasizes the need for social cohesion for sustainable growth and the development of the nation. Moon Jae-in's vision is that of an "innovative inclusive country that lives well together".

Challenges of Social Welfare Policy in Korea

The welfare system and social welfare policy are bound to change and are affected by changes in the capitalist economic and political system. However, it is not easy to predict the future of the Korean welfare system, which was born 60 years ago. The social insurance schemes, such as industrial accidents insurance, health insurance, national pension, and employment insurance, were introduced in the 1960s and expanded in the latter half of the 1980s. After the financial crisis in 1997, a basic livelihood security system was created. Also, various types of social services, such as free childcare, long-term care insurance, and vouchers, were introduced in response to the problems of low fertility and the need for social investment in an aging society. Cash benefit schemes, such as the basic old-age pension and the disability pension, are intertwined. However, overall, the Korean welfare system is fragmentary, with weak linkages between institutions, gaps in coverage, and low benefits. In other words, although Korea has succeeded in industrialization and democratization after World War II, it has yet to fully develop its social welfare policy. Recognizing this issue, the Moon Jae-in administration clearly defined the goal of establishing an inclusive welfare state in Korea, one designed to improve the quality of life, mitigate the problem in inequality, prepare for future technological innovations, and formulate policies for integration between generations.

The question remains how to realize these objectives. The Moon Jae-in administration's efforts to promote income growth were stymied by incompatible policies such as a minimum wage increase, shortening of working hours, and a transition of regular workers to the irregular economy. In addition, innovation growth was restrained due to limited support for policies promoting small to medium enterprises and regulatory reforms. Also, measures to restructure the governance of large corporations failed to properly implement the fair economy.

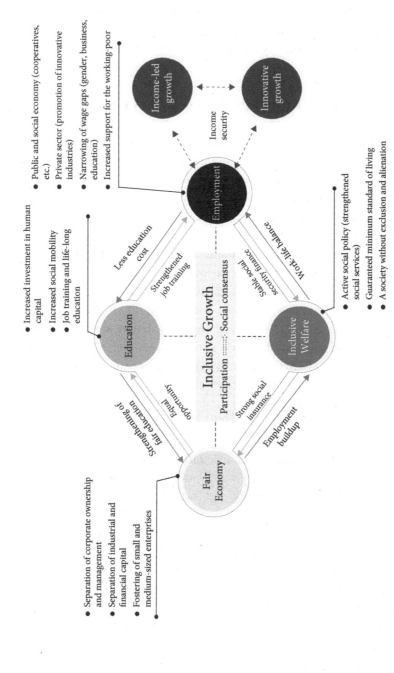

Figure 2.6 Golden rectangle model of inclusive growth and inclusive welfare.

To advance the objectives of the inclusive welfare state it is necessary to identify policy measures that are appropriate to the target and that strengthen the coordination between inclusive growth and welfare policies that support employment stability and economic dynamism. Several approaches for promoting the inclusive welfare state follow.

First, there is a need to broaden the discourse of inclusive welfare policy. For example, the objectives of income-driven growth should be extended beyond the self-employed and the working poor to encompass workers at all stages of the life cycle, particularly youth and the aged.

Second, it is important to establish the basis of the fair economy as one built on a progressive tax policy and social safety net for income-led growth.

Third, in order to create balanced jobs within the public and private sectors and to ensure a basic quality of life for low-income people such as the poor elderly, social welfare provisions for those in the lower-income classes should be more substantial than for those in the middle class.

Fourth, the household spending burden of medical care and gaps in health insurance, particularly in rural areas, should be addressed as quickly as possible. In addition, it is necessary to reduce the burden of educational expenses for households by promoting high school compulsory education and expanding scholarship for college students.

Fifth, the provision of unemployment benefits and the current emergency welfare support system should be integrated.

Sixth, it is necessary to strengthen the social service guarantee that prevents various social problems by supporting individuals and families who cannot meet their fundamental needs for an acceptable standard of health and well-being. The expansion of services will generate increasing public employment in this sector.

Finally, additional financial resources are necessary to realize the goals of the inclusive welfare state. These resources can be obtained through progressive tax reforms such as adjusting the corporate tax and the housing tax along with a mid- to long-term increase in the current value-added tax (VAT) from 10% (618 billion won in 2016, National Statistical Yearbook) to 15% during the mid term and 20% over the long term.

Conclusion

Building the inclusive welfare state is a work in progress, one that can be advanced through the various measures identified above, such as the expansion of public employment, promotion of education, institutionalization of cash allowance, and expansion of social services. Ultimately, however, it is imperative to build a structure in which the competitiveness of Korean industry depends on a wide range of skilled labor for upgrading the Korean industrial structure. In other words, as Professor Yoon Hong-sik (2018) pointed out, raising wages of workers in a society where productivity depends on the skill of those workers and universally responding to the social risks faced by these workers is not only good for workers but is also good for capital. It is important for the government to reform the industrial structure and increase consumption by easing income inequality and poverty.

References

Bank of Korea. (n.d.). Bank of Korea economic statistics system, each year. https://www.bok.or.kr/eng/main/main.do

Cho, H. S. (2018). Research on growth and inclusive growth. Research brief, no. 1. National Research Council for Economics, Humanities and Social Sciences.

European Union. (2010). Europe in figures—Eurostat yearbook 2010.

International Monetary Fund (IMF). (2017). Fostering inclusive growth. Staff Note for the discussion at the Meeting of G20. https://www.imf.org/external/np/g20/pdf/2017/062617.pdf

Kim, T. W. (2018). Presidential Directive Policy Planning Committee/Ministry of Relations. Moon Jae in government "inclusive state" vision and strategy.

Korea Institute for Health and Social Affairs. (2017). Annual report on poverty in 2017. https://www.kihasa.re.kr/en

Loungani, P. (2017). Inclusive growth and the IMF. iMFdirect. The IMF Blog. https://blog-imfdirect.imf.org/2017/01/24/inclusive-growth-and-the-imf

Loungani, P., and Ostry, J. (2017). The IMF's work on inequality: Bridging research and reality. The IMF Blog. https://blog-imfdirect.imf.org/2017/02/22/the-imfs-work-oninequality-bridging-research-and-reality/

National Economic Advisory Council. (2005). Changes in Korean economic development model and new prospects.

National Research Council for Economics, Humanities and Social Sciences. (2018). *Innovative inclusive state that live together well.* National Center for Research Strategies.

National Statistical Office (KOSIS). (n.d.). e-country index, each year. ·

National Statistical Office (KOSIS). (n.d.). KOSIS, each year.

Organisation for Economic Cooperation and Development (OECD). (2017a). How's life? 2017 Measuring well-being. https://www.oecd-ilibrary.org/economics/how-s-life-2017_how_life-2017-en

Organisation for Economic Cooperation and Development (OECD). (2017b). Social expenditure database. https://www.oecd.org/social/expenditure.htm

Organisation for Economic Cooperation and Development (OECD). (2014). Social expenditure update: Social spending is falling in some countries, but in many others, it remains at historically high levels.

Organisation for Economic Cooperation and Development (OECD). (2015). Online education database (educational finance indicators). https://www.oecd.org/education/database.htm

Statistics Korea. (2015). Korean Statistical Information Service (KOSIS).

Sung Kyung-ryung. (2018). The three great growth models and innovative inclusive states. Embedded Social Policy Forum, Policy Planning Committee.

World Bank. (2009). World Development Report 2009: Reshaping Economic Geography.

Yoon Hong-sik. (2018). Income-driven growth and legacy of the Korean welfare system. *Korean Social Policy, 25*(2), 243–280.

3

Welfarenomics

Inclusive Capitalism

Sang-Mok Suh

The Han River Miracle, characterized by high growth and low inequality, has come to a halt in recent times. Low growth, rising inequality, and growing social discontent have become the new characteristics of Korean capitalism. To remedy the situation Korea has to adopt a new development paradigm, viz. *welfarenomics*, which takes a more balanced view toward economic growth and social equity. While the government took a leading role in implementing the so-called *Park Chung-hee paradigm*, the new paradigm of welfarenomics requires close cooperation among the government, business sector, and civil society.[1]

Globally, capitalism has often faced crises due to random external shocks as well as internal shortcomings, but it has evolved into a better shape through its efforts for improvement. Capitalism 1.0, which began in the late 17th century, marked a historical turning point in terms of economic growth but resulted in urban poverty and the Great Depression in 1929. Capitalism 2.0, which began with the New Deal Program, led to the government assuming a more active role in social welfare. Capitalism 3.0, which began in the early 1980s, focused on the rationalization of expanded welfare programs. Capitalism 4.0, which got started in the aftermath of the 2008 financial crisis, is making new efforts to strike a balance between economic growth and social welfare. Welfarenomics, as presented in this chapter, can be a guiding paradigm in this age of Capitalism 4.0.

Welfarenomics is based on the perception that economy and welfare are the opposite sides of the same coin. It is an attempt to establish a new paradigm of capitalism and the welfare state by modifying the existing neoliberal market economy model to develop an inclusive capitalistic system that boosts "welfare economy" through "win-win capitalism" on the one hand,

Sang-Mok Suh, *Welfarenomics* In: *The Korean Welfare State*. Edited by: Kyungbae Chung and Neil Gilbert, Oxford University Press. © Oxford University Press 2024. DOI: 10.1093/oso/9780197644928.003.0004 and realizes "economic welfare: by enhancing the sustainability of the existing Western welfare state model on the other.

Since the French Revolution the left tends to support the welfare state and government intervention to achieve greater equity, while the right emphasizes economic efficiency and smaller government. Korea also has a long history of severe conflict between the left and the right. Since the Korean Peninsula is now divided into the communist regime in the North and the free democratic republic in the South, it is an urgent issue to reach a consensus among the differing sociopolitical groups in the South. Welfarenomics, which strikes a balance between economic growth and social justice, can become a new development paradigm on which the left and the right can agree.

Capitalism Under Serious Challenge in Korea

At the center of a typhoon, waves from different directions gather together and create triangular pyramid-shaped waves. Coming from various directions, these waves make it difficult for a vessel to set sailing targets. This is the current situation of Korean capitalism.[2]

Korea's economic growth rate is dropping at a rapid rate. The "Miracle of the Han River," which began in the early 1960s, brought about a 10% annual growth rate, but the growth rate started to decline from the late 1980s and now barely reaches 2–3% or less per year. In addition, as the job creation effect of Korea's export industries continues to fall, job shortages and youth unemployment are emerging as major social issues in the country.

Although the myth of Korea's economic development can be summed up as maintaining relatively good income distribution with high economic growth, recent years have witnessed worrying trends on account of worsening income distribution and intensifying polarization amid economic slowdown. Particularly since the 1997 foreign currency crisis, polarization in the labor market has become prominent, as shown by the sharp increase in the number of irregular workers, and all indicators of the income distribution level, including the Gini ratio and relative poverty rate, are getting worse.

The country's level of social stress is also on the rise. It turns out that 95% of Koreans think that the gap between rich and poor in Korea is widening over time; only 29% of the people think everyone is given equal opportunity in Korea (Hankook Research, 2010). As a result, the percentage of "happy people" is the lowest among the countries of the Organisation for Economic

Cooperation and Development (OECD), and Korea has the world's highest suicide rate. This is where Korea stands now. This is how a report by the McKinsey Global Institute (2013) describes the recent economic situation in Korea:

> It is increasingly apparent that the export-oriented growth formula that helped the large Korean conglomerates drive economic development and raise incomes is running out of steam. South Korea needs a new growth model that restores the financial health of middle-income families, raises consumption, and addresses social and structural problems that threaten the nation's long-term prospects. (McKinsey Global Institute, 2013)

Increasing social stress is evident in the negative perception most Koreans have of large conglomerates, *chaebol*. Issues of so-called economic democratization[3] surfaced during the 2013 and 2017 presidential elections, and various regulatory measures adopted in recent years against *chaebol* show how the political circle reflected public sentiment in the policymaking process. This is in line with what Porter and Kramer (2011) recently argued, asking for a new management paradigm as the capitalist system is challenged.

> The capitalistic system is under siege. In recent years, business increasingly has been viewed as a major cause of social, environmental, and economic problems. Companies are widely perceived to be prospering at the expense of the broader community. . . . This diminished trust in business leads political leaders to set policies that undermine competitiveness and sap economic growth. Business is caught in a vicious circle. However, if the purpose of corporate activities is to be redefined around the concept of creating shared value, a new wave of innovation and growth will arise to rejuvenate capitalism in crisis. (Porter and Kramer, 2011)

The so-called *Park Chung-hee Paradigm*, the basis of the "Miracle of the Han River," was made possible through skillful balancing of market liberalism and government intervention. However, rapid political democratization since 1987 shook the root of the Park Chung-hee Paradigm. As the authoritarian political system collapsed, industrial peace could no longer be sustained by governmental intervention. The emergence of strong labor unions and frequent labor disputes undermined Korea's global competitiveness, which eventually led to the foreign exchange crisis in 1997.

Economic reform policies prescribed by the International Monetary Fund (IMF) contributed greatly to curbing directed bank lending practices and improving the financial structure of big conglomerates and financial institutions in Korea but caused side effects such as low growth and economic polarization as well.

The role of the government is gradually diminishing as neoliberal policy trends are widely accepted across economic sectors. Reduced government functions and the growing influence of unions and social interest groups have given rise to polarized labor markets and deteriorating wage differentials. Simultaneously, the profitability-oriented management practices of conglomerates and financial institutions have resulted in sluggish investment in facilities and low economic growth. Stagnant construction activities are also contributing to further deterioration of domestic demand and polarization. As a result, Korean capitalism has been caught in a vicious circle of low growth and polarization.

Just as the country adopted a new paradigm that blended private business activities in the export sector with government interventionist policies through a 5-year development plan to escape the vicious cycle of low growth and poverty in the early 1960s, it is now time for Korea to seek a new paradigm of governance, one that will break through the pyramidal wave of low growth, polarization, and social stress.

Evolution of Capitalism and the Welfare State

Western capitalism has often faced crises due to random external shocks as well as internal shortcomings, but it has evolved into a better shape through its efforts at improvement. Kaletsky (2010) summarized the evolutionary process in terms of the following four stages: Capitalism 1.0, which began with the First Industrial Revolution in the late 18th century in the spirit of Adam Smith's classical liberalism, marked a historical turning point in terms of economic growth and industrial structure but resulted in urban poverty and the Great Depression in 1929. Capitalism 2.0, which began with the New Deal Program in the spirit of Keynesian economics, led to the government assuming a more active role, particularly in the field of social welfare. Capitalism 3.0, which began in the early 1980s in the spirit of neoliberal economics, reduced the size and rationalized the contents of welfare programs. Capitalism 4.0, which started in the aftermath of the 2008 financial crisis, is

Table 3.1 Evolution of Western capitalism

Stage	Period	Basic thought	Main outcome	Problem
Capitalism 1.0	Late 1800s–1929	Classical liberalism	Industrial Revolution	Urban poverty and depression
Capitalism 2.0	1930–late 1970s	Keynesian economics	Full-fledged welfare state	Government inefficiency
Capitalism 3.0	1980–2008	Neoliberalism	IT revolution and globalization	Financial crisis and growing inequality
Capitalism 4.0	After 2009	Pragmatism?	4th Industrial Revolution	Growing inequality and inhumanity?

Source: Kaletsky (2010).

making efforts to strike a balance between economic growth and social welfare (Table 3.1).[4]

> Democratic capitalism is a system built for survival. It has adapted successfully to shocks of every kind, to upheavals in technology and economics, to political revolutions and world wars. Capitalism has been able to do this because, unlike communism or socialism or feudalism, it has an inner dynamic akin to a living thing. It can adapt and refine itself in response to the changing environment. And it will evolve into a new species of the same capitalist genus if that is what it takes to survive. (Kaletsky, 2010)

Historically the social welfare sector has played the role of social innovator by solving social problems that arose during the progression of the Industrial Revolution. In the late 19th century, many private initiatives such as poverty studies, charity organizations, and community center movement started in the United Kingdom. Furthermore, the Bismarck government initiated the social insurance system in Germany, which disseminated to other parts of Europe quickly. In 1942, the UK's Churchill government published the Beveridge Report, which was the first comprehensive national strategy on social welfare that became the role model of the welfare state for other European counties. When the welfare state came under criticism in the 1990s, the UK's Blair government came up with "the Third Way" approach. With the rapid progress of technology since the 1990s, the wage differential has widened, resulting in a worsening of income distribution (Table 3.2).

Table 3.2   Evolution of the Western welfare state

Stage	Period	Basic thought	Main outcome	Problem
Before welfare state	Before 1880s	Utilitarianism	'Poor Law' to support the poor	Inhumane treatment of the poor
Birth of welfare state	1880–1945	New liberalism, Fabian socialism	Settlement movement, social insurance	Depression and mass poverty
Growth of welfare state	1945–1980	Beveridge Report	Full-fledged welfare state	Inefficiency of welfare programs
Restructuring welfare state	After 1980	The Third Way	Workfare, rationalization	Growing inequality

Source: Sang-mok Suh.

Further technological breakthroughs in the fields of artificial intelligence and genetic engineering have raised new concerns about the inhumane use of these technologies.

While the concept of capitalism as well as the welfare state have evolved over two centuries in Western developed countries, these have a relatively short history in Korea. The modern capitalism of Korea started with independence in 1945. However, despite its short history, the process of capitalistic development in Korea has been very dynamic and can be summarized in the following four stages: Capitalism 1.0, during the period of 1945–1960, pursued free democracy in politics and market principles in economic management but could not achieve its intended objectives due to the immature state of Korean society at the time. Capitalism 2.0, during 1961–1987, achieved remarkable progress in economic development by adopting an export-led development strategy, but political development was hampered under the military government. Capitalism 3.0, during 1988–2008, produced remarkable outcomes such as IT-led economic progress, enhanced international status through membership in the OECD and G20, and full democratization. Capitalism 4.0, which is under way since 2009, adopted an inclusive development strategy focusing on sustainability in economy, business management, and social welfare (Table 3.3).

The first characteristics of Korean capitalism is its dramatic achievement in a relatively short period of time. Korea has become the only country in the

Table 3.3 Evolution of Korean capitalism

Stage	Period	Basic thought	Main outcome	Problem
Capitalism 1.0: Weak gov't, weak economy	1945–1960	Liberalism, inward-looking economic policies	Institution-building for democracy and market economy	Vicious circle of low growth and poverty
Capitalism 2.0: Strong gov't, strong economy	1961–1987	Gov't-led strategy, outward-looking economic policies	Han River Miracle	Political authoritarianism
Capitalism 3.0: Democratic gov't	1988–2008	Democracy, neo-liberalism	IT-led economic growth, membership of OECD and G20	Growing inequality and social discontent
Capitalism 4.0: Sustainable capitalism	After 2009	Inclusive development	Sustainability in economy, business management and social welfare	Challenges from North Korea?

Source: Sang-mok Suh.

world, which achieved a status change from a developing country to a developed country as well as from an aid-receiving country to an aid-giving country after the Second World War. The second characteristics of Korean capitalism is its ability to develop its own recipe for economic development, namely, the Park Chung-hee paradigm combining the dynamics of private entrepreneurship and the military efficiency of economic planning. (Sang-mok Suh, 2013)

The level of social welfare in Korea has improved markedly, in parallel with rapid economic growth despite the fact that the government policy priority has been on economic development until very recently. Social welfare policies before 1960 centered around welfare institutions, particularly orphanages. Since 1961, the Korean government started to build a modern social welfare system comprised of pensions, health insurance, and public assistance programs. With the introduction of a long-term care system for the elderly in 2008, Korea had completed the process of constructing a modern social security system. Since 2009, Korean welfare policies have focused on improving the efficiency of the social welfare system, drawing lessons from other developed countries' experiences (Table 3.4).

Table 3.4   Evolution of the Korean welfare state

Stage	Period	Basic thought	Main outcome	Problem
Before welfare state	1945–1960	Minimum support for the poor	Welfare institutions such as orphanages	Dependent on foreign relief programs
Birth of welfare state	1961–1987	Economic growth first strategy	Gradual introduction of social security system	Unmet demands for social welfare
Growth of welfare state	1988–2010	Social development emphasized	Completion of the modern social security system	Growing inequality, low fertility
Strengthening welfare state	After 2010	Inclusive development, social solidarity	Improved Korean Model of welfare state	Crisis in social welfare finance?

Source: Sang-mok Suh.

There is a saying, "new wine must be put into new wineskins." In history, whenever capitalism faced crisis and solutions were needed, new theories and philosophies emerged to support the reinvention process. The First Industrial Revolution, which began in the late 18th century, was based on the classical liberal market economy principles presented by Adam Smith. Keynesian economics became the theoretical basis for expanding the role of government and the construction of the welfare state since the Great Depression of 1929. The neoliberal theories of Hayek and Friedman have become the foundation for welfare state reforms since the 1980s.

Therefore, in order to capture the two rabbits of economic vitality enhancement and alleviation of polarization which have emerged as new challenges for Korea and the world following the 2008 financial crisis, an overarching framework of integrated thinking encompassing economy and welfare is needed. We call it "welfarenomics," a term coined to refer to the integration of welfare and economics (Sang-mok Suh, 2013).

Welfarenomics is based on the perception that economy and welfare are the opposite sides of the same coin and that the 21st century is an era where new academic fields are created via interdisciplinary convergence. Welfarenomics is also an example of applying to economy and welfare the concept of "cooperative competition" or "co-opetition," which means competition and cooperation can be harmonized to create new synergies (Figure 3.1).

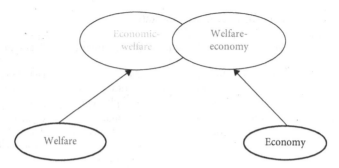

Figure 3.1 The concept of welfarenomics.

Co-opetition offers a theory of value. It's about creating value and capturing value. There's a fundamental duality here: whereas creating value is an inherently cooperative process, capturing value is inherently competitive.

Basically, welfarenomics is an attempt to establish a new development paradigm by modifying the existing neoliberal market economy model to develop an inclusive capitalist system that boosts welfare economy through win-win capitalism, on the one hand, and realizes economic welfare by enhancing the sustainability of the existing Western welfare state model on the other.

Welfare economy starts with strengthening the government's ability to formulate national strategies and can be achieved by enhancing the social values of businesses and helping civil society function better so that it creates an ecosystem of symbiotic development. In addition, economic welfare can take place by providing customized employment programs to the vulnerable based on the recognition that jobs are the best welfare, promoting social innovation in the process of implementing various social welfare policies, and establishing the tradition of welfare management through maximizing the social impact of welfare programs.

The concept of welfarenomics and policy proposals for its implementation would not only help Korea escape from the vicious circle of low growth and polarization, but also lead the argument between the right and the left over economic and welfare policies toward a more productive direction (Figure 3.2).

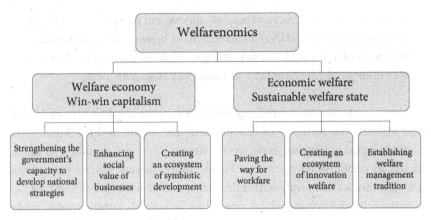

Figure 3.2 The structure of welfarenomics.

Sustainable (Creative) Welfare State

To turn Korea into a sustainable welfare state, the focus of discussion should be on how to implement the concepts of *workfare*, innovative welfare and welfare management. Unlike the old way of thinking that welfare is to extract more tax from the rich and distribute revenue to the poor, the primary goal of welfarenomics is to present the blueprint for a sustainable welfare state based on the belief that welfare contributes to economic growth by creating jobs for the vulnerable sectors of society. It is recognized that the vigorous activities of social entrepreneurs drive social innovation and set in motion a creative and sustainable new growth engine, generating social impact most effectively with various management techniques.

In light of the difficulties advanced economies have faced both internally and externally since the 1980s, the conventional Western welfare state model has already undergone a major revision. The United Kingdom has adopted the Third Way and a policy line of "welfare to work(workfare)" from the late-1990s; other developed countries have been making every effort to develop policies for workfare. Customized job programs for the underprivileged are being implemented, and many developed countries are actively working on setting up a new welfare-employment delivery system that can provide administrative supports for the programs.

I believe social democracy can not only survive, but prosper, on an ideological as well as a practical level. It can only do so, however, if social democrats
are prepared to revise their pre-existing views more thoroughly than most
have done so far. They need to find a third way. (Giddens, 1994)

However, in Korea, related departments such as the Ministry of Health
and Welfare, the Ministry of Employment and Labor, and the Ministry of
Gender Equality have separate service delivery systems, resulting in ineffi-
ciency in public welfare services. Furthermore, private welfare institutions
are reluctant to cooperate with each other, and services are not shared between public and private institutions either. To solve this problem at its roots,
a nationwide welfare-employment delivery system should be set in place.

As social innovation has become important, the role of social entrepreneurs
as innovators has been emphasized, and it has become imperative to foster
and develop the social finance market to support their activities. In the United
Kingdom, a special committee for nurturing the social finance market was established through concerted efforts by the government and the private sector
during 2000–2010. In the United States, private sector–led social venture capital activities have gained significant momentum. In recent years, the *social impact bond* (SIB) system has also been promoted in the United Kingdom, United
States, New Zealand, and Korea to enhance the social impact of public projects
and boost the social finance market at the same time.

Although Korea's social finance sector is at an early stage, it seems necessary for the government to pay more attention to and actively engage in
social finance market development, following the example set by the United
Kingdom in order to realize a sustainable welfare state. Among others, a
"Social Finance Development Council" consisting of experts and a specialized entity to promote research and exchanges in the field of social finance
should be established. Furthermore, the introduction and expansion of an
SIB system should be positively reviewed for the optimal social impact of
social welfare programs and the development of the social finance market.

There have also been attempts to apply business management principles to the field of social welfare. Efforts are under way to measure and
maximize the social impact of social welfare programs and other public
projects, and new public management theories are emerging to back such
efforts. Service purchase contract systems have become widespread, and
today's social welfare projects incorporate management evaluation systems
supported by balanced scorecards consisting of performance objectives in

several areas including finance, customer management, internal management, and growth potential.

An attempt has also been made to apply the concept of management efficiency to the field of social welfare in Korea, which, however, remains at its early stage. A management evaluation system for social welfare institutions has been introduced since 1998, and the e-voucher system was also put in place in 2007, to induce the social welfare sector to operate competitively. Under the Act on Social Security, revised in 2013, the government is required to come up with Master Plans for Social Security. The Korean Academic Society of Welfare Management was inaugurated in 2011 and has been leading research activities in this field. Nevertheless, apart from populist promises made during political campaigns to attract voters in the short term, governments should take the lead in providing a clear picture for a sustainable and creative welfare state and actively work toward shaping a national consensus on it.

Inclusive (Warm) Capitalism

There is a growing opinion that neoliberalism should be evolved to a higher level because neoliberal philosophy, the theoretical basis for reforming the ailing Western welfare state, has caused side effects such as polarization and global financial crises. Korea succeeded in overcoming the 1997 foreign exchange crisis quickly by earnestly driving IMF-directed neoliberal reforms across its financial and corporate sectors, but its polarization level has deteriorated, as in other OECD member countries.

The first prerequisite for *inclusive capitalism* is that the government changes the neoliberal position of minimizing its role as much as possible. Furthermore, the government's function to formulate strategies and put them into practice needs to be strengthened to resolve current issues such as unemployment and polarization. In particular, Korea enjoyed great success in establishing and implementing similar strategies during the Miracle of the Han River. Therefore, it seems very natural to redefine the role of government in implementing an approach that balances a liberal market economy and a government-led market economy (Giddens, 1994). In order to help the government function better in terms of strategy formulation in the economic sector, the Korea Development Institute (KDI) may serve as the secretariat of the National Economic Advisory Council, the body designated by the Korean constitution.

The second requirement of inclusive capitalism is that civil society plays a leading role in creating an ecosystem of symbiotic development. Until now, civic organizations in Korea have focused their activities on political agendas from the perspectives of rigid ideology. However, as the issue of democratization is more or less settled in Korea and communism is disappearing globally, civic organizations should lead Korean society to a path of symbiotic development through dialogue and cooperation rather than conflict and discord. To this end, educational activities should be organized systematically to cultivate a sound civic culture in Korea, the operation of civic organizations should be made more democratic and transparent, and active supports for civil society should be provided at the governmental and business levels.

The third and most important requirement is to help businesses direct their economic activities to create more social value. In Korea, companies have become better aware of their corporate social responsibility (CSR), but they need to adopt more concrete measures to fulfill their corporate social responsibility while increasing their economic value as well. The concept of CSR, first introduced by Howard Bowen in 1953, has become a standard paradigm in business management. Recently, the concept of CSR has evolved into the concept of *creating shared value* (CSV) by Porter and Kramer (2011) and is already being put into practice by many global companies. If Korean companies learn from these experiences and develop a new business model fit for them, their social value will be raised.

> In the operation of our economic system, the businessman occupies a position of great influence and leadership. Are businessmen obligated to consider social consequences when making their decisions? If so, do they have social responsibilities that transcend obligations to owners or stockholders? The answer to both these questions is clearly yes. (Bowen, 1953/2013)

Milton Friedman (1970), a leading theorist of neoliberalism, argues that "the social responsibility of a business is to increase its profits." This can be regarded as the perspective of "shareholder capitalism," in which businesses work for the interests of shareholders only, but this view is gradually changing even in the United States with its strong liberal tradition.

Unlike shareholder capitalism, *stakeholder theory* examines the role of a company from a broader perspective. According to this theory, the positions of indirect stakeholders such as the community and the country at large should be taken into account at the core of business management, not to mention the interests of direct stakeholders such as investors, workers, and parts suppliers. And this is a better business strategy from the medium- and long-term perspectives. Stakeholder Theory was first introduced by the Stanford Research Institute (SRI) in 1963, and the theory became widely known after Edward Freeman (1984) published a book about the findings of this research.

> The new narrative about business must also be one of "business in society."
> It needs to place a concern with ethics, responsibility, and sustainability on
> a par with profits. All are important and none can be ignored. More than
> ever, we need a story about "responsible capitalism." (Freeman, 1984)

As a business ecosystem theory, James Moore (1996) applied to industries the concept of *co-evolution*, suggesting that "a variety of creatures coexist, competing with one another as predators become extinct if their prey disappears in the food chain of the natural ecosystem." Moore divides the evolution of the business ecosystem into four phases—creation, expansion, leadership, and self-reproduction—and emphasizes that every phase needs simultaneous competition and cooperation. Therefore, if a company achieves harmony of competition and cooperation in the process of creating a new ecosystem, it will succeed; if not, it is bound to fail.

Since Korea has a long tradition of a government-led economy, the government's business policies are still largely interventional. The government provided extensive support in the areas of taxation and finance to foster export industries in the 1960s, and it facilitated the heavy chemical industry by selecting "promising" industries and giving them various benefits in the 1970s. In the process, as concentration of economic power deepened, the government started to regulate directly bank credits to conglomerates, and it has been implementing various taxation and credit policies to protect small and medium-sized enterprises (SMEs) since the 1980s. As polarization has worsened in recent years, regulations on conglomerates have been stepped up for the sake of "economic democratization," while SMEs are protected more than ever for the purpose of promoting "inclusive growth."

In the current era of globalization, Korea's big firms compete fiercely in the global arena, and countries around the world are doing their best to attract companies' investments. At this point, therefore, the industrial policy of the Korean government should be changed: these policies need to be directed at creating a new business ecosystem where companies can enhance their competitive edge through competition and cooperation, rather than regulating or artificially protecting business operations.

The new business ecosystem should pursue co-evolution, by which companies cooperate while competing freely, and management strategies to create shared value will be the key agenda in this ecosystem. Co-evolution and shared value creation is not a zero-sum game but a plus-sum game, which is similar to the concept of "co-opetition," where competition and co-operation coexist to create a robust and dynamic ecosystem that can survive fierce global competition.

To make this new business ecosystem happen, firms must begin to shift their business management practices before government action. If large corporations actively pursue CSV as their basic management strategy beyond CSR, people are bound to see them from a different viewpoint than they do now.

In particular, if the Federation of Korean Industries and the Korean Chamber of Commerce and Industry, which represent the private business sector in Korea, play a leading role in promoting CSR activities and boosting new CSV initiatives, it will help to change public sentiment about business and help companies forge new partnerships with the government, nongovernmental organizations (NGOs), and the community at large. Furthermore, the Korea National Council on Social Welfare, which plays the role of a bridge between the private sector and the government in the field of social welfare, can become an intermediary and facilitator to connect CSR activities to social welfare fields.

While companies strive to improve their social reputation by means of business operations based on a long-term and convergent perspective, as mentioned above, the government should change its existing anti-market and regulatory business policy to a market-friendly and plus-sum approach.

Beyond Left and Right

In Western developed countries, the distinction between the left and the right originated with the French Revolution. After the Revolution, French politics was divided into two groups: Jacobins, which advocated radical political reforms, sat on the left side of the Speaker's podium, while Girondins, which adopted relatively moderate political positions, sat on the right side. Since then, the left is referred to as a group of people who pursue radical

social reforms and the right as a group of people that tends to support relatively moderate social reforms.

In modern days, the left tends to support the welfare state and government intervention to achieve greater equity, while the right emphasizes economic efficiency and smaller government. *Beyond Left and Right* is a book by
Anthony Giddens (1994), a British leftist sociologist, in which he proposed
a new economic paradigm called "the Third Way" (Giddens, 1998) which
interweaves the right-wing principle of market competition in a globalized
world with leftist ideals of social solidarity and justice. For Giddens, the
Third Way is called the *social investment state*.

Korea has a long history of party politics from the beginning of the Yi
Dynasty in the 15th century, although it is not possible to divide Korean political parties during the Yi Dynasty in terms of the right and the left because
political factions at that time were based on personal connections rather than
political philosophies. After the fall of Yi Dynasty in 1910, Korean politics
were divided into two groups, a rightist group that took inspiration from
the independence movement in the United State and China and espoused
a Western philosophy of free market and democracy, and a leftist group that
led the independence movement in Manchuria and Korea under the influence of communism.

Right after independence in 1945, there was a severe conflict between
these two groups in the process of competing for political hegemony in the
new nation. Kim Il-sung formed a communist government in the North
with the help of the Soviet Union, while the right-wing political group led
by Rhee Syngman established a free democratic government in the South in
1948, with the help of the United States. Due to the totalitarian nature of the
North Korean government, only the extreme left can survive in the North,
while South Korean politics is divided into parties that pursue either rightist
or leftist views. At present, there are two criteria for separating the right from
the left in South Korea, namely their stance on communism and their degree of support for social welfare. The rightist camp consists of the Old Right,
who puts the highest priority on anti-communism, and the New Right, who
prefers market mechanism to guide the economy over government intervention. The leftist camp consists of the Old Left with an amicable attitude toward the North Korea communist regime and the New Left, longing for a
European-style welfare state.

Since democratization in 1987, the balance between the right and the
left was maintained until 2017. However, the impeachment of President

Park Geun-hye and a subsequent landslide victory by Moon Jae-in the 2017 presidential election broke the delicate political balance in favor of the left. As a result, the Moon Jae-in government maintained a strong leftist stance not only in economic policies and social welfare policies but also in foreign policies and inter-Korean policies. However, Yoon Suh-yeal from the concervative party won the 2022 presidential election. Thus, it is expected that most of leftist policies under the previous government will be abandoned in the Yoon Suk-yeol government. Thus conflicts between the right and left on the contents of government policies are likely to get intensified in the coming years.

Considering the current political situation in Korea, where the conflict between the right and the left is very intense, the concept of welfarenomics can provide a policy framework that can create consensus between both sides. Welfarenomics embodies most of the Third Way policy recommendations by Giddens, who tried to improve sustainability of the welfare state by linking social welfare programs to job opportunities for welfare recipients. Welfarenomics also incorporates the concept of not only business management but also social innovation in the implementation process of social welfare programs so that the rightist camp can accept the idea of the welfare state more easily.

Furthermore, welfarenomics emphasizes the social responsibility of business firms, which can make the concept of capitalism and a market economy more agreeable to the left. The transition from Shareholder Theory to Stakeholder Theory implies an attempt by the right to adjust capitalism in a way that is more acceptable to the left. Interestingly, Stakeholder Theory lends strength to the concept of CSR because it argues that CSR activities bring greater financial returns to a business firm in the medium- and long-term perspectives. The evolution from CSR to CSV further strengthens the argument that business firms can create both economic and social values at the same time. The emergence of the ESG concept, initiated jointly by UN Secretary General and a group of influential institutional investors, follows this spirit of CSR and CSV.

The concept of welfarenomics proposes a greater role for the government in the field of not only social welfare but also economic policy strategy-making, which is an important departure from the neoliberal viewpoint that proposes that the government assume only a minimal role. Furthermore, welfarenomics stresses the importance of creating an ecosystem of symbiotic development for civil society. Civil society has always played an important role in Western democratic society since the days of ancient Greece. Maintaining the tradition of civic empowerment in a democratic society is certainly an important element of the ideal society for the right as well as the left.

Notes

1. The author received his PhD in economics from Stanford University in 1974, and has led research activities and policymaking in the field of economics and social welfare for the past four decades. He conducted economic and welfare policy research at the World Bank and the Korea Development Institute and served as a member of the National Assembly and the Ministry of Health and Social Affairs in Korea as a policymaking expert in both the legislature and the government. During 2017–2022 Dr. Sang Mok Suh served as chairman of the Korea National Council on Social Welfare, representing the private social welfare sector in Korea. Currently he is global president of the International Council on Social Welfare (ICSW). In 2012, he published a book in Korean, *Welfarenomics*, which suggests the "road to a sustainable capitalism and welfare state," and this chapter is a summary of that book.
2. The current difficult situation is well described in the recent McKinsey report, "Beyond Korean Style: Shaping a New Growth Formula," 2013.
3. Under the Korean Constitution the term, "economics democratization" implies economic equity issues such as promotion of small-scale enterprises, preventing abuses of monopoly power, and achieving better distribution of income and wealth that may necessitate government policy intervention.
4. Hall and Soskice (2001), *Varieties of capitalism*, classifies capitalism into the following three categories: (1) liberal market economies, as in the United States and the United Kingdom, where wages are determined through the market mechanism; (2) coordinated market economies, as in Germany and Sweden, where wages are determined through the negotiation process between management and labor unions; and (3) government-led market economies, as in Korea under the Park Chung-hee regime, where the government plays a dominating role in managing the economy.

References

Bowen, H. (1953/2013). *Social responsibilities of the businessman*. University of Iowa Press.
Freeman, E. (1984). *Strategic management: A stakeholder approach*. Pittman.
Friedman, M. (1970, September 13). Social responsibility of business is to increase its profits. *New York Times Magazine*.
Giddens, A. (1994). *Beyond left and right: The future of radical politics*. Polity Press.
Giddens, A. (1998). *The third way: Renewal of social democracy*, Polity Press.

Hall, P. A., and Soskice, D. (2001). *Varieties of capitalism: The institutional foundations of comparative advantage*. Oxford University Press.

Hankook Research. (2010). Public Opinion Survey. Gyeonggi Welfare Foundation.

Kaletsky, A. (2010). *Capitalism 4.0: The birth of new economy*. Bloomsbury.

McKinsey Global Institute. (2013). Beyond Korean style: Shaping a new growth formula. https://www.mckinsey.com/featured-insights/asia-pacific/beyond-korean-style

Moore, J. (1996). *The death of competition: A new theory of competition*. Harper.

Porter, M., and Kramer, M. (2011). Creating shared value: How to reinvent a wave of innovation and growth. *Harvard Business Review*, Jan-Feb.

Sang-mok Suh. (2013). *Welfarenomics: The Road to a sustainable capitalism and welfare state* (in Korean). BookKorea.

PART II
THE POLICY PILLARS OF THE WELFARE STATE

4

The Income Security Systems in Korea

Kyungbae Chung

Introduction

Rapid population aging and family structural changes have increased the
need for the development of effective income security systems in South
Korea. Indeed, even though the public pension system was introduced late
in South Korea, coverage has been extended to the majority population in
a short period of time. However, a widespread coverage gap remains, along
with inadequate levels of benefits.

The public pension system of Korea consists of the National Pension (NP),
which is social insurance; the Special Occupational Pension for government
employees, military, and private teachers; and the Basic Pension, which is
public assistance. The Special Occupational Pension has achieved a high level
of adequacy on benefits, whereas the system's coverage is limited. However,
the coverage of the NP system is broad, but the actual number of insured persons is relatively low. Furthermore, in terms of the adequacy of benefits, the
income replacement rate has been reduced through pension reforms in 1997
and 2007 to enhance the program's long-term sustainability and mitigate the
risk of creating a financial burden on future generations caused by rapid population aging (Chung, 1995).

One of the reasons for the broad coverage gap in the national pension
system is that when the NP was introduced, the elderly aged older than 65
in that period were excluded. Furthermore, there were numbers of elderly
in the national pension system with a short actual contribution period. This
has raised the issue of initially excluding the majority of the elderly from the
public old-age income security system. Thus, poverty among the elderly became severe and has focused political discourse on the importance of closing
the coverage gap and reducing poverty. In response to this situation, the
Basic Old-Age Pension was implemented in 2007, targeting elderly citizens
aged 65 and older whose incomes were below 70% of the lower-income level

Kyungbae Chung, *The Income Security Systems in Korea* In: *The Korean Welfare State*. Edited by: Kyungbae Chung and
Neil Gilbert, Oxford University Press. © Oxford University Press 2024. DOI: 10.1093/oso/9780197644928.003.0005

(less than 60% in the first half of 2009). The Basic Pension was introduced in 2018, extending both coverage and the level of adequate income (Basic Pension Act [BPA], 2020).

The responsibility of the state to secure life after retirement for the older generation by providing an adequate level of benefit has been a critical issue due to population aging. Many countries have started to improve and develop their pension systems in accordance with their external and internal social situations, and it is important for countries to share and exchange experiences and information for improving these systems. In this context, this chapter aims to introduce the NP System and the Basic Pension System as central parts of the public pension system of Korea and also to discuss the issues surrounding and directions for improving the public pension system (ESCAP, 2015).

The Korean Employment Insurance System (EIS) is a compulsory social insurance system introduced in 1995. All employers and employees in participating enterprises must pay an insurance premium, which entitles workers to receive grants or unemployment benefits (UBs) from the Employment Insurance Fund. Work Injury Insurance (WII) was launched in 1964. Benefit levels of Korea's WII are considered fairly good compared to other countries. Ten types of benefits, including the medical care benefit, are provided.

The current basic security provided by the National Basic Livelihood Security Program (NBLSP) was introduced in December 2014. The livelihood security benefit, a core benefit of public assistance, is limited to persons 65 years of age and older or under 18 years of age, pregnant women, and persons with disabilities who are eligible for care in their home (National Basic Living Security Act [NBLSA, 2015]).

The ILO Convention: Minimum Standards for Human Rights

The International Labor Organization (ILO) states that social security is a human right, ensconced in a set of policies and programs designed to prevent and alleviate all forms of poverty and vulnerability throughout the life cycle. Typical social security systems consist of contributory social insurance, noncontributory taxation-based schemes, and social assistance programs. The ILO Social Security (Minimum Standards) Convention, 1952 (No. 102), sets out minimum standards for social protection with a focus on income security, mainly relating to income security except for "pregnancy care and disease treatment" and "medical care for disasters (accidents and illnesses) at work" (International Labor Organization [ILO], 2012).

Convention No. 102 was subsequently amended and supplemented in part before being massively complemented by the Social Protection Floors Recommendation, 2012 (No. 202). Based on a set of principles including "universality of protection based on social solidarity," the Social Protection Floors Recommendation emphasizes governments' responsibility for its implementation. In line with this, the UN Summit in September 2015 adopted 17 Sustainable Development Goals (SDGs), the first of which is to end poverty. Goal 1.3 of the SDGs provides for the "implementation of nationally appropriate social protection systems," including floors to prevent and reduce poverty (ILO, 2012; United Nations, 2015).

Korea has introduced in a timely manner a series of social security programs tailored to its needs and as proposed by the ILO since the 1960s. The pillar of Korea's income security system is the NP Plan, covering most Koreans excluding those working in special job categories such as government employees, soldiers, and faculty and staff of private schools. The pension plan began to be implemented as social insurance in January 1988, under the NP Act enacted in 1986. Its initial 3% insurance rate increased by 3 percentage points every 5 years, and the pace has remained flat for more than 20 years after reaching 9% in 1998. When it comes to benefit levels, the income replacement ratio estimated at 70% when the plan was introduced fell to 60% in 1998, 50% in 2008, and 40% in 2018, and the ratio is expected to drop further in 2028 unless special action is taken (NPA amendment, 2007).[1]

Structure of Old-Age Income Security

The Old-Age Income Security system consists of a pension system in the way of social insurance and a benefits system involving social assistance. The pension system is composed of NP; Special Occupational Pension for government employees, military, and private teachers; and Basic Pension. In addition, there is the NBLSP, providing benefits when household incomes are below the minimum living standard.

The Government Employees Pension system was introduced in 1961, and the Military Pension system was separated from the system in 1963.

The Private Teachers Pension system was introduced in 1975, and the NP was introduced in 1988. The NP was limited to workplaces with 10 or more full-time employees early on, but it has gradually extended to all citizens aged 18–59 residing in Korea (Organisation for Economic Cooperation and Development [OECD], 2017).

Because the coverage of the NP was below age 60, it has faced challenges in income security for those elderly who had no chance to be insured before its inception. In this context, the Basic Old-Age Pension was implemented in 2007 under the Basic Old-Age Pensions Act. Later, the Basic Pension was introduced in 2014, to provide benefits to elderly citizens aged older than 65 whose incomes are below 70% of the lower-income level by increasing the pension amounts and linking Basic Pension benefits to NP benefits.

The retirement pension, targeting workplaces with five or more full-time employees, was introduced in late 2005; it was developed from the retirement allowance system introduced in the 1950s. The effectiveness of the retirement pension system is limited due to limited selection between defined-contribution (DC), defined-benefit (DB), or retirement allowance in each company. Meanwhile, the private pension system has only supplementary role in securing old age income because of low incentive motivation (Chung, 2015).

The Status of the NP

When the NP system was introduced in 1988, it was limited to workplaces with 10 or more full-time employees. Later, coverage was extended to workplaces with five or more full-time employees in 1992, individuals in rural areas in 1995, and individuals in urban areas in 1999. Now, the system has been developed for all citizens aged 18–59 residing in Korea.

In the beginning, the contribution rate of the NP for workplace-based-insured person was set at 3% in 1988, but it was increased gradually by 3% every 5 years so that it reached 9% in 2004. For individually insured people, the contribution rate was set at 9% in 2004, increasing by 1% every year since 1999.

Regarding the sustainability of pensions, the income replacement rate is set at 70% for an average gross wage for insured persons with 40 years' contribution. However, it was largely reformed in 1997 and 2007 to enhance financial sustainability, under the influences of pension reforms of other countries in the late 20th century.

The first pension reform in 1998 aimed to decrease the income replacement rate of the NP from 70% to 60% and raise the pensionable age from 60 to 65 by 2033, from 2013. Furthermore, it became compulsory for an actuarial projection to be made of the NP Fund every 5 years under the NP Act. As a consequence of the first pension reform, the exhaustion of the national pension fund had been delayed to 2047.

The second pension reform occurred in 2007, to enhance long-term financial sustainability. The second pension reform gradually decreased the income replacement rate from 60% to 40% until 2028, without any changes in the contribution rate. As a result, the exhaustion of the national pension fund had been delayed to 2060. Furthermore, credits for childbirth and military service were also introduced during the second pension reform in an effort to close the coverage gap of the NP System (Chung, 2015, p. 182).

Characteristic of NP System

The NP System is a DB program. All the citizens aged 18–59 residing in Korea are covered under the NP, apart from those insured under the Special Occupational pension system, national pension beneficiaries aged between 55 and 59, military personnel, students aged less than 27, and beneficiaries of the NBLSP. This system was structured to provide a redistribution of income through the benefit formula.

The NP System is currently a partially funded system. The main financial source is contributions from insured persons. There is a subsidy from the government for management expenses and partial contributions from farmers and self-employed persons. The system is supervised by the Ministry of Health and Welfare but is managed by the NP Service.

Types of Insured Persons

The total number of insured persons in the NP System was 22,017,810 in late 2020, of whom 60% are included as workplace-based insured persons. Since the coverage of the NP was extended to the majority population of Korea (urban areas) in 1999, the overall number of insured persons has increased.

The number of workplace-based insured persons has increased, whereas the number of individually insured persons has decreased.

Meanwhile, there has been an increasing number of voluntarily insured persons aged 18–59. The number of voluntarily and continuously insured persons, which includes those previous members who continue their pension contribution past the age of 60, has also increased (see Table 4.1).

The Types of NP Benefit

There are three types of NP benefits (old-age pension, disability pension, and survivor pension) and three types of payments (disability lump-sum compensation, lump-sum refund, and lump-sum death payments). Eligibility for the old-age pension is based on members who have contributed for 10 years or more. The pensionable age for that pension was 60 at the beginning but will be raised to age 65 in 2033 through the gradual increase by 1 year every 5 years starting in 2013. The replacement rate was set at 50% in 2008, but it will be at 40% in 2028 through a gradual decrease by 0.5% every year.

The disability pension is paid upon occurrence of disability and disease during the coverage period once the diagnosis is confirmed (severity level of the disability is graded 1–3). The survivor pension is paid to bereaved family members when a beneficiary dies, and the amount is about 40–60% of the total amount of the old-age pension depending on years of contribution.

Disability lump-sum compensation is paid when the severity level of the disability is grade 4 and meets certain conditions. Lump-sum death payments are paid to the bereaved family members who do not meet certain conditions for a survivor pension. When a member has contributed for less than 10 years or emigrates, a lump-sum refund is paid, which amounts to the sum of total contributions plus interest (NPS Act, 2016).

Status of Beneficiaries

The total number of NP beneficiaries was 17,244,920 in late 2021, which includes those receiving pensions and lump sum allowances. There were 6,518,186 pension beneficiaries, among whom 82% received old-age pensions (Table 4.2). Approximately 97% of the beneficiaries of the lump-sum payments were paid with return allowances.

Table 4.1 The number of insured people under the NP system

	Total insured persons	Workplace-based insured Persons		Individually insured persons	Voluntarily insured persons	Voluntary and continuously Insured Persons
		Workplace	Insured persons			
'88	4,432,695	58,583	4,431,039	—	1,370	286
'90	4,651,678	72,511	4,640,335	—	8,274	3,069
'95	7,496,623	152,463	5,541,966	1,890,187	48,710	15,760
'99	16,261,889	186,106	5,238,149	10,822,302	32,868	168,570
'05	17,124,449	646,805	7,950,493	9,123,675	26,568	23,713
'10	19,228,875	1,031,358	10,414,780	8,674,492	90,222	49,381
'14	21,125,135	1,389,472	12,309,856	8,444,710	202,536	168,033
'19	22,216,229	1,949,286	14,157,574	7,232,063	328,727	497,866
'20	22,017,810	1,944,018	14,102,156	7,080,373	332,806	502,475

Source: NP Service, "The Statistics annual report of the NP," 2020,

Table 4.2 The number of NP beneficiaries

Year		2015	2017	2019	2020	Total
Total		4,028,671	4,692,847	5,163,110	5,588,154	17,244,920
Pension	Sum	3,832,188	4,475,143	4,961,143	5,388,022	6,518,186
	Old-age Pension	3,151,349	3,706,516	4,090,497	4,468,126	5,346,752
	Disability Pension	75,688	75,486	77,872	78,079	184,104
	Survivor Pension	601,151	693,141	792,774	841,817	987,330
Allowance	Sum	196,483	217,704	201,967	200,132	10,726,734
	Disability	2,597	2,916	3,028	2,904	83,956
	Return	179,937	201,278	186,921	184,342	10,428,965
	Death	13,949	13,510	12,018	12,886	213,813

Source: NP Service, "The Statistics annual report of the NP," 2021.

The NP Fund Financial Condition

The NP Fund started with 0.53 trillion Korean won (10,000 Korean won equals US$8.43) in 1988, climbing to 100 trillion won in 2013, and 743.2 trillion won in 2020, of which 70% was accumulated through pension contributions and the other 30% through investment return from fund management. The NP Fund will increase for the next 30 years (Ministry of Health and Welfare [MoHW], 2020a, 2020b) (see also Table 4.3).

The Stability of the Fund

Based on actuarial projections in 2008, it is estimated that the NP Fund will be depleted by 2060. If the contribution rate remains at 9%, the revenue-to-expenditure ratio will be decreased from 31.4 in 2008 to 0 in 2060 (see Figure 4.1). This projection highlights the necessity of pension reform to enhance the long-term sustainability of the public pension program (Table 4.4).

(*Optimality Analysis*): To maintain the NP System's sustainable objectives subject to constraints of replacement rate and contribution rate, it should be optimized by adjusting it toward the point where the individual insured mean income converges to the mean income of the entire insured population.

Table 4.3 The status of the NP Fund (in 100 million Korean won)

Year		2011	2015	2017	2019	2020.1
Fund balance		3,488,677	5,123,241	6,216,611	7,366,538	7,430,177
Revenues	Sum	4,193,275	6,385,779	7,852,750	9,450,964	9,535,673
	Contributions	2,708,842	4,034,222	4,842,429	5,764,165	5,805,417
	Invest return	1,477,651	2,341,820	2,999,390	3,374,776	3,718,195
	Others	6,782	9,737	10,931	12,024	12,061
Expenditure	Sum	704,598	1,262,538	1,636,139	2,084,426	2,105,496
	Pension Benefits	664,679	1,200,953	1,562,474	1,997,644	2,018,013
	Operation Expense	39,920	61,585	73,665	86,782	87,483

Source: NP Service, "The Statistics annual report of the NP," 2020.

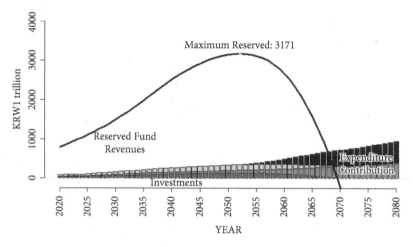

Figure 4.1 Long-term national pension projection.

Starting from a 70% replacement rate and applying the NPS formula [pension P = 2.4(1.75A) (1 + 0.05 × 20)/12 = 0.7], it will be converted to 40% by 2028, where A (the entire insured average income) and B (the individual insured average income) being equal, and where n = 20 contribution years, 2.4 is the policy coefficient, and 0.75 is the adjustment coefficient (see Table 4.5).

The Basic Pension

The Senior Citizen Pension was introduced in 1998, for those elderly who could not be insured but who had short contribution periods in the NP System. However, the beneficiaries of Senior Citizen Pensions were only 6% of elderly citizens at that time, and the adequacy of the benefits was miserably low.

For that reason, the question of public pension system adequacy was constantly raised as a critical issue. Even though the numbers of beneficiaries and adequacy of the benefit were expanded, problems remained with resolving elderly poverty. The Basic Pension was introduced in July 2014, to replace the Basic Old-Age Pension by strengthening the level and adequacy of benefits.

Characteristics of the Basic Pension: Financial Condition

The Basic Pension covers 70% of elderly aged 65 and older whose incomes are below a certain amount. The primary financial source is tax-financed,

Table 4.4 Long-term financial prospects of the NP Scheme (Actuarial Projection: NPS, In billion Won, %)

Year	Reserves	Total revenues			Total expenditures		Difference
		Revenues	Contribution	Yield (invest)	Expenditure	Pension	
2018	671,383	73,386	43,704	29,682	23,645	23,009	49,741
2020	780,610	84,745	48,028	36,717	29,190	28,500	55,556
2025	1,078,656	107,458	59,620	47,838	48,264	47,835	59,194
2030	1,378,515	132,884	71,537	61,347	73,509	72,985	59,375
2035	1,641,860	156,078	83,537	72,541	109,643	109,003	46,435
2040	1,776,319	174,861	95,926	78,934	163,722	162,941	11,139
2045	1,673,943	183,658	108,758	74,899	227,237	226,286	−43,580
2050	1,244,339	182,881	125,396	57,485	298,884	297,728	−116,004
2055	384,976	162,463	140,908	21,555	377,053	375,651	−214,590
2060	—	157,690	157,690	—	485,289	483,593	−327,599
2070	—	208,618	208,618	—	713,127	710,663	−504,509
2080	—	274,085	274,085	—	931,141	927,604	−657,056
2088	—	337,382	337,382	—	1,119,935	1,115,234	−782,553

Source: Long Term Projection of NP, 2018.

Table 4.5 Optimality of replacement rate[a]

Year	Policy tool	Entire average	Insured average	Excess of 20	Replacement
1988	2.400 ×	(A +	0.75 B) ×	(1+ 0.05n) =	70%
1999	1.800 ×	(A +	1.00 B) ×	(1+ 0.05n) =	60%
2008	1.500 ×	(A +	1.00 B) ×	(1+0.05n) =	50%
2009	1.485 ×	(A +	1.00 B) ×	(1+0.05n) =	49.5%
2020	1.320 ×	(A +	1.00 B) ×	(1+0.05n) =	44.0%
2021	1.305 ×	(A +	1.00 B) ×	(1+0.05n) =	43.5%
2025	1.245 ×	(A +	1.00 B) ×	(1+0.05n) =	41.5%
2028	1.200 ×	(A +	1.00 B) ×	(1+0.05n) =	40.0% Limit
≤	the same ×	(A +	1.00 B) ×	(1+0.05n) =	the same

[a] Optimality Analysis Center (OAC: Chung, Kyungbae): Long Term Projection.

with approximately a three to one proportion between the central and local governments. The Basic Pension benefits can be applied on top of the NP but are not paid to the beneficiaries and their spouses of the Special Occupational Pension. However, the benefits of the Basic Pension link to the NP income, equalizing part "A". If the monthly national pension receipt is 450,000 won or more (1.5 times the Basic Pension), it will be reduced. This is a system in which the Basic Pension, which is a maximum of 300,000 won per month, is reduced by up to 50% if the amount of A is 225,000 won or more.

The number of Basic Pension beneficiaries was 5,345,728 in 2019, covering 66.7% of elderly citizens aged 65 and older. The rate of beneficiaries of both the Occupational Pension and Basic Pension has reached 26.7% (MoHW, 2020a, p. 44; see also Tables 4.6 and 4.7).

The Basic Pension benefit is primarily funded from government sources. The central government covers about three-quarters of the cost depending on the size of the elderly population and regional conditions, and local government covers the difference, as shown in Table 4.8. The financial burden of the central government increases when the elderly population is high and regional economic conditions are inadequate.

Future Direction for Improvements

The public old-age income security system consisting of the NP and Basic Pension has become a reliable source of support to the elderly during

Table 4.6 Pension burden (PAYG) over gross domestic product (GDP)
(billion KW: %)

Year	Total income insured (A)	Pension Payment (B)	GDP (C)	Income insured over GDP (A)/(C)	Pension over GDP (B)/(C)	Pension burden (B)/(A)
2018	502,305	23,009	1,806,963	27.8	1.3	4.6
2020	549,469	28,500	1,984,946	27.7	1.4	5.2
2025	678,436	47,835	2,445,452	27.7	2.0	7.1
2030	811,739	72,985	2,924,580	27.8	2.5	9.0
2035	947,973	109,003	3,407,651	27.8	3.2	11.5
2040	1,091,203	162,941	3,928,053	27.8	4.1	14.9
2045	1,241,018	226,286	4,486,485	27.7	5.0	18.2
2050	1,434,787	297,728	5,096,405	28.2	5.8	20.8
2055	1,613,011	375,651	5,760,773	28.0	6.5	23.3
2060	1,805,740	483,593	6,454,771	28.0	7.5	26.8
2065	2,072,279	605,764	7,181,179	28.9	8.4	29.2
2070	2,390,572	710,663	7,966,870	30.0	8.9	29.7
2075	2,732,050	812,381	8,869,334	30.8	9.2	29.7
2080	3,141,781	927,604	9,909,947	31.7	9.4	29.5
2085	3,589,548	1,040,906	11,068,147	32.4	9.4	29.0
2088	3,868,136	1,115,234	11,816,028	32.7	9.4	28.8

Source: Long Term Projection of NP, 2018.

Table 4.7 Beneficiaries of the Basic Pension (Unit: persons, %)

Year	Elderly ≥65 (A)	Beneficiaries (B)	Ratio (B/A)
2014	6,520,607	4,353,482	66.8
2015	6,771,214	4,495,183	66.4
2016	6,987,489	4,581,406	65.6
2017	7,345,820	4,868,576	66.3
2018	7,638,574	5,125,731	67.1
2019	8,013,661	5,345,728	66.7

Table 4.8 Budget of the Basic Pension (Unit: 100 million Korean won, %)

	2014	2015	2016	2017	2018	2019
Total budget	69,001	100,090,	102,896	105,461	118,222	147,202
(Ratio)	(100)	(100)	(100)	(100)	(100)	(100)
Central Government	51,771	75,634	78,497	80,762	91,028	114,745
(Ratio)	(75.0)	(75.6)	(76.3)	(76.6)	(77.0)	(78.0)
Local Government	17,230	24,456	24,399	9,681	10,089	32,457
(Ratio)	(25.0)	(24.4)	(23.7)	(23.4)	(23.0)	(22.0)

retirement. However, it still faces various challenges, particularly in regard to the adequacy of old-age income and the relationship between the NP and Basic Pension. The primary purpose of the pension system is to prevent poverty among the elderly and to maintain their standard of living during retirement. The NP System has become a crucial old-age income security system for all citizens. There have been several social policy reforms aiming to solve the coverage gap because the actual contribution was meager due to payment exceptions and defaults.

NP Blind Spots and Support Policies

Those who are eligible to join the NP, but who do not actually pay insurance premiums fall into a sort of "blind spot" in the NP scheme. As of 2020, among the 2,2107,000 people eligible to join the NP Service, there were about 4,660,000 who were either exempt from payment or long-term delinquents, amounting to 14.7% of those who were eligible (Table 4.9).

Insurance Premium Support Policies

Premium Support System for Farmers and Fishermen
When the NP System was expanded to rural areas in 1995, the insurance premium support project for farmers and fishermen was undertaken due to the rapid increase in numbers of the aging population in rural areas and the relocation of young people from rural to urban areas leading to a deterioration of agriculture and fisheries. To minimize the damage caused by the Uruguay

Table 4.9 National pension excluded, as of 2020

18–59 population: 31,672,000 (A)				
Economically non-active: 7,826,000	Economically active: 23,846,000			
	NP insured: 22,107,000 (B) (B/A = 69.8%)			Occupational pensions: 1,739,000
	Payment exemption: 3,625,000 (C) (C/A = 11.4%)	Income declared: 18,482,000		
		LT delinquents: 1,035,000 (D) (D/A = 3.3%)	Contributors: 17,447,000	
Subtotal: 12,485,000			Subtotal: 19,187,000	

Source: Facts Book 2020, NP Service (adjusted based upon the final insured data as of 2020).

Round opening of the agricultural market in 1994, supports were provided to farmers and fishermen who were among regional subscribers to the NP Service. This relief method involved support up to 43,650 won within the limit of half of the monthly pension premium.

Durunuri Subsidy for Social Insurance Premium
Social insurance premiums, including for the NP and employment insurance, are subsidized up to 90% for workers employed in small businesses with fewer than 10 employees whose monthly average income is less than 2.1 million won. Newly insured 80–90% are differently supported depending on the size of the business, and the application period is limited to a maximum of 36 months. Since the basic purpose of the Durunuri social insurance premium subsidy is to encourage the social insurance enrollment rate of new subscribers, appropriate adjustments are necessary according to the financial situation of the NP Service.

Credit Support Policies for Unavoidable Circumstances
Credit support policies provide an incentive to maintain the mandatory subscription period for those who cannot participate in the labor market due to unavoidable circumstances. These credit policies allow 10 years (120 months), the minimum mandatory period to receive a pension, by adding up the periods without paying insurance premiums for certain groups.

Childbirth credit. According to the "birth credit" stipulated in Article 19 of the NP Act, pension credits of 12 months are provided for a second child and credits of 18 months for each additional child, up to a maximum of 50 months. When receiving the old-age pension without a separate application, the credit counting method checks the number of children of the beneficiary, adds the subscription period, and increases the pension amount by the added subscription period. The government pays 30% of the financial resources for additional maternity credit and the NP Fund pays 70%. Recipients with 12 months of maternity credit account for 27.5%, and, as of February 2020, a total of 1,488 beneficiaries receive credit for the old-age pension.

Military service credit. Military service pension credits of 6 months are given to military service members, conversion service members, full-time reserve personnel, and international cooperation volunteers. The 6 months' entitlement is acquired when the old-age pension is calculated. The financial resources for providing military service credits are fully borne by the central government.

Unemployment credit. A beneficiary of job search benefits pursuant to Article 37 of the Employment Insurance Act since 2016, the unemployment credit is applied by converting the daily wage into a monthly amount based on the "recognized income" stipulated in Article 45. At this time, a property or income test is conducted to select beneficiaries. The application period is within the period of receiving job search benefits, 3 to 8 months at a time, but only for up to 1 year of life per person. The central government pays 75% of the unemployment credit and the individual pays 25%. Of the 75% of the government's contribution, 25% comes from the Ministry of Employment and Labor's general account, 25% from the Employment Insurance Fund, and the remaining 25% from the NP Fund.

Relations Between the NP and Basic Pension

The NP is primarily introduced as social insurance and then the Basic Pension is provided as a supplementary benefit. The NP is structured to reallocate by income level via balancing out with the Basic Pension. The Basic Pension is connected to the NP average value (A-equalizing value) via deducting the Basic Pension. The Basic Pension of 301,500 won per month is provided to seniors 65 years or older, who are in the 70% lower-income bracket based on sum of their assessed income and property as follows:

Income assessment = [0.7 × (earned income − 960,000 won)] + other income

However, if the monthly NP receipt is 450,000 won or more (1.5 times the Basic Pension), it will be reduced. This is a system in which the Basic Pension, which is a maximum of 300,000 won per month, is reduced by up to 50% if the amount of A = 225,000 won or more.

Subsidiarity Principle of the Basic Pension

According to the National Basic Livelihood Security Act, the extremely poor, with a recognized income of 30% of the median income, will receive 548,349 won in the case of a single-person household. Among these basic livelihood security beneficiaries, senior citizens aged 65 or older who fall into the bottom 70% of the income bracket can receive an additional Basic Pension of 300,000 won. However, the sum of these two benefits will be reduced to the extent that it exceeds the limit of the recognized amount of income for livelihood benefits (combined income and property). The Basic Pension is transfer income that is subject to the "supplementary principle" stipulated in the NBLSP in accordance with the Enforcement Decree of the Act. The principle of subsidiarity is that the system provides support by supplementing only the amount that is less than the standard amount of the livelihood benefit set by the law.

The National Basic Livelihood Security Program

The NBLSP introduced in October 2000 is a public assistance program that provides a means-tested income benefit to lower-income households. The previous public assistance set in place in 1961 was modeled on the public assistance program of Japan but was considerably different in detail. In 1982, the Korean government attempted to improve the program by introducing a new system of self-support and education protections. However, it still remains a charitable, residual, and selective welfare system.

The livelihood security benefit, a core benefit of public assistance, was limited to persons 65 years of age and older or under 18 years of age, pregnant women, and persons with disabilities eligible for care in their homes. As a result, households facing crises such as the death of household heads, unemployment, and demolition could not receive livelihood security. These institutional inequities were revealed during the IMF crisis in 1997, leading to the program being reformed under the National Basic Livelihood Security Act.

The NBLSP established a minimum livelihood guarantee for all in need (Article 1 of the Act) and sees the right to the benefit as a fundamental human right by using the expression "beneficiary," not "protected person." However, it is not very different from livelihood security in that it is a residual and selective welfare program.

To become a recipient, a household's income must be less than the eligibility threshold (initially the minimum cost of living) and meet the requirement for dependents. Since July 2015, the eligibility threshold has been set at a certain percentage of the standard median income, not the minimum cost of living. The minimum security level for the livelihood benefit is 30% of the standard medium income, 40% for medical care benefits, 44% for housing benefits, and 50% for education benefits.

Household income is calculated as the sum of an appraised amount of income and an amount of income-converted assets. There are many complaints about this calculation of income, but more objections are raised to the criteria for the support of "obligatory providers," a relative responsible for rendering support to an eligible recipient. Many poor people are disqualified because they are unable to meet the strict criteria for the support of obligatory providers. In addition, NBLSP beneficiaries have to be available for and actively seeking work; they are required to accept training or employment in order to gain qualification for the benefit, with some exceptions.

Challenges and Assessments

In this section, we discuss the challenges facing the Korean NBLSP as well as its problems and assess its performance from a medium- and long-term perspective.

First, it is difficult to find a fundamental solution to the issue of the nonrecipient poor unless there is a significant increase of the Basic Livelihood Security budget, which is now small (relative to gross domestic product [GDP] in comparison) compared to other developed countries. Despite the new personalized benefit method, a number of poor people are still not covered by the benefit. The percentage of the poor eligible for government support amounts to roughly around 3% of the entire population.

Second, with a growing concern about the increasing rate of unemployment and the number of long-term jobless due to new technologies such as artificial intelligence (AI), attempting to protect the poor through the NBLSP

alone is unfeasible. Therefore, it is advisable to protect and support a new category of the impoverished based on displaced workers through other welfare
programs. As this new poverty class of people are qualitatively different from
the Basic Livelihood Security beneficiaries who are accustomed to living
as long-term benefit recipients, it is necessary to design a separate system
for them.

Third, considering the free-ride and moral hazard issues with the system
in Korea, with almost no stigma attached to receiving benefits, their negative impacts need to be minimized when setting the minimum security level
(selection standard), which is expected to continue to rise, and defining
beneficiaries. In Japan, despite the small-scale basic security budget, significant stigma, and less concern about moral hazard, the Public Assistance
(equivalent to the NBLSP in Korea) budget has increased more rapidly
than that for other sectors. Recent reductions have been introduced to rein
in growing public assistance spending by lowering the livelihood security
standards that greatly affect various social security benefits.

Fourth, efforts are needed to secure the long-term sustainability of the
system, despite its being financed by taxes. Deepening polarization in the
income distribution caused by the universal use of AI may drive a sharp increase in the number of the Basic Livelihood Security recipients and related
budgets in the future.

Fifth, if the coverage and related budget of the NBLSP are expanded, it may
be inevitable to consider adjusting functions of the Basic Pension financed
by the same taxes. Japan spends more money on basic security than does
Korea and can still afford to provide better basic security because its Basic
Pension accounts for merely 50% of the government budget. Nevertheless,
the country has attempted to reduce the basic security budget under a 3-year
plan since 2018.

Sixth, prospective beneficiaries should be informed about the responsibility of the state and its limitations, as well as of various self-support
strategies for their old age; the country needs to provide support for them to
prepare for lives after retirement on their own.

The Employment Insurance System

The Koreans strived to introduce an unemployment insurance scheme as economic development progressed, but most people feared the side effects of

unemployment insurance. Particularly, the unemployed receiving UBs are likely to choose leisure rather than looking for a job. Most Koreans opposed the negative effect of not lowering the unemployment rate. In response, the Korean government chose not to solve the problem through cash benefits, but to prevent unemployment itself by stimulating economic growth and labor market efficiency. In this respect, the government decided to call the program the *Employment* Insurance System rather than the *Unemployment* Insurance System. The Employment Insurance Bill was passed unanimously on December 1, 1993, and the law went into effect on July 1, 1995.

The Korean EIS is a compulsory social insurance system in which employers and employees of all firms must pay premiums into the Employment Insurance Fund to receive subsidies or UBs. Like the German and Japanese models, Korea's EIS includes a series of active labor market policy (ALMP) measures. In order to prevent abuse by the unemployed who receive UBs, which prolongs unemployment status and reduces the supply of labor, entitlements are strictly supervised. At the same time, various incentives for early reemployment and vocational training are provided (Yoo, 1999).

The first clause of the Korean Employment Insurance Law (see Box 4.1) stipulates the principal purpose of fostering economic and social development by (1) preventing unemployment and promoting employment in conjunction with the development of and improvement in vocational knowledge, skills, and capabilities; (2) strengthening the development of job skills of the labor force and efficient job placement services; and (3) providing financial assistance to displaced workers. With those goals in mind, the Korean EIS has created four basic programs: the Public Works Program, vocational programs, the Employment Stabilization Program (ESP), and the Job Skills Development Program (JSDP).

Outline of the Employment Insurance System

The labor market policy in Korea consists of six programs that aim to promote employment by providing UBs, wage subsidies, and social support for the low-income unemployed, but which are conditional on job-seeking activities. The employability promotion programs are ALMP measures; these include vocational training, public employment services, and job creation. The first four programs are basically under the umbrella of EIS.

Box 4.1   First Clause of the EIA

---

1. (EIA Act, Article 1)
Object of Employment Insurance System

The purpose of this Act is to ensure that the employment insurance system operates effectively to prevent unemployment, to promote employment, to develop and improve the vocational skills of workers, to enhance the State's vocational guidance and job placement services, to support the livelihood of unemployed workers and job seeking by providing unemployment benefits, thereby contributing to sustained economic and social development (EIS = UB + ALMP)

   To achieve the purposes prescribed in Article 1, employment insurance programs (hereinafter referred to as "insurance programs") shall be carried out for employment security and vocational skills development programs, unemployment benefits, child care leave benefits, maternity leave benefits, etc.

Only wage subsidies, vocational training, and public employment services for persons with disabilities are covered by the Disability Special Program, which is financed by an employment levy for persons with disabilities. The Public Works Program, which provides temporary jobs to the low-income unemployed, is financed by tax revenues and partially supported by the Employment Insurance Fund. Vocational programs for insured employees are financed by the Employment Insurance Fund, while for other, it is financed by tax revenues (Yoo, 1999; see also Table 4.10).

Unemployed people who are eligible for UBs can receive such benefits if they meet the eligibility requirements. Those who are not eligible for UBs or have exhausted these benefits may receive social assistance as a last resort if their income falls below the minimum wage, but with the requirement of job search.

The Employment Stabilization Program (ESP) aims to prevent large-scale layoffs and rapid transfers. When a company undergoes a major employment adjustment due to industrial restructuring or rapid change in technology, the ESP allows workers to change direction by providing reskilling and training for new environments to inform, guide, and help job seekers adapt to the new labor market.

Table 4.10 Duration of job-seeking allowance (Unit: days)

Age	Insured employment period				
	Less than 1 year	1–3 years	3–5 years	5–10 years	10 years or more
Less than 30 years old	90	90	90	150	180
30–50 years old	90	120	150	180	210
50 years or older, disabled	120	150	180	210	240

Seven days waiting duration of JSA.

Basis for the period of job-seeking allowance: Article 48 of the 'Employment Insurance Act' (receiving period and number of receiving days).

The Job Skills Development Program (JSDP) seeks to promote and stimulate lifelong vocational training and vocational skills development. JSDP aims to improve labor productivity, job security, worker marketability, and corporate competitiveness by providing financial incentives for individual companies to invest in employee training (Employment Insurance Act [EIA], 2017).

UBs aim to stabilize living conditions and promote early reemployment of displaced workers by providing unemployment compensation. For those who are taking vocational training for reemployment, those who have found new employment in a relatively short period of time, or those who are actively seeking work, there are financial benefits provided by the EIS. This financial incentive system seeks to encourage recipients of UBs to participate in retraining programs and actively seek new employment. Maternity and parental leave benefits, implemented in 2001, were included in the EIS to subsidize the costs of motherhood (Yoo, 1999).

Financing Rules and Contribution Rates

The Employment Insurance Fund (EIF) is financed jointly by employees and employers. The contribution rate varies among the EIS programs. The component of UBs is funded by contributions in equal proportions from both the employee and the employer. ESP and JSDP are programs for which only the employer is responsible for all costs. For the components of UB, EIS funds may also be used to pay maternity and parental leave benefits. The administrative costs of EIS are covered by the government from the general budget.

Each component of EIS has its own rate of contribution. The sum of contribution rates in each program cannot exceed 3% of the total payroll. The contribution rate of each program is determined within the limit of contributions, considering the financial situation of the Employment Insurance Fund and the future prospects of the economic and labor markets.

When the EIS was first introduced on July 1, 1995, the contribution rates were 0.6% (0.3% from employees and 0.3% from employers) for the UB, 0.2% for the ESP, and a differentiated rate between 0.1% and 0.5% of the total payroll based on the size of the firm for the JSDP. However, the 1997 financial crisis resulted in a high unemployment rate. It was anticipated that this high unemployment rate would prevail for several years and that expenditures for UBs and active labor market programs would also remain high. Also, those newly covered by the EIS in 1998 were expected to increase the UB expenditures by becoming eligible for UBs from April 1, 1999.

In the light of cost factors, the Korean government raised the contribution rate of each program from January 1999. As of 1999, the contribution rate for the UB is 1.0% (0.5% from employees and 0.5% from employers), and that for the ESP is 0.3%. The contribution rate for the JSDP is between 0.1% and 0.7% of the total payroll, depending on the size of the firm Table 4.11).

Table 4.11 Employment insurance (EI) contributions by the firm size (%)[a]

EI programs and size of enterprises		Total	Employer	Employee
Unemployment, maternity, and parental leave benefits		1.30	0.65	0.65
Firm size	Less than 150 employees	0.25	0.25	—
	SMEs with more than 150 employees	0.45	0.45	—
	More than 150 but less than 1,000 employees	0.65	0.65	—
	More than 1,000 employees	0.85	0.85	—

SMEs, small and medium sized enterprises: firms with 300 employees or less in transportation, warehousing, communication, construction industries.

[a]Basis for employment insurance premium: Article 142 (Determination of premium rate) of the Act on the Collection of Premiums for Employment Insurance and Industrial Accident Compensation Insurance.

Employment Insurance Fund

The EIF has a separate account for each major component of the EIS: the ESP, the JSDP, and the UB. The EIF is managed by the Ministry of Labor. Reports on the financial state of these account and annual management plans are submitted to the Employment Insurance Committee, comprised of trade union representatives, employer representatives, government officials, and specialists from academia.

Economic circumstances can change suddenly and often severely, producing sharp fluctuations in the level of unemployment. Thus, unemployment is subject to greater volatility compared to other contingencies of the social insurance programs. EIS revenue increases in boom years and decreases in recession years. In contrast, EIS expenditures decrease during economic upturns and increase sharply during periods of recession. As a result, the financial state of the EIF varies counter-cyclically, experiencing amplified fluctuations during economic cycles. Therefore, the EIF has to dispose of reserves to meet serious economic downturns and high unemployment rates.

The EIS has gone through continuous changes over time, including coverage extension, lengthening of benefit duration, etc. Also, its financial structure seems to experience great change before its expenditure pattern is stabilized if daily employees are covered by the EIS and maternity protection is financed by the EIF. It is thus difficult to set the optimum level of the Korean EIS reserve fund. The reserve should not be unnecessarily high, so as not to distort the economic activities of the private-sector economy, but it should not be so low as to risk depletion of the fund and default on benefit liabilities.

Wage Subsidy Programs

The employment stabilization system is intended to prevent unemployment and promote reemployment amid changed economic conditions. According to rapidly changing technological levels, each company must adapt to the new economic environment and continuously modify its skill-intensive qualitative structure.

Globalization accelerates competition in labor market. Technological progress compels the labor market to adapt employment flexibility in a cold-blooded manner. Economic policies to deal with the resulting large-scale unemployment, protect livelihoods, and reduce income inequality are top priorities.

With large-scale unemployment, most marginal workers are the primary victims. Therefore, the major purpose of the ESP is to balance efficiency and equity in the process of employment adjustment and labor market flexibility. To this end, companies are phasing out large-scale layoffs, reimaging them as opportunities for reskilling. When hiring disadvantaged workers such as the elderly, female heads of household, and the long-term unemployed, encouragement subsidies are provided to firms.

There are several types of wage subsidies, and they are broadly classified into two categories: *employment adjustment subsidies* and *employment promotion subsidies*. Employment adjustment subsidies are intended to assist employers in their efforts to retain employment despite temporary financial difficulties. The employment promotion subsidy supports business owners who promote employment of the underprivileged, such as the elderly and female heads of household. The employment promotion subsidy consists of the employment promotion subsidy for the elderly, the female employment promotion subsidy, the employment promotion subsidy for the long-term unemployed, and the employment facilitation subsidy (EIA, 2017).

Employment Adjustment Subsidies

Economic changes in particular cause firms to continually alter employment levels to correspond with their levels of production, thus creating the problem of employment adjustment. Article 16 (i) of the Employment Insurance Law states, "The Ministry of Labor may assist the employer who has stabilized employment by taking proper measures for employment maintenance such as a temporary shutdown, reduced working hours, employment maintenance training, dispatching of employees, leaves of absence or relocation of employees in an effort to adjust to the changing economic environment and industrial structure" (Article 16). The Employment Insurance Law promotes unemployment prevention by offering assistance to the employer who has contributed to the stabilization of the labor market by hiring displaced workers in the process of employment adjustment.

Reflecting these goals and objectives, the Enforcement Decree of the Employment Insurance Act stipulates that employers with stable employment through temporary shutdown, reduction of working hours, employment maintenance education, dispatched workers, leave, and relocation are specified as having specific means of employment adjustment. Employers who have contributed to such employment stability can receive an employment maintenance subsidy. To be eligible for this assistance, employers must meet the certain conditions: (1) in the course of employment adjustment, some layoffs are inevitable; (2) the employer took appropriate measures to maintain employment to ensure continued employment; (3) the employer reported its employment maintenance plan to the Labor Administration and took measures to maintain employment according to the plan; and (4) no employee reductions shall be made during the period in which the employment maintenance measures are implemented (EIA, 2017).

Employment Facilitation Program

The employment facilitation program is a wage subsidy for employment of the disadvantaged. This program is composed of grants to promote employment of the elderly, female heads of household, and the long-term unemployed. Since enforcement of the employment insurance program in July 1995, conditions and standards for the employment promotion support system frequently changed, accompanying changes in the labor market such as changes in the unemployment rate and utilization trend of detailed programs.

Only the grants to promote employment of the elderly existed in the early stage of enforcement, but the grants to promote reemployment of women/ the elderly were instituted starting in the late 1997 to support reemployment of women and the elderly. The grant to promote employment of unemployed female heads of household was established in the next year to support unemployed female heads of household. The grant to promote employment of the long-term unemployed was introduced in 1999, to promote prompt reemployment of the increasing numbers of the long-term unemployed, leading to the current system of the grants to promote employment for disadvantaged groups (i.e., elderly, women and the long-term unemployed; see EIA, 2017).

Actively Seeking Work

A person claiming UBs must show that he or she is actively seeking work. Claimants are expected to report every other week on their reasonable efforts to search for a job. Reasonable efforts for seeking work will vary according to previous occupation, skills, and knowledge of the claimant. Public employment offices help claimants in their active job search efforts by providing job opening information, job guidance, and counseling services. A claimant is considered to be inactively seeking work if he or she has never responded to job offers and never accepted the job placement or job counseling services of the public employment office.

Nationwide Job-Seeking Allowance

The National Job Seeker's Allowance (NJSA) is designed to support a wide range of job search efforts by qualified individuals by subsidizing transportation and lodging expenses. The search must begin with a recommendation from a public employment office, and claimants must meet all of the following eligibility requirements: (1) the job search process must begin with a recommendation from a public employment office; (2) prior to the start of the national job search, the waiting period for job seekers must be expired; (3) the prospective employer is unwilling to finance the expenses incurred or pays less than the total cost; and (4) the distance between the job seeker's residence and the prospective employer's business location must exceed 50 kilometers. The allowance includes lodging and transportation by rail, car, and ship. If the prospective employer pays the cost, the insured job seeker must report it so that the prospective employer is reimbursed for any amount not covered (EIA, 2017).

Vocational Training Promotion Allowance

The Vocational Training Promotion Allowance (VTPA) is a supplement to NJSA, instituted to facilitate vocational training of qualifying unemployed workers as recommended by the public employment office. The training must take place within the UBs period. Days of absence and NJSA suspension are subtracted from the duration of VTPA. Employers can conduct initial training, advanced training, and job change training. Each type of training can be conducted in the form of off-JT or OJT. All training courses must satisfy the conditions stipulated in the Vocational Training Promotion Act, such as by providing training materials, facilities, and training period. If the employer directly provides training for the employed or prospective job seekers or entrusts it to another institution, the EIF subsidizes some or all of the training costs (Kim, 2001).

Challenges in the Labor Market

The gap between job openings and applications has widened greatly, and supply and demand imbalances among sectors are highly likely to continue for some time. Labor market mismatch has negative impacts, such as a rising unemployment rate, sluggish recruitment, and falling labor productivity. The Korean labor market also faces mismatch as a major problem. Problems of mismatch include youth unemployment, increases in women's activity, employment of the elderly, and skill mismatch. The widening of the gap between workers includes an increase in irregular workers, long-term unemployment, and a decrease in job security. However, only three issues are discussed here (OECD Employment Outlook, 2015).

The first important issue is that youth unemployment is high and is gradually increasing. Although the youth unemployment rate is the highest among all age groups, the actual number of job seekers is likely to be much higher than official statistics because there are not many discouraged young people and more than 80% of high school graduates go on to college. The high percentage of young people receiving higher education directly impacts social productivity and fertility and is the major cause of Korea's serious fertility problem. As new professional and semi-professional jobs are transformed through labor-saving technologies, job creation is very limited.

The second issue is related to women's employment. Women's desire to enter the job market shows a remarkably increasing upward trend. Contributing factors are the expansion of women's educational opportunities, the development of the childcare system, and changes in social attitudes. However, most female workers currently belong to the secondary labor market, so that gender wage inequality is still large compared to other countries. Although some working conditions have improved in recent years, there exists still widespread gender discrimination.

The third issue concerns the deterioration of the employment structure. As the proportion of irregular workers has risen significantly, the income gap between workers is widening. This trend of an increasing proportion of irregular workers in the labor market is also observed in many developed countries. In Korea, not only the wage gap, but also the exclusion of irregular workers from social insurance is serious. The institutional devices to protect these irregular workers from the wage gap and provide basic protection for social security needs to be improved in terms of active labor market policies (Cho, 2008).

The Work Injury Insurance

Introduction: The Industrial Accident
Compensation Insurance

The Industrial Accident Insurance Act was enacted in 1963 as a social insurance system that applied to workplaces with 500 or more employees. After a 2018 amendment, it has been applied to all workers in workplaces with one or more employees. The insurance premium must be paid compulsorily in full by the employer. Since 2021, the insurance premium rate is set at 1.53% of employee wages. Unlike private insurance, a no-fault liability principle is applicable to compensates for all accidents regardless of negligence (Lee, 2016).

Korea's Industrial Accident Insurance (WII) benefit level is evaluated to be relatively generous compared to other countries. As for the rehabilitation program, as the Industrial Accident Insurance Act was recently amended in 2000, 10 types of benefits are provided, including medical benefits, psychosocial services, and vocational rehabilitation, to help workers recover and return to society (Kim, 2002).

Types of industrial accident compensation insurance benefits are described here. Medical care benefits are paid to workers when they are injured in work-related situations. Industrial accident victims receive medical care services at the Industrial Accident Insurance Medical Institution. If an occupational injury or disease can be cured with medical treatment within 3 days, medical care benefits are not paid. Suspension benefits are paid for the period of being injured or unable to work due to work-related medical treatment, and the amount paid per day is equivalent to 70/100 of the average wage. The disability benefit is paid to a worker when he or she has a physical disability after recovering from a work-related injury. Workers with disability grades 1 through 3 receive a disability compensation annuity (Industrial Accident Compensation Insurance Act [IACIA], 2018, 36-1).

Challenges and Assessments

In Korea, more than 55 years have passed since the Industrial Accident Act was enforced. Knowledge about how the system operates has been accumulated, but the insurance premium rate is still high compared to other countries. For example, in Japan and Germany, industrial accident insurance premium rates continue to decline. The reasons for this discrepancy are that (1) probably due to a lack of safety awareness in Korea, the accident rate is high; (2) authorities fail to take timely action to institute appropriate institutional reforms; and (3) above all, safety management administration is inefficient.

First, Korean administrative authorities neglect industrial accident management, and occupational safety officers neglect measures that would prevent industrial accidents in advance. Many inspectors respond sympathetically to employers' complaints rather than enforcing the Industrial Accident Insurance Act, and as a result, there is little motivation to improve safety. Article 1 of the Industrial Accident Insurance Act, amended in 1986, stipulates that the Act contributes to the protection of workers by carrying out projects for accident prevention and the promotion of workers' welfare. The function of occupational accident insurance is not to reinforce preventive measures, but merely to set the goal of "fair compensation for workplace accidents" after accidents occur.

The normative framework of the legal system appears to be similar to that of Japan and Germany, but the precautionary measures against industrial accidents and safety awareness to cope with risks are very insufficient in Korea compared to other countries. Regarding workplace management, companies and workers must be made aware of the need to take precautionary measures in accordance with recommended safety standards. Administrative authorities responsible for supervision are essential for prior inspection and strict management. Due to the weakness of safety culture including all these factors, industrial accident prevention is very low. The United Kingdom and Singapore, which have lower industrial accident compensation insurance benefits than Korea, have a much lower accident rate than Korea. Korea needs to make more efforts to improve occupational safety in advance of accidents.

Second, the number of deaths and serious accidents due to industrial accidents in Korea is also due to the lukewarm response of stakeholders. Employers want simple procedures to cut costs and shorten the time needed for tasks; thus, affected workers choose short temporary measures to reduce the time required for tasks and do not comply with safety recommendations. The apathetic responses of parties with an interest in the workings of industrial accident insurance, such as the Occupational Safety Agency, ultimately cause accidents, along with the implicit obstruction of supervisors and employers.

Third, Korea's average industrial accident insurance premium rate is as high as 1.65% (2019), which is much higher than Japan (0.45%) and Germany (1.16%). Among the three countries, Germany has the most comprehensive coverage for industrial accidents with a correspondingly higher insurance premium rate. Contrastingly, Korea's insurance premium rate is higher than other countries not because it provides comprehensive compensation, but because of the higher expense of serious accidents. Industrial accident insurance in Korea is characterized by a high recurrence of serious accidents and an ineffectiveness of accident control management.

The WII system in Korea has low operational performance coupled with a high premium rate. The system's long-term financial stability is vulnerable compared to the other four income security systems (NP, Basic Pension, NBLSP, and Employment Insurance). Institutional reformation is needed to promote financial stability and improve protection coverage; this should begin by reviewing the overall structure and management system (OECD, 2000).

Note

1. Replacement rate formular changes. The replacement rate of the national pension benefit started at 70% in 1988. However, in order to stabilize the pension finances, it was decided to reduce the replacement rate to 40% in 2028. Article 51 of the NP Act was amended to change the constant of the basic pension formula from 2.4 to 1.2. The replacement rate will decrease by 1.5% annually over 20 years, reaching 40% in 2028. The progressively decreasing schedule is stipulated in Annex 20 as amended on 23 July 2007.

References

Basic Pension Act (BPA). (2020). https://elaw.klri.re.kr/eng_mobile/viewer.do?hseq=57227&type=sogan&key=10

Cho, J. (2008). Employment problems with irregular workers in Korea: A critical approach to government policy. Pacific Affair, 81(3), 407–426.

Chung, K. B. (1995). *The NP Fund Projection Model*. NPS.

Chung, K. B. (2015). The NP History. NPS. Constitutional Court Decision on NP Fund Protection, pp. 165–181.

Employment Insurance Act (EIA). (2017). https://elaw.klri.re.kr/eng_mobile/viewer. do?hseq=41240&type=sogan&key=6

ESCAP. (2015). Income security for older persons in the Republic of Korea.

Industrial Accident Compensation Insurance Act (IACIA). (2018). https://elaw.klri.re.kr/ eng_mobile/viewer.do?hseq=41243&type=new&key=

International Labor Organization (ILO). (2012). R202, Social protection floors recommendation, 2012 (No. 202).

Kim, C. H. (2001). Vocational training in Korea. Korea Research Institute for Vocational Education & Training (KRIVET).

Kim, H. K. (2002). *Industrial accident compensation insurance in Korea.* KLI.

Lee, S. H. (2016). *Employment insurance scheme of Korea.* Korea Employment Information Service (KEIS).

Ministry of Health and Welfare (MoHW). (2020a). *The Basic Pension statistics.*

Ministry of Health and Welfare (MoHW). (2020b). *The Statistics annual report of the NPS.*

National Basic Living Security Act (NBLSA). (2015). https://elaw.klri.re.kr/kor_service/ lawView.do?hseq=45557&lang=ENG

NPA amendment. (2007).

NPS Act (NPA). (2016).

Organisation for Economic Cooperation and Development (OECD). (2000). Pushing ahead with reform in Korea: *Labor market reform and SSN.* OECD.

Organisation for Economic Cooperation and Development (OECD). (2017). Pension at a glance. *OECD.*

United Nations. (2015). *Sustainable development goals.* United Nation.

Yoo, K. S. (1999). The employment insurance system in Korea. KLI.

5

National Health Insurance in Korea

Hyoung-Sun Jeong

Introduction

T. H. Marshall emphasized social rights as the foundation of the social welfare system. These social rights are inherent in social legislation. The "fundamental rights to life" were first stipulated by the German Constitution of
the Weimar Republic (Die Weimar Verfassung) in 1919, and were inherited
in all modern countries through World War II. And Germany was the first
nation in the world to adopt an old-age social insurance program in 1889,
designed by Chancellor, Otto von Bismarck. In the same vein, in 1935, the
United States enacted Social Security, and, after World War II in England, the
welfare state "from cradle to grave" based on the Beveridge Report in 1942
was born (Brohmer and Hill, 2020; Hooghe and Oser, 2015; Klausen, 1995).
Korea's Framework Act on Social Security, which legislated social rights in
the Constitution, stipulates that Social Security includes Social Insurance,
Public Assistance, and Social Welfare Services. Social Insurance is financed
by contributions from the insured, while Public Assistance and Social Welfare
Services are financed by general taxes, the former being accompanied by a
means test. Korea's National Health Insurance (NHI) is one type of Social
Security, but, from the point of view of the health system, NHI is also an inte-
gral part of Korea's health system that provides the main financial resources
to secure healthcare to the people. Korea's health insurance was very similar
to the Japanese system at the time it was introduced in Korea. This is similar
to how Japan followed Germany's Bismarck-type social insurance. However,
with the achievement of universal health coverage (UHC) in 1989, and the
creation of an integrated NHI in 2000, Korea's health insurance is developing
a unique look, different from Japan's system. As hundreds of health societies
across the country were integrated into one organization, economies of scale

Hyoung-Sun Jeong, *National Health Insurance in Korea* In: *The Korean Welfare State*. Edited by: Kyungbae Chung and
Neil Gilbert, Oxford University Press. © Oxford University Press 2024. DOI: 10.1093/oso/9780197644928.003.0006

were achieved in terms of management and operation of the system. The foundation for health insurance policy to be consistent and systematic with health policy at the national level has been laid.

Health insurance as a social program in Korea began in 1977, when large-scale workplaces with 500 employees or more were required by law to form workplace health insurance societies. Since the mid-1960s, there have been cases in which employee health insurance cooperatives and self-employed health insurance cooperatives have been operated on a trial basis, but these were voluntary organizations. The background to the implementation of the system is that the economic foundation was established through the third Five-Year Economic Development Plan (1972–1976), the need for social security in medical care was relatively increased due to the postponement of the national pension system, and the Park Chung-hee administration, which continued to prolong its dictatorship, was conscious of competition with North Korea, which advertised free medical care.

The introduction and expansion of health insurance were led by the government. Under the authoritarian government of the time, the expression of interest at the high policy level and the impetus of the Ministry of Health and Social Affairs officials were important. The system of the neighboring country, Japan, served as a reference in making specific policy drafts in the process of introducing and expanding the system. The system and experience of Japan, which has a similar legal system and cultural background, provided the best information for Korea to reduce trial and error in the early stages of system introduction. However, it did not mean that the Japanese system was transplanted en bloc (Jeong and Niki, 2012). For example, in the case of payment method, fee-for-service was adopted as in Japan, but, unlike Japan, hospitalization fees were not subdivided into hospital room fee, standard nursing fee, and patient wear rental fee. Unlike Japan, where the co-payment rate differs depending on the type of insurance or whether the insured person or dependent is the patient, the same co-payment rate was applied to all subscribers, differing only on whether they are inpatient or outpatient, clinic or hospital.

Formation of Public Health Insurance

In 1977, the first year of the introduction of public health insurance, the number of covered population was 3.2 million, which was 8.8% of the total

Table 5.1 Expansion of public health insurance-covered population,
1977–1990

Year	1977	1980	1985	1990
Total population (A)	36,412	38,124	40,806	42,869
Covered population (B)	3,200	9,226	17,995	40,180
A/B (%)	8.8%	24.2%	44.1%	93.7%
Workplace Societies	3,140	5,381	12,215	16,155
Civil Servants etc.	·	3,780	4,210	4,603

Source: National Health Insurance Service (NHIS) and Health Insurance Review and Assessment Service (HIRA) (2007). Medical Aid Program beneficiaries are not included.

population. In January 1979, health insurance for civil servants and private school staff began, covering an additional 2.9 million people. In July of the same year, as health insurance was expanded to workplaces with 300 or more employees, 21.2% of the entire population benefited from it. At this stage, it was important to diversify financial risks and maintain appropriate management and operation costs. Considering this, a plan to group societies by region was adopted. In 1981, health insurance was expanded to workplaces with 100 or more employees, in 1983 to workplaces with 16 or more, and in 1988 to workplaces with 5 or more (see Table 5.1).

As health insurance applied to employed workers, the benefits provided became known, and the exclusion of self-employed people and non-workers from these benefits became a factor of social conflict. The application of health insurance was a great benefit in that the insurance fee for medical service was lower than the general fee, in addition to the fact that the employer paid half of the insurance contribution. Even in 1977, when health insurance was first implemented, the insurance fee was set much lower than the fee in the marketplace, and the gap between the two was gradually widening throughout the 1980s. The Chun Doo-hwan government, supported by the military, needed to supplement its lack of political legitimacy by addressing the people's social dissatisfaction. Accordingly, in 1981, a pilot project of local health insurance was started. Among the six pilot areas, one was an urban area and all the others were rural.

In January 1988, health insurance was expanded to rural areas. Insurance subscriptions were made on a household basis. One hundred thirty-four societies were organized by county. Because it was a large-scale project that was different from the gradual expansion of workplace societies, a lot of preparation work was required. After many twists and turns, in July 1989, 110 urban health insurance societies were established at the city and district levels, and insurance benefits began to be provided to nearly 10 million urban area insured persons. As a result, universal health insurance was achieved 12 years after the start of health insurance as social insurance (Ministry of Health and Welfare, 2022).

The achievement of universal health insurance in such a short period of time is a great success story internationally. How could these gradual reforms have been possible within such a short period of time that, in the experience of Western countries, could be called radical reforms? The rapid economic growth of the 1970s and 1980s is often cited as the cause (Kwon, 2009). Economic growth and the subsequent increase in people's ability to pay insurance contributions are, of course, necessary conditions for UHC. However, considering that the United States, which was already more economically advanced than Korea, the question deserves examination. The US economy is in a difficult situation because high medical expenses adversely affect other sectors of the economy; thus although economic power may be a necessary condition for achieving UHC, it is not a sufficient condition. In Korea, several factors worked together, including the lessons learned from Japan's health insurance system, the president's political leadership, and the bureaucracy's technical leadership. Militarily trained presidents tried to find justification for their power in social integration, and the authoritarian political culture up to that time made all walks of life move in the direction they suggested. Administrative technocrats have also been leading academics and ordinary people as both conformers and beneficiaries of this authoritarian culture. Especially in the 1970s and 1980s, when health insurance was introduced and expanded, their roles stand out (Jeong, 2011).

Governance of Integrated National Health Insurance

Integration of Societies

The separatism-integrationism debate surrounding the health insurance system in Korea has continued for a long time, having both political and ideological aspects. Separatists emphasized competition among autonomous societies, and integrationists emphasized equity through consistent operation at the national level. Conservative groups in Korean society tended toward the former, while progressive groups leaned toward the latter. This was a key issue in Korean health insurance throughout the 20 years from the early 1980s to the early 2000s, and it was a topic of debate so extensive that almost all social groups and interest groups expressed their views and got involved.

The expansion of insurance to workplaces with 300 or more employees, scheduled for 1979, led to the question of determining the appropriate size of a health insurance society. At this time, the government decision to abolish and merge health societies with fewer than 3,000 members was made, and the consolidation work began, but the decision was overturned again. In 1980, a plan to unify the Workplace Societies Association and Health Insurance Management Corporation for Civil Servants and Private School Staff was discussed. Because this viewpoint was called "integrationism," the opposing side began to be called "separatism." Even within the Ministry of Health and Social Affairs, the majority of public officials opposed the integration plan. It was promoted only by a small number of bureaucrats within the Ministry of Health and Social Affairs and was stopped at the direction of the president. This is the so-called First Integration Debate under the Chun Doo-hwan government. However, in this process, a change was made that unified the health insurance review organization under the new Federation of Health Insurance Societies and integrated the computer system there. In 1983, some officials who promoted the integration plan within the Ministry of Health and Social Affairs were removed, which led to the recognition that integrationism was in line with the democratization movement against the military government at the time. One such official, Lee DH, returned as vice minister in 1988, but he failed to integrate health insurance societies; another, Cha HB, returned as minister in 2000, and completed the integration reform of health insurance societies as well as a separation reform for drugs (Jeong, 2005).

In 1988, when health insurance for rural areas was implemented, dissatisfaction with health insurance broke out everywhere. In particular, farmers protested against excessive health insurance contributions, and they returned insurance certificates or burned contribution bills in various parts of the country. Progressive health and medical organizations active after the 1987 democratization movement intervened in this issue and presented a bill to integrate and unify health insurance societies. Officials of the Ministry generally wanted to create 110 city and district societies in urban areas but met with opposition from the ruling party under the majority opposition parties, which insisted on establishing province-level societies. Following the sit-in of the three opposition party headquarters by civic groups, an emergency meeting of the leaders of the three parties was held, and finally, in March 1989, a law containing the contents of the integration was unanimously passed by the National Assembly. However, as the press continued to criticize the increasing burdens on employed workers, President Roh Tae-woo finally exercised his veto power. In July 1989, universal health insurance was eventually implemented in the form of a number of societies. After that, the political reorganization led to the disappearance of the majority opposition parties, and the integration movement came to an end. This was the "Second Integration Debate" under the Roh Tae-woo administration (70 Years of Health and Welfare Compilation Committee, 2015).

In 1993, when President Kim Young-sam's civilian government departed, discussions on integration reappeared. It was civil society organizations that played a central role in the movement to unite existing societies into one insurer. In 1997, under a lame-duck president, the integration bill passed the National Assembly. At the end of 1997, President Kim Dae-jung, who achieved the first power change between the ruling and opposition parties in Korea, selected health insurance integration as one of the top 100 national tasks. The integration work was carried out in two stages. The first stage, which started in October 1998, was the process of integrating the finances of 227 local societies and integrating the local societies and the Corporation for Civil Servants and Private School Staff into one insurer, the National Health Insurance Corporation (see Table 5.2). In the second stage, the National Health Insurance Corporation and 142 workplace societies were integrated into the National Health Insurance Service (NHIS), and the Health Insurance Review and Assessment Service (HIRA) was established as a separate organization in charge of review and evaluation functions.

Management and Operation: NHI

Korea's integrated NHI is operated under a system in which the Ministry of Health and Welfare (MoHW) and the High Committee on Health Insurance Policy (hereafter, High Committee) under it make policy decisions, and the NHIS and the HIRA execute them. MoHW, as manager of the health and health insurance system, plays a role in determining health insurance-related policies and overseeing the overall health system. As the single payer

Table 5.2 Number of health insurance societies before integration, 1978–1999

Year	Total	Workplace societies	Civil servants, etc.	Local societies	Others
1978	600	592			8
1979	612	603	1		8
1980	432	423	1		8
1981	197	185	1	3	8
1982	164	146	1	6	11
1983	168	146	1	6	15
1984	171	146	1	6	18
1985	170	144	1	6	19
1986	171	144	1	6	20
1987	182	153	1	6	22
1988	313	154	1	140	18
1989	409	154	1	254	
1990	409	154	1	254	
1991	421	154	1	266	
1992	421	154	1	266	
1993	420	153	1	266	
1994	417	150	1	266	
1995	373	145	1	227	
1996	373	145	1	227	
1997	373	145	1	227	
1998	143	142	1		
1999	141	140	1		
2000	1				

Sources: National Federation of Medical Insurance (NFMI) (1991) and National Health Insurance Corporation (NHIC) (2000).

of NHI, NHIS manages the eligibilities of policyholders, imposes and collects insurance contributions, and pays for insurance benefits. The HIRA reviews bills from medical institutions and pharmacies and evaluates the adequacy of their services.

The MoHW operates the High Committee for Health Insurance Policy Deliberation chaired by the Vice Minister. The High Committee was created in 2002 in response to the huge deficit of health insurance in the early 2000s; it comprises eight representatives of subscribers (labor unions, consumer groups, etc.), eight representatives of providers (Korean Medical Association,

Korean Hospital Association, Korean Pharmaceutical Association, etc.), and eight representatives of public interest (MoHW, NHIS, HIRA, academic experts, etc.). The chairperson does not participate in resolution discussions, but has the deciding vote in case of a tie. Thus the High Committee is a dispute resolution structure in which the government is supposed to act as a mediator between conflicting stakeholders. The functions of the High Committee are, first, to set the standards of benefits; second, to set the insurance fees; and third, to set the insurance contribution rate. All important decisions on the NHI are made by this High Committee (see Figure 5.1).

NHIS has 16,441 employees spread across its main headquarters, six regional headquarters, and 178 branch offices, as of the end of 2022. NHIS has a board of directors and a Financial Management Committee. The board of directors is composed of 15 members, including the chairperson, and it deliberates and decides on major issues such as business operation plans, budgets, and settlement of accounts. The Committee, composed of 10

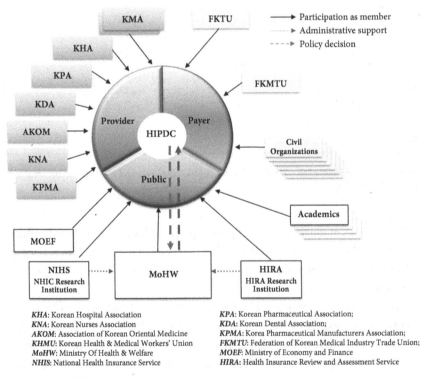

KHA: Korean Hospital Association
KNA: Korean Nurses Association
AKOM: Association of Korean Oriental Medicine
KHMU: Korean Health & Medical Workers' Union
MoHW: Ministry Of Health & Welfare
NHIS: National Health Insurance Service

KPA: Korean Pharmaceutical Association;
KDA: Korean Dental Association;
KPMA: Korea Pharmaceutical Manufacturers Association;
FKMTU: Federation of Korean Medical Industry Trade Union;
MOEF: Ministry of Economy and Finance
HIRA: Health Insurance Review and Assessment Service

Figure 5.1 High Committee on Health Insurance Policy.

members representing workplace subscribers, 10 members representing local subscribers, and 10 members representing the public interest, deliberates and decides on major matters related to the finances of NHIS, such as conversion rate contracts and disposition of deficits in insurance contributions. However, since most of the important matters affecting NHI finance are deliberated and resolved by the High Committee under the MoHW, the role of the Financial Management Committee is limited to that extent. In addition, since 2011, NHIS has been in charge of notifying, receiving, and managing arrears in the four major social insurance contributions, including not only health insurance, but also pension, employment insurance, and industrial accident insurance contributions.

HIRA has 3,711 employees spread across its main headquarters and 10 regional headquarters, as of the end of 2022. HIRA was established in July 2000 as an institution whose main task is to review and evaluate the appropriateness of health insurance benefit costs. In addition to health insurance, HIRA's review and evaluation have been expanded to include medical expenses under the Medical Aid Program, National Veterans Program, and automobile insurance. HIRA has a board of directors composed of 15 members, including the chairperson, to deliberate and decide on major issues such as business plans and budgets. The Medical Review and Evaluation Committee under its umbrella, consisting of 1,090 members or less (90 full-time and 1,000 part-time), performs duties such as developing review and evaluation standards and deliberating matters related to review and evaluation (Health Insurance Review and Assessment Service, 2021).

Eligibility for NHI

Eligibility for health insurance entails the obligation to pay contributions and the right to receive benefits. Currently, the eligibilities of subscribers do not attract attention because all citizens who are not recipients of the Medical Aid Program are automatically enrolled in the NHI. However, changes in health insurance eligibility requirements during the formation of NHI affected the right to receive insurance benefits as well as the method of imposing and collecting insurance contributions. Although health insurance integration has been achieved, eligibilities are still managed in two separate categories: those for workplace subscribers and those for local subscribers. This is because the eligibility management method and contribution charging method are structurally different between the two categories. Workplace subscribers include the insured person (employee) and his or her dependents, whereas, in the case of local subscribers, all household members become subscribers. Workplace subscribers pay a contribution only on income, but local subscribers pay a contribution not only on income but also on property.

Scope of Dependents

The biggest issue surrounding eligibility management is the scope of dependents of workplace subscribers. According to the National Health Insurance Act, a dependent is a person whose income and property are below a certain standard while maintaining a livelihood mainly by a person insured at work. At the time of the introduction of the system in 1977, only direct descendants centered on the patrilineal line were recognized. In 1981, this definition was expanded to the lineal ascendant of the spouse (male) of the female insured, and, in 1982, it was expanded to grandparents and parents living together with unmarried women. In 1985, it was extended to the lineal ascendant of the female spouse, and, in 1987, it was extended to the spouse of the lineal descendant and the siblings of the insured person. Even after that, the scope of dependents continued to expand, and, in 1995, it was expanded to include stepparents, stepchildren, natural parents, biological children, maternal grandparents, maternal grandchildren, and collateral blood relatives within the third degree, such as uncles, aunts, and nephews.

Local subscribers are managed by household, so insurance contributions are levied on all household members with income, but spouses, parents, brothers, sisters, etc. of workplace subscribers are not charged once they are recognized as dependents. This raised the issue of fairness. Moreover, in the face of the financial crisis of health insurance in 2000, the atmosphere in which the number of dependents was expanded to increase the number of employee subscribers reversed, and those who were recognized as dependents began to be excluded. In 2000, collateral blood relatives within the third degree were excluded from dependents. In 2001, dependents with business and rental income were converted to local subscribers and levied contributions, and, in 2002, dependents with an annual income exceeding 5 million won were excluded. Also, married children, grandchildren with parents, and daughters-in-law with husbands who do not live with the workplace subscriber were excluded from dependents. In 2006, dependents were excluded if their annual interest and dividend income exceeded 40 million won.

In 2010, brothers and sisters whose property exceeded 300 million won; in 2011, all dependents whose property exceeded 900 million won; and, in 2013, all dependents whose income exceeded 40 million won were excluded. In 2014, dependents whose rental income exceeds 20 million won per year were excluded. The most recent reforms, in 2018 and 2022, excluded dependents with an annual income of more than 10 million won as well as property exceeding 540 million won, dependents with a total income of more than 20 million won, and siblings aged 30–65 with a property of more than 180 million won. Although reform has continued for decades, more than one-third of the entire NHI population is still receiving insurance benefits as dependents (18.1 million people out of 5.1 million people covered by the NHI as of the end of 2021) without the burden of paying insurance contributions. As shown in Table 5.3, although the dependency ratio has decreased over the past decade, the reduction in the number of dependents is still recognized as an issue for continued improvement in terms of equity.

Incorporation of Workplaces with Fewer than 5 Employees

In 2001, workers at workplaces with fewer than 5 employees and daily workers with more than 1 month of employment, which had been managed as local subscribers, were converted to workplace subscribers. From 2003 to 2006, workers at voluntary workplaces with fewer than 5 employees (15 industries including restaurants, etc.) and part-time workers working more than 80 hours a month were incorporated as workplace subscribers. In 2010, the number of workplace subscribers was expanded to include part-time workers who work more than 60 hours a month. The expansion of the scope of coverage for workplace subscribers has contributed to enhancing equity among workers in paying insurance contributions (Jeong, 2010).

Financing Sources of NHI: Contributions and Subsidies

The main sources of finance for NHI are insurance contributions collected from subscribers and employers, and government subsidies. Government

Table 5.3 Changes in the number of dependents and dependency ratio 2010–2021 (Unit: million persons)

Year	2011	2012	2013	2014	2015	2016	2017	2018	2019	2020	2021
Dependents (A)	19.9	20.1	20.4	2 0.5	20.5	20.3	20.1	19.5	19.1	18.6	18.1
Employees (B)	13.4	14.0	14.6	15.1	15.8	16.3	16.8	17.5	18.1	18.5	19.1
Dependency ratio (B/A)	1.5	1.4	1.4	1.4	1.3	1.2	1.2	1.1	1.1	1.0	0.9

Source: NHIS (accessed on March 1, 2023). National health insurance statistical yearbooks. http://www.nhis.or.kr

subsidies are financed from both the government budget coming from general taxation and from a Health Promotion Fund coming from tobacco tax. Workplace subscribers are charged insurance contributions at a certain percentage of their remuneration, with subscribers and employers each paying half. Local subscribers (farmers, fishermen, and urban self-employed) are charged insurance contributions according to points calculated based on property in addition to income. As for the government subsidy for health insurance, 14% of the expected total contribution is to be supported from general taxes and 6% from the Health Promotion Fund.

The insurance contribution of workplace subscribers is relatively simple to calculate as it imposes a certain percentage (6.99% in 2022) of regular remuneration at work. In the past, insurance contribution rates were different for each insurer (society), but since 2001, when they were integrated into NHIS, the contribution rates have been the same nationwide. The upper limit of the monthly contribution amount for 2022 is 7,307,1000 won and the lower limit is 19,5000 won. For income other than regular wages at work exceeding 20 million won, insurance contributions are imposed on it additionally. In the past, workplace subscribers were charged insurance contributions only for their regular remuneration (earned income). However, as the source of income for workplace subscribers has diversified, in 2012, additional insurance contributions were imposed when annual income other than remuneration exceeded 72 million won. In 2018, the target of additional insurance contributions was expanded to cases exceeding 34 million won per year, and, in 2022, expanded again to cases exceeding 20 million won per year.

Local subscribers are also charged contributions based on their income, but considering the fact that there are incomes that are not ascertainable compared to workplace subscribers, contributions are imposed based on an assessment score that takes property into consideration as well. There are also differences in the method of determining the income subject to contributions. For the wages of workplace subscribers, contributions are levied on the total wages before deduction, but for business income of local subscribers, contributions are levied on income after deducting necessary expenses. However, as the conditions for determining income have improved, criticism on imposing contributions on property is growing day by day. Accordingly, two reforms were carried out in 2018 and 2022, the main content of which is to reduce the share of levies on property. In the future, reforms in the direction of eligibility based on income and reduction of the scope of dependents will continue.

Another source of funding for NHI is government subsidies. The government subsidy, which started when local health insurance was introduced in 1988, was provided with the intention that the government subsidizes insurance contributions instead of employers, which only workplace subscribers have. It is for this reason that the "constant rate subsidy for local insurance finance" method was maintained until the revision of the National Health Insurance Act at the end of 2006. In 2002, the national treasury provided 40% of the total insurance benefit costs and operation costs for local subscribers, and the health promotion fund provided the remaining 10%. This method of subsidizing half of the budget for local subscribers has changed since 2007. An amount equivalent to 14% of the total expected annual revenue from insurance contributions is subsidized from the national treasury, and an amount equivalent to 6% is subsidized from the National Health Promotion Fund (up to 65% of the expected annual revenue of the Fund is from tobacco taxes). Thus, government subsidy is not limited to supporting existing local subscribers. However, increases in the government subsidy did not keep pace with the increase in benefit expenditures, resulting in a decrease in the share of government subsidies.

Health Insurance Reimbursement

Payment Methods

The payment method for medical services in the NHI is based on the fee-for-service method. During discussions about the introduction of the health insurance system, application of a capitation-based payment was also mentioned, but it was difficult to choose an alternative other than fee-for-service method to attract people who were familiar with the price of medical services determined in a free market economy. In a fee-for-service system, the amount of compensation (which is the sum of treatment activities such as diagnosis, examination, and treatment provided by a medical institution) is determined ex post facto (retrospectively) and is paid. This has the advantage providing accurate compensation, but it is likely to cause misuse and abuse of medical care, increase medical expenses, and increase the difficulty of price management for each service. To overcome these limitations of the fee-for-service system, various payment methods have been proposed around the world, with the representative argument that a comprehensive and prospective payment system will induce efficient medical behavior of medical providers.

In Korea, the diagnosis-related groups (DRG) Payment Method Introduction Review Council was formed in 1995, and it recommended a pilot project applying K-DRG. The pilot project was conducted three times from 1997 to 2001, and, from 2002, it was applied as a payment method for health insurance to medical institutions that wanted it. Initially, eight disease groups were covered: tonsil surgery, lens surgery, anal surgery, hernia surgery, appendectomy, hysterectomy, vaginal delivery, and caesarean section, but in 2003, vaginal delivery was excluded. However, the institutional limitations that began in the form of voluntary participation continued for nearly 10 years after that. As a result, tertiary general hospitals (originally, 15 had participated in the pilot project), withdrew one by one, and, by 2009, none remained. Hospital-level medical institutions favored the DRG-based payment method because the prices of DRG items were raised in line with the price of fee-for-service items, and this price is raised every year. Price reductions in drugs or treatment materials were not reflected, so DRG-based payment actually had the effect of raising fees. However, the medical community as a whole was strongly opposed to DRG-based payment, believing that this bundling payment method could ultimately be abused to suppress medical expenses.

The Health and Medical Future Committee, temporarily established in 2011 by the MoHW, recommended the gradual expansion of the DRG-based payment method as one of its 10 policy recommendations. The High Committee accepted this recommendation and voted on the agenda to compulsorily apply the DRG-based payment to small hospitals and clinics from July 2012 and to other big hospitals from July 2013. Along with this, included in the High Committee agenda was a roadmap to expand the system by preparing an integrated model after evaluating the so-called new DRG-based payment method, which was being tested as a separate track from the DRG-based payment method. With the implementation of DRG-based payment, the number of institutions applying it and the number of patients subject to it increased significantly, and there was no problem with the quality of medical care (Choi et al., 2019).

On the other hand, from 2009, as an alternative to overcome the limitations of the DRG-based payment limited only to seven simple disease groups, the so-called new DRG-based payment, which combines the DRG-based payment (standard fee + per diem fee) and fee-for-service payment, was introduced. The pilot project was applied in 2009 to 20 disease groups in one hospital belonging to NHIS, which was expanded to 550 disease groups in 2012. The expansion of the applicable disease groups was accompanied by the expansion of the applicable hospitals. In the pilot project in 2012, it was applied to 550 disease groups in 40 regional hub public hospitals. Since 2018, it has been expanded to private hospitals that want to participate, and, as of the end of 2020, pilot projects are under way for an additional 98 hospitals (46 public hospitals, 52 private hospitals) and 567 disease groups. Although the new DRG-based payment method is being implemented in the form of a pilot project, payment for treatment is actually made. While watching the progress of the project, continuous corrections and supplements are being made. For example, in the process of implementing a pilot project, if the proportion of outliers to which the fee-for-service system is applied is too high, the range of the normal group is adjusted (Kim and Lee, 2021).

Price Setting of Medical Services

Under the National Health Insurance Act, which came into effect on July 1, 2000, the price of services is determined by contract and the scope, method, and procedure of benefit service and the upper limit prices of medicines and treatment materials are stipulated by Ordinance of the MoHW. The target of concluding a contract is the unit price per point of the relative value score of each service (i.e., the conversion index). The relative value score of each service and the upper limit price of both medicines and treatment materials are announced by the Minister of Health and Welfare.

In 1977, when health insurance was applied to some citizens for the first time and then expanded, dissatisfaction from medical providers was great. There were many complaints about the low prices of the services set by health insurance, but there were also complaints about the wide imbalance between the services. After lengthy discussions and research to resolve these complaints, the methods adopted in 2001 were to set a relative value score and contract the conversion index, with reference to the US Resource-Based Relative Value Scale (American Medical Association, 2023).

Research on the development of relative value scores, which began in 1997, calculated relative values based on the resource inputs of each medical service. The results were reflected in the first relative value scores announced in 2001. However, in fact, it was not easy to make relative scores by objectively examining the amount of resource inputs for so many services. In fact, the announced relative value scores did not deviate much from the existing line of appropriately scoring the price for each service. In response to this criticism, research for the first reformation of relative value scores has been conducted since 2003. After about 3 years of research, a plan to classify doctors' workload, practice cost, and risk and reflect them in the relative value scores was proposed. However, due to severe conflicts between clinical departments regarding scores, no agreement was reached on the proposal. In the end, under the condition that the total score of relative value considering frequency for each clinical department was fixed at the existing value (i.e., while maintaining financial neutrality), the relative value score of individual services was adjusted (Kang and Lee, 2007).

The research for the second reform of relative value scores began in 2010. This focused on adjusting the score imbalance between five service types including surgery, treatment, functional test, specimen test, and imaging tests. However, the results were reflected much later, between 2017 and 2020. Currently, research for the third reform, which started in 2018, has been completed: it recommends moving in the direction of lowering the overall additional rate and raising the relative score of surgery and treatment by the same saved amount.

The annual revision of the conversion index is made through annual negotiations between seven provider organizations and NHIS, following guidelines determined by its Financial Management Committee. A single conversion index was applied between 2001 and 2006, before the system of individual contracts for each type was created in 2007, and the contracts at that time were made between the NHIS and the Provider Association Council. In the annual conversion index contracts from 2001 to 2023, there were only four years (2006, 2014, 2017, and 2018) when all contracts were concluded without being passed over to the High Committee.

Health Insurance Benefits

In principle, the benefits of NHI are in-kind, but some medical expenses are exceptionally reimbursed in cash. Benefits in kind include benefits for diseases, injuries, childbirth, etc. as well as health checkups of subscribers and their dependents. Benefits in kind are provided by the insurer, NHIS, but patients pay part of the cost as co-payment when using medical care. The co-payment rate is 20% of the total medical expenses for inpatients and 30–60% for outpatients.

With the achievement of UHC in 1989, Korea's health insurance has already achieved a "breadth" of benefits (World Health Organization [WHO], 2010). However, the annual number of days and items covered were limited, and, even in the case of items to be covered, the co- payment rate was set relatively high at 50%. Such a low level of benefits helped settle the health insurance system by not increasing the financial burden of insurers in the process of introducing it, but, on the other hand, access to medical care varies greatly depending on households' ability to pay, and the low-income class in particular suffers from excessive medical expenses.

Awareness of these problems by policy authorities and academics has been the driving force behind a series of progressive moves to secure "depth" and "height" in health insurance benefits, along with the support of sustained economic growth. Until 2000, elimination of the limit on the number of benefit days, and, since then, an expansion of the scope of benefits and a reduction of out-of-pocket burdens have been the main contents and goals of reform. The first two correspond to the "depth" of the benefit, and the last corresponds to the "height" of the benefit. As benefits continued to expand over a long period of time, most essential medical services were covered in the Korean NHI.

Expansion of Benefit Items

Until the mid-1990s, the Korean NHI had a limit of 180 days per year for the allowable benefit period. Since 1995, the allowed period has been increased by one month per year, and, in 2001, the period limit was finally removed. However, even before that, the expansion of insurance benefits was progressing by making various exceptions to the limit on the number of days of benefits.

The expansion of insurance benefit items was steadily promoted throughout the entire process of introducing and expanding the health insurance system. In the same context, health insurance was applied to the field of oriental medicine in 1987, and to drugs purchased at pharmacies in 1989. In the 1990s, new medical technologies, new drugs, and new materials for treatment continued to be developed, and, as the people's demand for them increased, the scope of health insurance benefits continued to expand. In 1993, laparoscopic surgery and intraocular lens for cataract surgery were covered, and, in 1996, computed tomography (CT) was included in insurance benefits. In 1997, prosthetic equipment for the disabled became the subject of benefits, with up to 80% of the purchase cost subsidized within the upper limit set by the insurer. From 1997 to 1999, insurance benefits were expanded to include single-photon emission CT (SPECT), autologous hematopoietic stem cell transplantation, percutaneous endovascular stent insertion, and processing costs using PACS.

Health checkups were provided to subscribers and their dependents aged 40 or older in 2000, gamma knife surgery in 2004, magnetic resonance imaging (MRI) in 2005, meals for inpatients in 2006, and proton therapy in 2011. In the field of dentistry, dental fillings were covered by insurance in 2009, dentures for the elderly in 2012, and tartar removal in 2013.

Cost-Sharing by Patients

When health insurance was first introduced in 1977, individual insurance societies were able to set their respective insured's co-payment rates within 40% of outpatient medical expenses and 30% of inpatient medical expenses. In the 2000s, the co-payment rate was actively lowered. However, with the pursuit of sophisticated cost-sharing policies that appropriately utilize the price function of co-payment, there are some items with a partially increased co-payment rate. As of 2022, the co-payment rate is 20% of inpatient medical expenses, 30–60% of outpatient medical expenses, and 30% of pharmaceutical expenses. The expansion of benefits seen above also means that the number of items in which the co-payment rate is reduced from 100% to 20–60% increase, but the achievement of the height of benefits here indicates that the co-payment rates for the items covered are lower.

In 2001, outpatient co-payment rates for rare or intractable diseases such as cancer and Parkinson's disease were lowered to 20%. In 2005, the co-payment rate for mental illness was lowered to 20%, and the co-payment rate for high-severity diseases such as cancer was lowered from 20% to 10%. Conversely, in 2009, the co-payment rate for outpatients at tertiary general hospitals rose from 55% to 60%. This was a measure to induce demand suitable for the medical delivery system. In 2010, the co-payment rate for cancer and cardiovascular and cerebrovascular diseases fell again to 5%. Even after that, the number of rare or incurable diseases for which co-payment rates were reduced continued to expand.

In 1995, co-payment was reduced for seniors aged 70 or older who visited a doctor's clinic due to a simple illness with the medical expenses below a certain amount. In 2018, the cost-sharing method for seniors was elaborated. If the total medical expense is less than 15,000 won, a fixed amount of 1,500 won is co-paid; if the total is between 15,000 and 20,000 won, 10% of co-payment rate is applied; if the total is between 20,000 and 25,000 won, 20% of co-payment rate is applied; and if the total exceed 25,000 won, the same co-payment rate of 30% as non-senior persons is applied. Meanwhile, the expansion of benefits for seniors has been applied to dentures and dental implants. Complete resin-based full dentures were provided to seniors aged 75 or older in 2012; partial dentures in 2013; and dental implants in 2014, with a 50% co-payment rate applied to all of them. In 2015, the age of benefit coverage was extended to 70 years of age, and coverage was extended to metal-based full dentures. In 2016, the age was lowered to 65 or older. The co-payment rate for dentures was lowered in 2017, and the co-payment rate for implants was lowered in 2018 from 50% to 30%.

To create a sophisticated payment system (Organisation for Economic Cooperation and Development [OECD], 2004), a method of differentiating co-payment rates according to the degree of necessity and selectivity/optionality of benefit items was introduced. This is the so-called selective benefit method, introduced in 2013. The main targets are medical services and treatment materials with high selectivity/optionality but some degree of necessity, or those that are expensive and thus lack cost-effectiveness. For these services, health insurance is applied, but the co-payment rate is as high as 50–90%. In this sense, the selective benefit method is a method of applying differentiated co-payment rates. This method has several advantages. First, the patient's financial burden can be reduced by setting an appropriate public price for services that have been neglected as uninsured. Second, it is possible to manage the quality of healthcare provided through review and evaluation of medical expenses.

In 2004, the out-of-pocket ceiling system was introduced, which refunds the excess amount to the patient if the out-of-pocket amount exceeds 3 million won for 6 months. In 2007, the upper limit was lowered to 2 million won. In 2009, the ceiling began differ depending on the income level. The lower 50% of earners are capped at 2 million won per year, the middle 30% of earners at 3 million won, and the top 20% of earners at 4 million won. In 2014, the income range was widened from 1.2 million to 5 million won and subdivided into seven stages, and the ceiling was changed every year to reflect the national consumer price index. Even after that, work to adjust the ceiling to increase fairness continues, such as lowering the ceiling to 10% of annual income in 2018. In the ceiling system, the "post-refund," but the "advance payment" method is sometimes applied. Advance payment is made when the total amount of co-payment exceeds the ceiling of the highest grade, the patient pays only up to that point, and the excess is paid directly to the medical institution by the NHIS. Medical expenses covered by the out-of-pocket ceiling system are limited to medical expenses covered by the NHI, and expenses for non-covered items are not applied.

Benefit Expansion for Drugs and Treatment Materials

In 2021, health insurance drug expenses amounted to 21.2 trillion won, accounting for 24.1% of total health insurance expenditures, and treatment materials accounted for 4.2 trillion won, accounting for 4.8%. According to health data from the Organisation for Economic Cooperation and Development (OECD), pharmaceuticals and other medical consumables account for 20.0% of total current health expenditure in 2021, which is higher than the average of 18.1% in OECD member countries (OECD, 2022).

Under the NHI, drugs that are evaluated as sufficiently cost-effective are listed on the benefit list and covered. Treatment materials, when approved by the Ministry of Food and Drug Safety (MFDS), are compensated by being included in the medical service or are reimbursed at the price actually purchased, with the upper limit price set by the HIRA and listed separately on the benefit list. If they are classified as non-reimbursable, the patient pays the full amount. The difference between drugs and treatment materials is that the former can be sold as non-reimbursable drugs without applying for benefit registration, whereas in the latter the case must be referred to the HIRA for a decision on benefit or non-reimbursement and the results followed.

As for medicines, since 2007, the Positive List (formulary) system has been applied, in which only drugs that have been recognized as cost-effective are covered. HIRA determines the therapeutic and economic value of the applied new drug through economic evaluation, etc. Once evaluated as reimbursable, the pharmaceutical company negotiates a price with NHIS again, and, if the negotiation is successful, the agreed upper price is listed in the health insurance formulary. Drugs that were already on the formulary at the time of the system change were recognized as they were. However, these drugs are reviewed for inclusion through a reevaluation process.

In 2013, the Risk Sharing Agreement (RSA) was introduced for expensive anticancer drugs or treatment materials for rare and intractable diseases, for which there is no alternative but cost effectiveness was difficult to prove. Drugs are listed on the insurance formulary under the condition that pharmaceutical companies share part of the health insurance finances. Types of risk sharing include refund, total amount limit, usage per patient limit, and refund with conditional continuous treatment. As of August 2021, RSA applied to 95 items and 54 ingredients.

Health insurance reimbursement for treatment materials at actual purchase price started in 1999, when a total of 2,616 items in 12 large categories were listed in 2000. After that, the number of items listed increased rapidly, and, as of 2022, there are 2,408 intermediate taxa under 17 major taxa, and a total of 27,384 items under these. The upper limit price of treatment materials reimbursable by the NHI is determined by examining the manufacturing or import cost of each item plus selling and administrative expenses, operating profit, wholesale margin, and value-added tax. As in the case of drugs, the upper limit price is adjusted through on-site investigation and reevaluation of the actual transaction price.

Impact of Benefit Expansion: Public Share

From 1977, when health insurance was introduced, to 1989, when universal health insurance was achieved, the focus was on expanding the covered population. In this process, the share of health expenditures financed by public money has increased rapidly. In the 1990s, the number of days covered by health insurance and the number of covered services continued to expand, resulting in a double-digit annual increase in public finance. The increase in government finances following the health insurance financial crisis in 2001 and measures to strengthen health insurance coverage, which began in earnest in 2005, maintained an increasing trend in the 2000s. In the 2010s, as non-covered medical expenses increased rapidly, the proportion of publicly financed expenses remained the same because publicly financed medical expenses had also increased rapidly. The amount of health insurance benefits, which was 16.6 trillion won in 2005, increased nearly threefold to 39.0 trillion won in 2014, but the non-benefit out-of-pocket burden also showed a similar increase from 6.8 trillion won to 16.4 trillion won. In 2017, as a large amount of public finance was invested as a measure to strengthen protection (so-called Moon Jae-in Care), the share of public finance tended to rise slightly. However, efforts to increase the total public share have also shown that there are side effects that cause total health expenditures to explode. There is a need for more sophisticated compensation methods, such as the differential imposition of co-payment rates.

Impact of Benefit Expansion: Financing of NHI

Until July 2000, when hundreds of health insurance societies were integrated into the nation- wide NHIS, the financial situation of each society was confined to that society. However, after integration, the finances of NHI became a national political issue. Health insurance finance, which was divided into three groups of local, workplace, and public officials and teachers as subscribers in the early stages of integration, lasted three years and has been integrated and operated without distinction since July 2003. A huge reform for the integration of health insurers and another one called the "separation of prescribing and dispensing," which took place almost simultaneously in Korea, extremely deteriorated the finances of the NHI, resulting in a deficit of 1.1 trillion won in 2000 and 2.5 trillion won in 2001 (Jeong, 2005).

In May 2001, the government announced sweeping fiscal stabilization measures and expanded government subsidies. Thanks to this, from 2002, the size of the current year's deficit decreased to 760 billion won, and, in 2003, this turned into a surplus of 1.1 trillion won. In 2004, the NHI paid off all of its bank debt and showed a surplus, and, in 2005, it recorded a surplus of 1.2 trillion won. Due to the expansion of benefits for severe diseases, including cancer, which was promoted from 2005, NHI expenditure increased by 17.7% in 2006 and 14.3% in 2007. The government implemented measures to rationalize spending again, and, as a result, the rate of increase in spending decreased to 7.9% in 2008, and NHI recorded a surplus of 1.4 trillion won. In 2009, the rate of increase in the contribution rate was frozen, and, as a result, the current account was almost balanced. The economic downturn in 2010 reduced the income base of insurance contributions, resulting in a current-term deficit of 1.0 trillion won.

The MoHW, which experienced a large health insurance current deficit and cumulative balance deficit in the early 2000s and a current deficit in

2010, has made every effort to achieve a current surplus over 2010s. As a result, the current surplus continued from 2011 to 2017. The progressive Moon Jae-in administration, which entered into force in 2017, strongly promoted the so-called Moon Jae-in Care, which expands the level of health insurance benefits, resulting in a deficit of 3.3 trillion won in 2018 and 2.9 trillion won in 2019. When COVID-19 broke out in 2020, government expenditures to prevent transmission and compensate for losses in medical institutions increased, but patients' medical use rather decreased, resulting in a decrease in NHI's expenditure to support treatment costs. As a result, in 2020 and in 2021, the NHI turned a surplus. In 2021, NHI revenue was 81.7 trillion won and expenditure was 79.0 trillion won, recording a surplus of 2.8 trillion won and cumulative reserves of 20.2 trillion won (see Table 5.4). This result is due to continued higher-than-necessary increase in contribution rates. In 2001, when the current NHI structure was created, the health insurance contribution rate was 3.4%, but it has continued to rise to 4.21% in 2004, 5.08% in 2008, 6.07% in 2015, and 6.99% in 2022.

Conclusion: Sustainability and Challenges

The primary goal of the health system is to maintain and improve the health status of all citizens. To this end, healthcare policies aim to secure public access to quality healthcare services. The average life expectancy of Koreans is 82.7 years currently, which is one of the longest among OECD member countries, and the infant mortality rate is 2.7 per 1,000 live births, lower than the OECD average of 3.5. However, since resources cannot be invested indefinitely to achieve these goals, the procurement and input of finance must be done efficiently. The scale of Korea's total current health expenditure was 25 trillion won in 2000, less than 4% of gross domestic product (GDP), but, in 2022, it is expected to surge to 209 trillion won, 9.7% of GDP. This exceeded the average of around 9% for OECD member countries (see Figure 5.2). The average annual growth rate over the past decade (2011–2022) is 9%, which is a high rate of growth rarely seen in other economic sectors. The problem is that there is no sign that this increase will stop due to the increase in the number of geriatric and chronic diseases due to rapid population aging and the introduction of new drugs and new medical technologies. A bigger problem is that there is no mechanism in place to control all of these expenditures throughout the Korean health system.

Table 5.4 Trends in the NHI's finances: revenues and expenditures, 2010–2021 (Unit: trillion won)

Year	2010	2011	2012	2013	2014	2015	2016	2017	2018	2019	2020	2021
Revenue	33.9	38.8	42.5	47.2	50.5	53.3	56.5	58.8	62.7	69.2	75.1	81.7
Contributions	28.5	32.9	36.4	39.0	41.6	44.3	47.6	50.4	53.9	59.1	63.1	69.5
Gov. subsidies	4.9	5.0	5.3	5.8	6.3	7.1	7.1	6.8	7.1	7.8	9.2	9.6
Others	0.6	0.8	0.7	2.4	2.6	1.9	1.8	1.6	1.7	2.3	2.8	2.7
Expenditures	34.9	37.3	39.2	41.3	44.8	48.2	53.7	58.0	66.0	72.1	73.6	79.0
Benefits	33.7	35.8	37.6	39.7	42.8	45.8	51.0	54.9	63.2	69.0	71.2	−76.7
Operating costs	0.7	0.6	0.6	0.6	0.6	0.6	0.7	0.7	0.8	0.9	0.9	0.9
Others	0.5	0.8	1.0	1.0	1.3	1.8	2.1	2.4	2.0	2.2	1.6	154.8
Balance	−1.0	1.5	3.3	5.9	5.8	5.1	2.7	0.8	−3.3	−2.9	1.5	2.8

Source: NHIS (accessed on March 1, 2023). National health insurance statistical yearbooks. http://www.nhis.or.kr.

Total Health Expenditure
/GDP

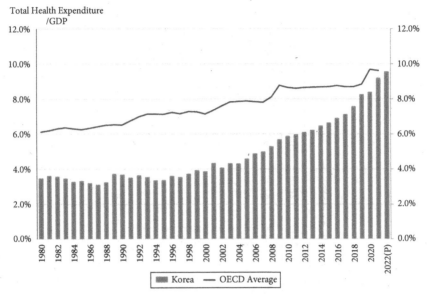

Figure 5.2 Trends in total health expenditure's share of gross domestic product (GDP).

Source: OECD (accessed on March 1, 2023). OECD Health Statistics 2022. http://stats.oecd.org.
Note: Data of the year 2022 are preliminary.

The same is true in terms of NHI spending. Total finance for NHI benefit, which was 37.4 trillion won in 2011, increased rapidly to 85.1 trillion won in 2022 (an average annual increase of 7.8%). NHI is operated so that revenue and expenditure are balanced over the course of a year. Insurance contributions of NHI subscribers determine the size of total revenue and insurance benefits determine the size of total expenditure, and the difference is linked to the financial situation of the NHI. The current NHI in Korea is structured to determine revenue in line with the scale of expenditure. However, the latter is determined at the interface between the patient's medical use and the provider's medical provision. In the current NHI system, the mechanism to control the scale itself is not sufficiently prepared.

Securing a mechanism for managing total health and NHI expenditures will be the number one task for Korea's health and NHI system in the future. To achieve this, the Korean government is promoting detailed policies such as rationalization of the fee structure, sophisticated adjustment of the co-payment rate, reduction of pharmaceutical expenses, prevention of financial leakage, and reduction of health system operating expenses. Alongside these, fundamental institutional improvements, such as the reorganization of the NHI payment system, should be pursued with a long-term perspective. The NHI conversion index contract method and relative value score system should be completely overhauled. To reduce the public's burden of medical expenses beyond the NHI, we must focus on supervision of non-insured items. At the same time, the supplementary nature of private insurance must be socially agreed upon, publicly declared, and realized in real policies so that private insurance does not interfere with the performance of public insurance. Above all, citizens, the medical community, insurers, and the government must put their heads together and reach a social consensus that securing financial sustainability is the number one challenge for Korea's health system and the NHI.

References

70 Years of Health and Welfare Compilation Committee. (2015). *70 Years of Health and Welfare*. Ministry of Health and Welfare of Korea. 2, 1–485.

American Medical Association. (2023). US Resource-based relative value scale. https://www.ama-assn.org/about/rvs-update-committee-ruc/rbrvs-overview

Brohmer, J., and Hill, C. (2020). 60 Years German basic law: The German Constitution and its court-landmark decisions of the Federal Constitutional Court of Germany in the area of fundamental rights. *Malaysian Current Law Journal Sdn Bhd.*

Choi, J. W., Kim, S. J., Park, H. K., et al. (2019). Effects of a mandatory DRG payment system in South Korea: Analysis of multi-year nationwide hospital claims data. *BMC Health Services Research, 19*(1), 1–9.

Health Insurance Review and Assessment Service (HIRA). (2021). 2021 Health Insurance Review and Assessment Service's functions and roles. https://repository.hira.or.kr/handle/2019.oak/2523

Hooghe, M., and Oser, J. (2015). TH Marshall's concept of political and social citizenship in public opinion. The dual structure of democratic ideals in Europe. *14th Dutch-Belgian Political Science Conference*, June 11–12, 2015. Maastricht.

Jeong, H. S. (2005). Health care reform and change in public–private mix of financing: A Korean case. *Health Policy, 74*(2), 133–145.

Jeong, H. S. (2010). Expanding insurance coverage to informal sector populations: Experience from Republic of Korea. *World Health Report*, 1–38.

Jeong, H. S. (2011). Korea's National Health Insurance: Lessons from the past three decades. *Health Affairs, 30*(1), 136–144.

Jeong, H. S., and Niki, R. (2012). Divergence in the development of public health insurance in Japan and the Republic of Korea: A multiple-payer versus a single-payer system. *International Social Security Review, 65*(2), 51–73.

Kang, G. W., and Lee, C. S. (2007). The refinement project of health insurance relative value scales: Results and limits. *Health Policy and Management, 17*(3), 1–25.

Kim, H. J., and Lee, J. Y. (2021). Changes in public hospital employees' perceptions following the introduction of the new diagnosis-related groups (DRG)-based payment system in the Republic of Korea. *Quality Improvement in Health Care, 27*(2), 30–44.

Klausen, J. (1995). Social rights advocacy and state building: TH Marshall·in the hands of social reformers. *World Politics, 47*(2), 244–267.

Kwon, S. (2009). Thirty years of national health insurance in South Korea: Lessons for achieving universal health care coverage. *Health Policy and Planning, 24*(1), 63–71.

Ministry of Health and Welfare. (2022). *White Paper 2021.* Ministry of Health and Welfare of Korea (pp. 687–688).

National Federation of Medical Insurance (NFMI). (1991). *Medical Insurance Statistical Yearbook of 1990.*

National Health Insurance Corporation (NHIC). (2000). *National Health Insurance Statistical Yearbook of 2001.*

National Health Insurance Service (NHIS) and Health Insurance Review and Assessment Service (HIRA). (2007). *Statistical booklet on 30 year-history of Korean National Health Insurance.* p. 8.

National Health Insurance Service (NHIS) and Health Insurance Review and Assessment Service (HIRA). (n.d.). National Health Insurance Statistical Yearbooks. Each year. https://www.nhis.or.kr/nhis/together/wbhaec06300m01.do

Organisation for Economic Co-operation and Development (OECD). (2004). Towards High Performing Health Systems (pp. 1–125). OECD.

Organisation for Economic Co-operation and Development (OECD). (2022). OECD Health Statistics 2022. https://stats.oecd.org

World Health Organization (WHO). (2010). The world health report: Health systems financing: the path to universal coverage. https://apps.who.int/iris/handle/10665/44371

PART III
POLICY CHALLENGES OF A RAPIDLY AGING SOCIETY

6

Long-Term Care

Experience and Challenges

Jaeeun Seok

Introduction

In 2008, Long-Term Care Insurance (LTCI) for older adults became a core component of South Korea's social care system. The methods for providing LTC to older people includes long-term hospitalization services at nursing hospitals, care services provided to middle- and lower-income people who are ineligible for LTCI benefits, and dementia care services for those with cognitive impairment. In addition, tax funds are applied to provide an activity support system for the disabled.

LTCI for older adults is a universal social insurance system that guarantees extended support and services for those 65 and older who require long-term care and those 64 and under who need long-term care for geriatric diseases. An accreditation review determines eligibility for this insurance, and benefits are provided according to a six-level system starting with mild cognitive impairment. In 2021, 10.2% of individuals older than 65 in South Korea were awarded LTCI. Long-term inpatients in nursing hospitals totaled 2.9% of the elderly population, and 0.5% of the older adults were local elderly care service beneficiaries. The overall social care receipt rate in the nation is 13.6%. The total expenditure on social care benefits was approximately 20 trillion won or 1% of the gross domestic product (GDP). Within this, LTCI benefits amounted to 11 trillion won (0.53% of GDP), 8 trillion won was spent on nursing hospital admissions for long-term inpatients, 400 billion won on care services for older adults, and 200 billion won for dementia care programs (National Health Insurance Service [NHIS], 2021; Seok et al., 2020a).

Jaeeun Seok, *Long-Term Care* In: *The Korean Welfare State*. Edited by: Kyungbae Chung and Neil Gilbert, Oxford University Press. © Oxford University Press 2024. DOI: 10.1093/oso/9780197644928.003.0007

LTC services are provided with in-kind benefits, and cash benefits are strictly limited. Beneficiaries of LTC can freely choose the type of benefit they prefer. Instead of a standardized care management system controlling care provision, recipients are empowered to select the type of service, care mix, and provider based on their needs and preferences. Seventy percent of beneficiaries currently use home-based care, and 30% choose institutional care.

Almost all of the providers of LTC services are found in the private sector. Individual proprietors operate more than 80% of the service entities among private operators. Because all applicants who met minimum standards are allowed to enter the market as LTC providers without additional restrictions, an oversupply of providers developed quickly. The excess of small-scale providers has hindered the development of service quality. In particular, home-based care providers do not perform the role of service managers. Instead, they simply connect service recipients to care workers. Meanwhile, 20% of home-based care is provided by family members who are formal care workers.

Social insurance contributes to financing most LTC services, and the government bears the administrative and benefit costs for low-income people. Service recipients provide a predetermined portion as out-of-pocket (OOP) expenses. Users of home-based care services are expected to reach 15% of the service costs, and users of institutional care should bear 20% of the cost of services and the total cost of meals. About 50% of beneficiaries are exempted from this or pay only a tiny portion as OOP expenses based on their income level.

With the country projected to become a super-aged society by 2025, South Korea's social care system for older adults, including LTCI, faces significant challenges. First, there is a need to improve LTC services to ensure dignity and quality of life for older adults. Home-based care should be significantly strengthened to support aging in place. It is also necessary to improve the quality of institutional care. Second, the social care system needs to be reorganized to make it more cost-effective to ensure sustainability. LTC costs and medical costs for older adults are expected to increase sharply in the coming years. In particular, South Korea faces an issue known as *social hospitalization*, in which many LTC recipients are hospitalized for an extended period in nursing hospitals. LTC and healthcare systems should be revised to eliminate unnecessary social hospitalization for their fiscal stability.

Background

In 2000, when South Korea first met the criteria of an aging society, a government-led public–private committee was formed to institutionalize LTC properly. In this regard, a 3-year pilot project was carried out from 2005 to 2007. Eventually, the Long-Term Care Insurance Act for the Elderly was enacted in 2007, and LTCI for older people was implemented in 2008. South Korea's introduction of universal public LTCI with a 10% aged population was quite preemptive compared to Germany and Japan, where public LTCI was introduced at 17–18% (Seok, 2010).

Respect for seniors has long been one of the core principles of the Neo-Confucian philosophy that has formed deep roots in South Korean society. People are expected to take good care of their ailing parents. At the same time, however, the foundation for family caring capacities, such as the nuclear family system and a sense of support, has been undermined. A care gap has emerged due to a shift toward a more individualistic lifestyle. Extreme events such as the suicide of elders, homicides committed by caregivers, and murder-suicides occasionally still occur based on multilayered modern pressures which stand in stark contrast with the aspirations of traditional ethics. In particular, since there was no governmental LTC service available in South Korea, the steep increase in the cost of medical care for older adults due to so-called social hospitalization and its economic burden on the family had to be addressed. There was a need to alleviate the care burden on the family and establish a cost-effective social system optimized for LTC needs.

The introduction of a LTC system for older adults was a campaign promise of President Roh Moo-Hyun and had strong backing from citizens. This was a meaningful institutional development in South Korea since, unlike in Germany or Japan, no such system or service had been previously available to the general public.

With the introduction of LTCI for older adults, South Korea's LTC policy for older people shifted from tax-based residual service to a universal system based on social insurance. Beyond simply increasing the number of beneficiaries of LTC services, the entire system of providing the services was transformed. Social insurance financing was newly created, and the payment method shifted from the subsidy method to payment based on service performance. Furthermore, introducing a market system with diverse competing service providers meant beneficiaries could select their service providers and purchase services.

Characteristics of the Policymaking Process

The most prominent characteristic of the policymaking process underlying Korea's LTCI system for older adults is the leading role played by the government in establishing the system. The government began reviewing the institutionalization of LTC before the public expressed any such need. An institutional framework was discussed using a public–private committee made up of private-sector experts and government officials as a platform, but the policy design was eventually led solely by the government and the influence of civil society was minimal during the introduction of the system.

The committee discussed several issues regarding the framework for the system: social insurance versus tax-based social services, a nationally standardized system versus a regionally flexible system, more lenient versus more stringent eligibility to be evaluated at moderate to severe levels of need, healthcare services to be included versus social care alone, allowing versus prohibiting cash benefits, public provider-centered versus private provider-centered delivery of services, service providers with specific qualifications versus diversified service providers, and whether or not to introduce a care management system. In particular, there was relatively fierce debate over adopting a centrally standardized social insurance system or a community-based tax system and providing a care management system.

The Public Long-Term Care Committee that met in 2003 and 2004 suggested a tax-based community service method, generous coverage that would apply to 12% of older adults, and the introduction of a care management system. However, the South Korean government eventually chose the social insurance model, stricter conditions of eligibility for severe compared to moderate level of need, and a social care–oriented and private provider-based system. It allowed diversified service providers but banned cash benefits. It also decided not to adopt a care management system.

Unlike Germany and Japan, South Korea had to establish service providers and train service personnel from scratch since no formal services had been available until then. Fearing that it might be "insurance without services," the government paid considerable attention to attracting private service providers before introducing the system. To lower entry barriers for private providers, the government streamlined national standards for qualification in terms of personnel and facilities to the degree possible.

As a result, the government could attract private providers, and trained care workers were available upon the system's introduction. However, a surplus of providers and many care worker training institutions caused confusion and unintended side effects.

Policy Design and Current Status

South Korea enacted the Long-Term Care Insurance Act for the Elderly in 2007 and has been implementing the LTCI system for older adults since July 2008.

Qualifications

LTCI is available for people 65 years of age or older who require LTC. Those younger than 64 with geriatric diseases such as dementia, cerebrovascular disease, and Parkinson's disease also are eligible. As in Japan, persons with disabilities who are younger than 65 are subject to a separate tax-based assistance system for the disabled. In designing the Korean system, the government reviewed Germany's national LTCI, which serves the disabled within a single system. However, it accepted the opinion of representatives of the disabled who argued that a separate system is needed to respond to the unique situations experienced by the disabled and focus on assistance with activities. When a person with a disability becomes older, they then become eligible for LTCI for older adults instead of the disability activity assistance system. However, complaints have been raised about the reduction in benefits resulting from this system change, and improvement measures are being considered.

LTCI for older adults is a form of social insurance based on contributions. However, it is a socially integrated system that covers the care burden for low-income families who have difficulty paying for social insurance. In their case, the government bears the cost of benefits for low-income people.

Qualification for LTC is determined through a standardized professional review process called Long-Term Care Accreditation that systematically evaluates applicants' related needs. The reviewers exclusively consider the degree of need for care. Individual circumstances such as the type of cohabitation; status of family caregivers, if any; and housing status are not reflected in the review process. A function evaluator from the National Health Insurance Service (NHIS) visits the applicant to evaluate the mental and physical condition of the applicant using a standardized tool for the evaluation of LTC needs. The measure consists of 52 items divided into five areas, including activities of daily living, cognitive impairment, problem behaviors, and nursing and rehabilitation treatment needs. Following a tree analysis based on data mining, an accreditation score is calculated considering the degree of dysfunction and required service time. The accreditation score and a doctor's opinion are submitted to the Long-Term Care Rating Committee, which then decides whether the applicant is eligible and determines the level of accreditation.

When the system was introduced in 2008, LTC accreditation was granted at three levels of severity. However, in 2014, it was expanded to a five-level system. In 2018, it was further developed into a six-level system that includes a cognitive support level that encompasses mild dementia regardless of LTC accreditation score. The most severe is Level 1, and Levels 5 and 6 (cognitive support) are grades of mild dementia with a low degree of physical dysfunction.

Initially, there were only 210,000 beneficiaries of LTC, all with severe care needs, accounting for 3.1% of those aged 65 and older. When the scope of accreditation was expanded in 2014 and 2018, the number of beneficiaries soared. By 2021, the number of LTC recipients reached 920,000, or 10.2% of those aged 65 and older. The beneficiary rates rose by 3.3 times from 2008, when the system was introduced. The proportions of each level within the system are 5.8% at Level 1, 11.2% at Level 2, 29.3% at Level 3, 42.2% at Level 4, 9.5% at Level 5, and 2.0% at the cognitive support level (National Health Insurance Service, 2021; see Table 6.1).

South Korea is notable for the substantial number of older adults hospitalized for extended periods in nursing homes covered by health insurance. Among all the cases of long-term hospitalization lasting more than 1 year in nursing hospitals, 89.1% are people aged 65 and older. Most of these patients suffer from cognitive impairment and poor physical function but have low medical needs, a situation described as "social hospitalization." The introduced self-pay cap system to strengthen health insurance coverage incentivizes older adults to stay in nursing homes over extended periods. Treatment in nursing hospitals accounts for 45% of the total reimbursement for the maximum OOP expenses, and 64% of people have the total OOP costs reimbursed (National Health Insurance Service, 2019; Kim, 2019; Seok, 2020a). There are 320,000 beds in South Korea's nursing hospitals, and the inpatient rate of people older than 65 is 81.5%, or approximately 250,000

Table 6.1 Changes in long-term care recipients and finances

	2010	2012	2014	2016	2018	2020	2021
Share of population older than 65(%)	10.8	11.5	12.4	13.2	14.3	15.7	16.6
Share of population older than 80(%)	1.9	2.1	2.4	2.8	3.2	3.6	3.9
Share of long-term care certified person (B/A, %)	4.6	5.4	6.2	7.1	8.4	9.7	10.2
Expenditure on long-term care insurance (1 billion won)	2,589	2,911	3,740	4,707	6,676	9,344	10,959
Long-term care expenditure as a percentage of GDP(%)	0.19	0.20	0.24	0.27	0.35	0.48	0.53

Source: Korean Statistical Information Service (KOSIS),
https://kosis.kr/statHtml/statHtml.do?orgId=301andtblId=DT_111Y002andcheckFlag=N; and
National Health Insurance Service (NHIS), The long-term care insurance (LTCI) statistics yearbooks.

individuals. If 920,000 (10.2%) among those eligible for LTC are added to the 250,000 (about 2.9%) hospitalized in a LTC hospital, the rate of social care reaches 13.1% (National Health Insurance Service, 2021).

In addition, local governments in South Korea operate a tax-based senior care service that provides a 50% home-based LTC benefit to 50,000 people (0.5%) from middle- and lower-income families who failed to pass the LTC eligibility examination. This senior care service includes services to check on older adults' well-being and link them to resources to prevent lonely deaths among older people living alone.

As of 2021, 13.6% of the total elderly, or 1.22 million people, are receiving social care in Korea: 10.2% through LTCI, 2.9% at nursing hospitals and 0.5% through elderly care services supported by local governments (Statistics Korea, 2022; National Health Insurance Srevice, 2021).

Major countries of the Organisation for Economic Cooperation and Development (OECD) had an average social care rate of 14.2% in 2019, with an average rate for the aged demographic at 17.3%. Based on South Korea's rate of elderly population (assessed at 16.6% in 2021), the social care rate of 13.6% is similar to that of other OECD countries. However, the country has a higher rate of social hospitalization in nursing hospitals, an issue that needs to be addressed.

Benefits

Like the system followed in Japan, LTC in South Korea is based on in-kind benefits. In very exceptional cases, cash benefits are allowed as allowances for the family caregiver (150,000 won per month, equivalent to 15% of home-based care benefits). Cash benefits are prohibited for the following three reasons:

Concerns about the misuse of pay
Concerns that focus on cash benefits might discourage formal services from being developed in a situation where infrastructure has not been developed sufficiently
Concerns that the choice of cash benefits might eventually lead to the burden of care being imposed on family members, especially women

LTC benefits-in-kind are broadly divided into institutional care and home-based care. Institutional care includes care facilities and communal homes. In contrast, home-visit care, home-visit bathing, home-visit nursing, day and night care, short-term care, and welfare supplies belong to the home-based care category.

As in Germany, LTC benefits in South Korea focus on assisting elderly persons with activities of daily living through physical and housekeeping support. Medical services for LTC beneficiaries are linked through health insurance. For users of institutional care, medical services are provided through commissioned doctors and partner hospitals. Recently, there have been efforts to provide home-based medical services to users of home-based care.

LTC beneficiaries are free to choose between institutional care and home-based care. Thirty percent of users select institutional care, and 70% are users of home-based care. The proportions of institutional care and home care by level are 51.1% versus 48.9% for Level 1, 53.3% versus 46.7% for Level 2, 34.8% versus 65.2% for Level 3, 19.5% versus 80.5% for Level 4, 5.4% versus 94.6% for Level 5, and 0.3% versus 99.7% for the cognitive support grade (NHIS, 2021).

Only those in Levels 1 and 2 were freely allowed institutional care in the early stages of implementation due to a lack of facility infrastructure. Those in Level 3 were allowed to elect institutional care minimally. Currently, however, institutional care can be selected regardless of level. As a result, as of 2020, about 70% of institutional care users are in Levels 3 and 4. The portions of institutional care by level are 35.1% for Levels 1 and 2, 69.2% for Levels 3 and 4, and 1.5% for Levels 5 and 6. For home-based care, they are 13.2% for Levels 1 and 2, 80.5% for Levels 3 and 4, and 11.9% for Levels 5 and 6 (NHIS, 2021).

Even among those with the same level of LTC accreditation, the benefit amount for institutional care differs from that for home-based care. There are preset institutional care benefit amounts for each accreditation level. The standard benefit amount is applied for institutional care at Level 3 or lower. For home-based care, an upper limit on benefits is set for each accreditation level, and beneficiaries can only use services within their limit. A maximum of 1.6 million Korean won per year can be used to avail care equipment apart from the limit for home-based care benefits, and only home-based care beneficiaries are eligible.

Under the principle specified in the Long-Term Care Insurance for the Elderly Act that home-based care takes priority, the out-of-pocket expense level for home-based care (15% of the benefit-cost) is set lower than that for institutional care (20% of the benefit-cost). However, institutional care benefits are higher at 145% of home care benefits. Institutional care benefits include related housing costs. Even among those assigned to the same level, there is a significant difference in the benefit amount, service period, and scope of service provision between institutional care and home-based care. For these reasons, institutional care tends to appear more attractive to users (Seok et al., 2020b). The institutional care benefit covers housing expenses and hiring of nutritionists and cooks, but food costs are not covered. South Korea should eliminate the incentives to use institutional care, as was done in Japan and Germany, by excluding both housing and meals from benefits and making these the users' responsibility (Seok et al., 2020b).

Although users of home-based care enjoy the right to mix services, most employ only a single service. Eighty-two percent of home-based care beneficiaries use only one service (home-visit care, in most instances). Since home-based care service entities mainly provide only a single type of service, many are reluctant to cater to users who wish to use their service only partially. In addition, home-visit care service is offered according to the packages/systems that the provider has developed. The situation is far from a user-centered service, with a uniform provision of 3 hours per day. Since there is no care-management system to organize and manage the services in a user-centered manner, the burden of care on users and their families remains heavy. LTC beneficiaries are driven toward institutional care and nursing hospitals due to the unfavorable provision of benefits in home-based care compared to institutional care, the insufficiency of the home-based care benefit, and the rigidity of the system for the provision of home-based care services (Seok et al., 2020b).

Service Provision System

Adoption of Quasi-market Mechanism

LTCI for older adults is a form of universal social insurance. The Ministry of Health and Welfare is in charge of the policy, and the NHIS is responsible for its management and operation. The NHIS collects insurance contributions and pays service costs, screens and determines eligibility for benefits, and evaluates the quality of services. Local governments are responsible for designating, managing, and supervising LTC institutions and granting certification to LTC workers (Kim and Kwon, 2021).

South Korea has adopted a quasi-market mechanism for its LTC delivery system. The government has established an LTC market in which service providers in various operating entities compete freely, and recipients have the right to choose their service providers. The government eliminated price competition by imposing standard service prices; however, service providers are expected to improve their service quality to attract more users (Yi and Seok, 2019a, 2019b).

This quasi-market mechanism focuses on resolving the lack of accountability in the delivery system by making service providers more responsive to service users' needs (Gilbert et al., 2009). However, the South Korean care management system does not formally or professionally intervene in the usage of services. Thus the role of addressing fragmentation and discontinuity by selecting types of benefits suitable for beneficiaries and the task of coordinating an appropriate service mix is left entirely to service users. According to Gilbert et al.'s (2009) assessment, South Korea's LTC delivery system policies are based on egalitarianism rather than professionalism and enable an open rather than a closed system (Seok, 2010).

The government is in charge of financing and creating a quasi-market, and it also plays the role of both regulator and evaluator. The provision of services is generally designed to be handled by private providers. The government sets national minimum standards for each type of benefit to ensure service quality and allows suppliers who meet these standards to register as service providers. Low minimum standards were imposed to actively attract private suppliers during the introductory stage. A low-threshold policy was adopted so that providers who meet the criteria could participate as service providers as long as they registered as a LTC entity. The government allowed any operating entity to participate, whether individuals, for-profit private operators, or non-profit private operators. Control of the total number of providers to suit service demand was not considered (Seok et al., 2015; Seok, 2017) (Figure 6.1).

Home-Based Care Provision

Weak, small institutions dominate the home-based care delivery system due to the oversupply of home-visit care providers. The existing proportion of individual operators is overwhelming at 80–90%. Every year, approximately one-third of these providers go out of business, but another one-third enter the market, reflecting the extreme volatility in the sector. This unhealthy market culture promotes expedient, illegal attempts to gain clients and exaggerated claims to attract users. Home-visit care providers play the role of intermediary between users and care workers, while the part of managing services and care workers is essentially neglected. In addition, the risk of instability in the home-visit care market resulting from unstable service demand is mainly passed on to care workers in the form of tenuous employment and income (Seok et al., 2016).

The service mix rights granted to service users have proved virtually useless. Because most home-based care organizations provide only a single type of service, a user-centered service mix across multiple organizations cannot function in practice. In addition, home-visit care services are offered in a provider-centered manner. A longitudinal study using administrative data on recipients who had initially chosen home-based benefits shows that those living together with family members were more likely to leave an institution

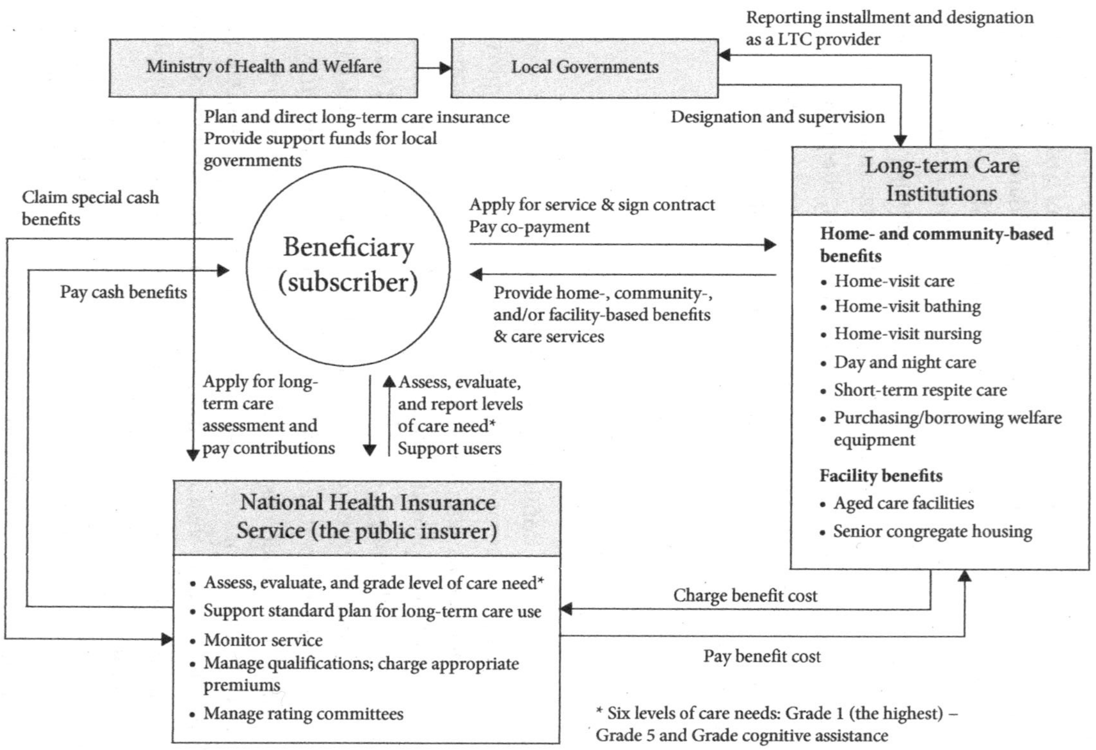

Ministry of Health and Welfare
Local Governments
Reporting installment and designation as a LTC provider
Plan and direct long-term care insurance
Provide support funds for local governments
Designation and supervision
Long-term Care Institutions
Home- and community-based benefits
• Home-visit care
• Home-visit bathing
• Home-visit nursing
• Day and night care
• Short-term respite care
• Purchasing/borrowing welfare equipment
Facility benefits
• Aged care facilities
• Senior congregate housing
Claim special cash benefits
Beneficiary (subscriber)
Apply for service & sign contract
Pay co-payment
Provide home-, community-, and/or facility-based benefits & care services
Pay cash benefits
Apply for long-term care assessment and pay contributions
Assess, evaluate, and report levels of care need*
Support users
National Health Insurance Service (the public insurer)
• Assess, evaluate, and grade level of care need*
• Support standard plan for long-term care use
• Monitor service
• Manage qualifications; charge appropriate premiums
• Manage rating committees
Charge benefit cost
Pay benefit cost
* Six levels of care needs: Grade 1 (the highest) – Grade 5 and Grade cognitive assistance

Figure 6.1 The delivery system of Long-Term Care Insurance.
Source: Kim and Kwon (2021, p. 24).

or nursing home sooner than those living alone (Seok and Yi, 2017). Because the burden of care on the family has still not been relieved, there are many cases where older adults give up their home life for a nursing hospital or institutional care despite preferring to remain at home.

Meanwhile, family caregivers, who were not considered in the policy design, account for 20% of those engaged in home-visit care services. At one time, the proportion reached as high as 40%. A family care worker is a family member qualified to be a caregiver who provides services to their family members. On paper, family care workers are employed by home-visit care service providers and receive wages. In reality, however, their salaries tend to be recognized as a sort of cash benefit paid through the Family Caregiver Allowance. The government has attempted to curb the number of family care workers because it is challenging to monitor the services provided. To this end, the hours of accredited service provided per day by family care workers is limited to 60–90 minutes, which is one-third of the general limit (Seok et al., 2020b).

Provision of Institutional Care .

The types of facility services are divided into aged care facilities with a capacity of 10 or more per facility and senior congregate housing with five to nine people or less per housing unit. There are roughly 180,000 aged care facilities operating in South Korea and about 20,000 elderly care homes. The total capacity of institutional care facilities is 2.2% of the population aged 65 and older. The average number of people in a given aged care facility is 48, and the median number is 29. The middle and median quota for each home for senior congregate housing is 9. In case the entity operating a nursing facility for the elderly is an individual, the size of the facility is typically small. In the case of a corporation, the size of the facility tends to be relatively large.

The capacity fill rate for institutional care facilities is 85.6%. Due to the aggressive expansion of nursing hospitals, active creation of demand, and policy support based on the health insurance copayment cap system, LTC institutional care facilities are undergoing a management crisis.

Aged care facilities in South Korea are operated by individuals (66.7%), corporations (30.4%), public organizations (2.6%), and other entities (0.3%). Senior congregate housing is managed by individuals (91.3%), corporations (8%), public organizations (0.3%), and other entities (0.4%).

Table 6.2 Long-term care facilities and workforce

	2010	2012	2014	2016	2018	2020
Beds in residential long-term care facilities (beds)	116,782	131,761	150,579	168,356	180,428	200,379
Residential long-term care facilities (place)	3,751	4,326	4,871	5,187	5,320	5,763
Home-based care facilities (place)	11,228	10,730	11,672	14,211	15,970	19,621
Long-term care workforce (persons)	245,074	251,131	290,573	341,424	417,974	500,521

Source: National Health Insurance Service (NHIS), The long-term care insurance (LTCI) statistics yearbooks.

The facility standards for institutional care facilities are based on a rule of four people per room. As for the workforce employed at elderly care facilities, there should be one direct-care worker per 2.5 beneficiaries, one nursing staff per 25 beneficiaries, and one social worker per 50 beneficiaries. In the case of care workers, considering three shifts per day, a 52 hour-work week, and statutory paid leave, the number of older adults assigned to each care worker should be 7–8 during the day and 20 at night. This means the work is labor-intensive, and it is not easy to guarantee the quality of service. In response, there is currently a plan to elevate the workforce standards to reduce the number to 2.1 beneficiaries per direct-care worker within 3 years (Table 6.2).

Regulatory Efforts in the Long-Term Care Market

Given the difficulties experienced by the LTC market, the government has reshuffled its regulations on the LTC service market (Jung et al., 2014; Seok, 2017). In 2018, the government strengthened the rules on entry and exit of service providers to boost the number of reliable providers in the LTC market. Furthermore, the system was shifted from a registration system to a designation system by raising the standards for provider entry examinations. To filter out bad operators with repeated entries and exits, the government also incorporated service history and a reputation inquiry into the review and qualitative evaluation of the LTC institution operation plan. In addition, the government allowed each local government to manage the number of service institutions under its jurisdiction in line with the demand and supply in the region. In addition, a system (effective in 2025) for redesignating service providers every 6 years has been introduced. This redesignation system will make it possible to expel poor performers by considering the results of the reputation and service evaluations conducted every 3 years. However, the operation of an entrance examination and designation system for new suppliers over the past 3 years in Seoul shows that 95.5% of the applicants are being redesignated. Thus these strengthened measures have not yet yielded results, and the impact on creating a healthy LTC market may not be significant.

To prevent LTC institutions from passing their risk of instability on to workers through reductions in labor costs, the government has introduced a regulation that requires a certain percentage of service expenditures to be devoted to labor costs.

The government discloses the results of the service quality evaluations on LTC institutions conducted by the NHIS every 3 years to resolve information asymmetry. The evaluation score of an institution is set as an absolute score so that institutions can be compared objectively. The government publishes an overall score and ratings in five quality-management categories.

To improve service usage behaviors of beneficiaries who are biased toward home-visit care, the government temporarily increased the upper limit of benefits by 50% for using day-/night-care benefits. As a result, several day- and night-care facilities were established, and an increase in day- and night-care users was observed. The upper limit for day and night protection has been adjusted to a 20% premium.

In addition, the government mandated that a visiting social worker be deployed to manage service cases and oversee quality control for home-visit care service providers. A visiting social worker should be assigned to home-visit care institutions with 15 or more beneficiaries, and one visiting social worker should be deployed for every 30 beneficiaries.

To prevent care institutions from avoiding patients with cognitive impairment and as a means to improve dementia services, the government installed dementia-specialized facilities with trained personnel and higher facility standards for each benefit type and also prepared special subsidy rates for dementia care. Benefits in the range of 110–123% of the conventional subsidy are provided to dementia specialist rooms at aged care facilities, 124%

is allowed to dementia-specialist senior congregate housing, and 126% is offered to day- and night-care facilities dedicated to dementia.

Care Workers

A care worker certification system was created for direct LTC services in preparation for introducing LTCI. In the early stages of introducing the system, care workers were trained through a 240-hour course (80 hours of in-class sessions, 80 hours of practice, and 80 hours of on-the-job training) offered at private educational institutions.

These private educational institutions were only sparsely regulated, and the quality of education was not ensured at an adequate level. In April 2010, the government amended the law to switch the registration system to a designation system for education institutions training care workers. In addition, the National Qualification Examination for Care Professionals (held at least once a year, with a minimum required passing score of 60/100) was introduced. Care worker licenses are now issued only to those who have passed the national exam after taking a training course.

So far, 2 million people have acquired a nursing care professional license, but the number of people currently working in the field is roughly 500,000 (25% of licensees). More than 95% of these care workers are women, and the average age of care workers is 58 (Lim et al., 2019). A significant proportion of care workers are aged 65 and older. LTC institutions struggle to hire caregivers: the farther they are from Seoul and its surrounding areas, the more severe the labor shortage they experience.

The government has regulated institutions to guarantee proper working conditions for care workers. It is trying to prevent abuse of the dispatch and service job system by providing a clause stating that workers must conclude an employment contract directly with the head of the institution. In addition, it is recommended that employers secure the four major social insurances for care workers and comply with the Labor Standards Act.

It was found that the most significant challenge for care workers, both for home-based and institutional care, was low wages. However, most home-visit care workers work under a no-contract wage payment system that links wages to service performance. They may be placed in poor working conditions with no guarantees of employment or income. In addition, the poor public reputation of the care work profession results in low self-esteem, and the ample supply of qualified workers increases the risk of job loss (Jeon, 2010; Kwon et al., 2018; Seok, 2020). In the case of care workers serving at a care institution, the labor burden is significant because each caregiver has to attend to seven or eight people during the daytime.

In addition, more should be done to provide a safer environment for care work. Many care workers experience musculoskeletal disorders throughout their careers, but these conditions are seldom recognized as an occupational illnesses. Sometimes they are even exposed to risks of violence and sexual assault (Seok, 2020).

Education and capacity-building are not provided systematically to care workers. However, with the amended law that requires local governments to create support centers for care workers, such centers are being established in respective regions, providing job training, personal support services, and protection of rights and interests.

The outlook for the professional development of nursing care workers is not promising. There is no promotion system for experienced caregivers. However, in 2017, a long-term service incentive system was introduced that offers financial incentives to care workers working at the same institution for more than 60 hours per month for a period longer than 36 months.

Service Unit Cost

Long-Term Care Service Fees refer to the service price set by government policy and granted to providers in exchange for services. The price is an important policy signal that the government delivers to service providers and users in the LTC service market. The service fee impacts service providers' decisions to participate in the market and their behaviors. It also affects service use decisions and the usage behavior of recipients.

South Korea's Long-Term Care Fees are based on a comprehensive fee system for each type of benefit. The inclusive fee system is not a method for calculating the fee for respective service activities but a method in which fixed service prices are set for each service unit, per day, per case and hour. For institutional care, it is a daily fee; for home-visit care, an hourly service fee; and for home-visit bathing, a service fee per case.

Long-Term Care Fees are calculated by adding labor and management costs. Labor costs consist of the labor of the direct service personnel. The input varies depending on the accreditation grade and overhead labor cost (which remains the same regardless of the accreditation grade of clients). Based on a study of service time for each type of care worker (which is input differently according to the accreditation grade of the clients involved), the relative information of the direct service workforce's labor cost by the severity of patients' needs is derived and used as the basis for the differential rate of subsidy. Private suppliers are dissatisfied with this system since the price does not consider profit, facility investment, or facility depreciation (Seok, 2008).

Accordingly, in Korea's system for LTC payments to providers, the differential rate reflects the number of service resources required. In the case of institutional care and day- and night-care, a differential comprehensive flat-rate system has been adopted that reflects the number of service resources needed based on the accreditation grade of LTC. In the case of institutional care, the Grade 3 fee is applied to Grade 3 and below. In the case of day- and night-care, a differential comprehensive flat-rate system is used based on the LTC accreditation grade and hours of usage.

In the case of home-visit care, a differential comprehensive fee system has been applied according to hours of use regardless of the LTC certification level. After 120 minutes, the per-hour rate for home-visit care declines; this is intended to reduce the current 3–4 hours of service time per visit. Recently, to prevent home-visit care providers from shunning the most severe cases, a plan to reflect the difficulty of care is being considered for the most severe grades (Grades 1 and 2).

The institutional care fee is 145% higher than the cap for home care benefits. Some argue that this gap is inappropriate since different social resources are provided to institutional care and home care for the same accreditation level, which causes people to abandon home-based care. A plan is being considered to allocate the same levels of social resources to the same LTC accreditation level regardless of the service being used (Seok et al., 2020b).

Financing

The social insurance method was selected to finance the Long-Term Care Service in South Korea. Before introduction of the system, a taxation method was also considered. However, the government eventually chose social insurance, following in the footsteps of historical institutionalism in other countries. The fact that Japan and Germany also introduced LTC systems based on social insurance and that it is more challenging to collect tax stably than to collect social insurance contributions played a significant role in the government's decision.

LTCI for older adults is essentially equivalent to health insurance. Its structure provide social solidarity and intergenerational support. The entire nation pays social insurance, but a relatively small number of LTC beneficiaries receive the benefits.

The funding for LTCI draws on insurance contributions, payroll contributions on behalf of the recipients of low-income medical benefits, and government subsidies. Grants to LTCI account for 67% of the funding; the cost of medical benefits is 20%, and national subsidies make up 13%. The central and local governments pay the payroll contributions on behalf of low-income medical benefit recipients. The national subsidy covers 20% of income from contributions to LTCI.

Individual insurance contributions are calculated by multiplying the health insurance contribution by the contribution rate to LTCI. The NHIS collects integrated LTC and health insurance contributions but manages them separately as different accounts.

Funding for LTC expanded rapidly by 5.1 times, from 2 trillion won in 2009 to 10.9 trillion in 2021. During the same period, the number of accredited LTC beneficiaries reached 930,000, a 4.3-fold increase from 220,000 in 2009 (NHIS, 2021). The main contributor to the growth in financing is the rise in the number of persons recognized as requiring LTC (80%). In contrast, the increases in benefits and payments extended to providers were influential. When South Korea enters the super-aged society phase in the future and, given the more rapid aging, potentially progresses toward an ultra-super-aged society, funding for LTC will increase exponentially. Therefore, securing the sustainability of the LTC system is a critical task ahead for policymakers.

Copayment by Service Users

LTCI in South Korea imposes a copayment on service users. To encourage the use of home-based care, the level of OOP expenses was set at 15% of the service costs for home-based care and 20% of the service costs for institutional care. In addition, the cost of food must be entirely borne by the user when they avail of institutional care. High-end facilities offering rooms that accommodate one or two people rather than the standard of four people per bedroom are allowed to charge additional housing costs.

In the case of low-income people, OOP expenses can be exempted or reduced. Currently, beneficiaries of LTC are divided into four groups: the exempt group, 60% exempt group, 40% exempt group, and the entire-payment group. The exempt groups make up 50% of all beneficiaries (Seok et al., 2020a). From the introduction of the system until 2018, recipients of public assistance were fully exempted, and the lowest income group paid 50% of their OOP expenses. The scope of exemption from copayments was greatly expanded with the revision of the law in 2018. Public assistance recipients are still fully exempted from copayments, but now the lowest income group receives a 60% exemption, and the second-lowest group is allowed a 40% exemption.

Challenges

Rapid Super-Aging and Sustainability

South Korea is facing increasing pressure regarding the sustainability of the LTCI system in its rapid progress toward an ultra-super-aged society. Fiscal expenditures on LTC have shown an average annual growth rate of 20% over the past 5 years, the highest among Korean social insurances. Accordingly, there have been rising concerns over pending financial challenges for LTCI. The advance toward a super-aged society means increasing demand for LTCI and a high number of people suffering cognitive impairment. Even when only a natural increase in demand is considered and the current insurance level is maintained, the social expenditure required for LTC is expected to reach 6% of GDP in 2060 from 0.9% in 2021 (. In addition, as the post-Korean War baby boom generation with significantly higher levels of education and living standards than the previous generation joins the elderly population, the pressure to improve the quality of LTC services and scope of coverage is bound to increase. Thus financial expenditures for LTC and concerns over its sustainability will grow, making it critical to cost-effectively reorganize the social care system for older adults, including LTCI (Seok et al., 2020a).

Reorganization of the Social Care System for Older Adults

South Korea must implement several reforms to provide a people-centered sustainable care system that supports human dignity and cost-effective social care (Seok et al., 2020a, 2020b).

First, the system faces a sustainability crisis due to the surge in medical expenses for older adults resulting from the medicalization of nursing care, as exemplified by the social hospitalization phenomenon. A restructuring of nursing hospitals and their functions is needed to address this. Furthermore, the current institutional measures that encourage hospitalization should be replaced. Although such a change is difficult due to resistance from nursing hospitals and the backlash from users who have no options beyond nursing hospitals, the government has recognized it as a necessary reform to ensure the sustainability of the social care system.

Second, institutional reforms are needed to improve the sufficiency, continuity, and flexibility of long-term home-based care services so that people can age in place.

Third, the government must develop a policy of expanding the role of emergent community care in local communities to delay entry into LTC as long as possible through appropriate aging management and healthy aging. In this regard, South Korea has been reviewing the integrated care policy led by local governments since 2018. A pilot project for integrated community care (2020–2022) is under way in 16 cities and counties.

Reinforcement of the Home-Based Care Benefits and Changes in the Service Provision System

The government is reviewing the feasibility of shifting to the principle of allocating the same social assistance for different types of care provided to the same level of need by bridging the gap between the benefits provided for institutional care and home-based care. Moreover, to make home-based care services more people-centered, the government is working to improve policy measures regarding the case management and coordination system, enhance the quality of home-based care services for critically ill patients to raise it to the level of institutional care, and make the provision of services more people-centered. In addition, the government will introduce a comprehensive home-based care benefit in July 2022 that integrates case management customized for each user with the LTC home-based benefit.

Second, the supply system should be improved so that LTC home-based care service providers can implement people-centered service case management. Transitioning from single-service providers to those offering multiple services should allow a more people-centered service mix actually to work. Furthermore, service providers should be scaled up through measures such as the fee policy. To encourage the fiscal stability of home-based care service providers, their proportion of permanent workers should be increased, and providers' management capacity needs to be strengthened.

Improvement of Long-Term Institutional Care Services

First, the incentive to choose institutional care over home-based care should be removed. As practiced in Germany and Japan, it is necessary to have service users pay for housing and food. There is also a need to reorganize the allocation system for social care resources so that only LTC recipients who are more eligible for institutional care, such as those with severe diseases or severe cognitive impairment, can use institutional care services.

Second, LTC institutions need to be made more people-centered. The COVID-19 pandemic demonstrated that the institutional standard of four-person rooms increases vulnerability to infection. It should be improved, and enough personal space provided to ensure dignity. Thus it is necessary to increase the number of private rooms and shift institutions to a more home-like unit care structure. Furthermore, the quality of service needs to be enhanced by reducing the number of care recipients per caregiver. Institutional services should become more people-centered to respect individuality and the right to self-determination.

Third, various institutions should be developed to improve the facility environment substantially and address diverse needs, and discriminatory pricing should be allowed. In this context, it is appropriate to approach the provision of service workers and customized services from the perspective of LTC policy and the residential environment from the standpoint of housing policy.

Fostering Long-Term Care Workers

Ensuring a sustainable LTC workforce is emerging as an important challenge. Institutions are having difficulty hiring and retaining care workers such as nurses, social workers, physical therapists, occupational therapists, nutritionists, and care workers to go out into the field. Unlike other developed countries, South Korea maintains barriers to immigration, such as language and qualification tests, so the proportion of migrant workers among frontline care workers remains insignificant. However, most private caregivers at nursing hospitals are migrant workers, such as ethnic Koreans from China.

Improving the treatment of care workers to ensure a stable workforce is directly related to LTC costs, which explains why the task has proved difficult (Seok, 2020). The government is trying to make progress by raising social awareness of care work as essential labor. In addition, it has set up Long-Term Care Worker Support Centers in each region to support worker well-being, education, and protection of rights and interests. Their professional prospects have been strengthened by introducing a promotion system and enhancing related education.

References

Gilbert, N., and Terrell, P. (2009). *Dimensions of social welfare policy* (7th ed.). Pearson.

Jeon, B. Y. (2010). Problems of long-term care worker for the elderly and search for alternative model and policy improvements in Korea. *Korean Social Policy Review, 17*(3), 67–91.

Jung, H. Y., Jang, S. R., Seok, J. E., and Kwon, S. M. (2014). Quality monitoring in long-term care in the Republic of Korea. In V. Mor, T. Leone, and A. Maresso (Eds.), *Regulating long-term care quality: An international comparison (health economics, policy and management)* (pp. 385–408). Cambridge University Press.

Kim, H. S., and Kwon, S. M. (2021). A decade of public long-term care insurance in South Korea: Policy lessons for aging countries. *Health Policy, 125*(1), 22–26.

Kim, Y. H. (2019). Financial sustainability and intergenerational fairness of long-term care insurance in Korea. *Health and Social Welfare Review, 40*(4), 149–177.

Kwon, H. J., Jeon, H. S., and Ko, J. W. (2018). Why do care workers return to work?: The institutional relations and precarious work. *Korean Journal of Social Welfare. 45*(3), 179–212.

Lim, J. M., Lee, Y. K., Kang, E. N., Lim, J. Y., Kim, J. H., Park, Y. S., Yoon, T. H., Yang, C. M., and Kim, H. S. (2019). A mid- to long-term plan for the supply of long-term care workers in a changing population structure. Research Report 2019–24. Korea Institute for Health and Social Policy.

National Health Insurance Service (NHIS). (2021). 2020 long-term care insurance (LTCI) statistics yearbooks. NHIS.

OECD. (2022). OECD Health Statistics 2022. https://www.oecd.org/els/health-systems/health-data.htm

Seok, J. E. (2008). The unit cost of care services in long-term care insurance in Korea. *Korean Journal of Social Welfare Studies 39*, 253–286.

Seok, J. E. (2010). Public long-term care insurance for the elderly in Korea: Design, characteristics, and tasks. *Social Work in Public Health, 25*(2), 185–209.

Seok, J. E. (2017). A study on rationalization of regulation for strengthening the publicness of long-term care services. *Health and Social Welfare Review, 37*(2), 423–451.

Seok, J. E. (2020). Vulnerability and social challenges of long-term care workers revealed in the COVID-19 phase. *Korean Journal of Social Welfare, 72*(4), 125–149.

Seok, J. E., Kim, Y. H., Moon, B. G., Jang, S. R., and Seo, D.M. (2020a). *In-depth financial evaluation on long-term care.* Ministry of Economy and Finance.

Seok, J. E., Kim, Y., Nam, H., and Choi, S. (2020b). *Development plan for long-term care policy in super-aged society.* Ministry of Health and Social Welfare. (prism.go.kr)

Seok, J. E., Lim, J. G., Jeon, Y. H., and Choi, S. H. (2015). *A reform plan on strengthen regulations on long-term care providers.* Ministry of Health and Social Welfare. (prism.go.kr)

Seok, J. E., Park, S. J., Kwon, H. J., and Choi, S. H. (2016). *A reform plan on reinforcement of home service of long-term care insurance for aging-in-place.* Ministry of Health and Social Welfare. (prism.go.kr)

Seok, J. E., and Yi, G. (2017). Analysis on the staying at-home of the qualified recipients of long-term care for aging in place. *Health and Social Welfare Review, 37*(4), 5–42.

Statistics Korea. (2022). Statistics on the aged. Statistics Korea. 2022 (kostat.go.kr)

Yi, G. J., and Seok, J. E. (2019a). Does the higher the competition in the long-term care market, the better the service quality? *Health and Social Welfare Review, 39*(4), 425–255.

Yi, G. J., and Seok, J. E. (2019b). Analysis of the impact of marketization of long-term care provision: Focusing upon the effects on cost and service quality. *Korean Social Security Studies, 35*(1), 103–128.

7

Inclusive Community Care Policies in Korea

Young-shin Jang[*]

Transition to Community Care

Korea transitioned into an aged society as the nation's population of people aged 65 and older accounted for more than 14% in 2017. The figure is expected to reach 20% by 2026, making it a super-aged society. Due to the rapid aging of Korean society, demand for care services for the elderly and the disabled is rising quickly.

An important characteristic of this aged society is the increase in the population requiring care. The number of elderly people who need care services in place of the usual family safety net is increasing year by year in Korea. As of 2017, 21.7% of the elderly are older than 80, and their numbers are increasing. The number of the elderly living alone was 23.6% in the same year, up 3.9 percentage points from 2008; this number is also increasing at a rapid pace every year. On the other hand, households where parents live with children decreased by 3.9 percentage points to 23.7%, while those of solely elderly couples remained in the 40–50% range. What are the difficulties faced by elderly couples living alone? Nursing problems if they are sick accounted for the greatest proportion of problems (19.0%), followed by economic uncertainties (17.3%) and psychological anxiety or loneliness (10.3%). The elderly are generally in poor health compared to the young. Prevalence rate of chronic diseases among them is 89.5%. Furthermore, 73.0% of these elderly are patients suffering more than two diseases, with an average of 2.7 chronic diseases.

---

[*] The author received a PhD in social welfare from Lutheran Seminary in Japan in 2012, and currently serves as the head of the Policy Research Division at the Korea National Council on Social Welfare. This chapter is a summary of "Why Community Care?" chapter 1 of a book published by the Council in 2019, which suggests directions for the community care system in Korea.

Young-shin Jang, *Inclusive Community Care Policies in Korea* In: *The Korean Welfare State*. Edited by: Kyungbae Chung and Neil Gilbert, Oxford University Press. © Oxford University Press 2024.
DOI: 10.1093/oso/9780197644928.003.0008

In addition, 21.1% of the elderly have depression, 83.5% were taking medications for 3 months or longer at the time of survey, and 19.5% of them need better nutrition, with 39.3% requiring special attention (Korea Institute for Health and Social Affairs, 2018). Because Koreans tend to increasingly live alone or with their spouse in their old age, and as the elderly and their children alike have weakening norms of cohabitation, the need for public systems is increasing.

The Korean government has made great efforts to expand care services by introducing a long-term care (LTC) system for the elderly in 2008, and the range of care services has also grown significantly (as noted in Chapter 6). The numbers of elderly who use long-term care insurance (LTCI) due to physical needs and the cost of their medical care are both soaring. The rapid aging of the population in Korea is the result of an increase in the number of elderly persons. In 2017, the number of LTC recipients was nearly 590,000, which represented 8% of the entire elderly population of 7.31 million, and the number of care service locations was 20,737. Compared to 10 years ago, the number of recipients has doubled, while the number of institutions has increased five-fold.[1] Given that the demand for care is expected to continue to soar, unfortunately, unnecessary hospitalizations or admissions to residential care facilities stand to increase as well. About 48% of long-term inpatients in nursing hospitals are not in need of medical care but seek "social hospitalization" due to other factors such as the absence of caregivers (Hwang Do-gyeong et al., 2016). Services in large facilities and hospitals are provided according to regulations and are effective for treatment and care, but these have limitations when it comes to alleviating the sense of loss that residents feel in unfamiliar living environments. It is normal for them to wish to return to their communities after care or treatment, but this is not always easy due to family care issues and lack of various home care services.

The move to establish a community care system is a preemptive measure to respond proactively to changes in Korea's social landscape, such as growing social hospitalization due to the aging population, the identified need of the disabled to avoid living in a care services facility, a growing demand for mental health welfare services, and the need to protect children. Therefore, heralding the era of US$30,000 in national income, Korea needs to take its welfare system to the level of advanced countries by adopting community care, and it is time to change the paradigm (Choi Gyun, 2018).

Community Care in Other Countries

One of the main drivers of community care policy in Korea and other developed countries is changing demographics. Because of the rapid increase in the number of elderly, care issues have become commonplace, and the quality of life and choices of those who are given care must be ensured. Another factor is the sustainability of the social security system given the surge of social insurance expenditures in line with the aging population.

Sweden turned to community care in the early 1970s, Britain in the early 1990s, and Japan in the mid-1990s. It took 20 years for Sweden to implement full-fledged community care since the country started discussions about it. For Britain, it took 15 years to do so since the 1990 legislation. In comparison, Japan established its community care system under the third amendment of the Nursing Care Insurance Act in a short span of 12 years.

Sweden

In Sweden, which experienced rapid population aging, elderly care developed early. Home care services began to be provided widely from the 1950s and became widespread as universal public services already in the 1970s. The ideal characteristics of elderly care can be summed up in terms of universality, generosity, public interest, and trust in public services. In other words, elderly care is a service that everyone can avail regardless of income, it is a generous service requiring a relatively large amount of money and manpower, and it is structured as a public service provided directly by local governments. Based on trust in the public sector, the system has evolved into a framework by which a professional workforce, such as care managers, exercises broad discretions in assessing care needs and managing the quality of services.

Since the 1990s, Sweden has found solutions to deal with changes in social service requirements through localization and marketization. In 1992, the Swedish government implemented *Adel Reformen* as an alternative to meet elderly welfare needs by streamlining its resource allocation practices without any further increase in public financial burden. Based on the new system, healthcare services were provided by the central government and metropolitan municipalities and social services by the municipalities. Localization through Adel Reformen eventually led to increased demand for social services instead of reducing demand for healthcare services to reduce the overall proportion of public care burden. To cope with the increased demand for social services within limited resources, municipalities were forced to concentrate on those with needs for critical care services, and people with minor care needs relied on informal care or private-sector services.

The Adel Reformen has the following characteristics: first, all elderly welfare services were transferred to the basic municipality, the *Kommun*, along with the required funds. This made nursing homes or care facilities that were mostly large in scale become smaller. One of the reasons for this was the fact that there were not many elderly people under the jurisdiction of local municipalities who needed critical or substantial care enough to be accommodated at these facilities. In addition, since home care services can reduce costs to the welfare budget more so than residential care services, Sweden greatly expanded home care services. Second, it shifted the basic direction of resources allocation for elderly welfare. Sweden started with a universal welfare policy that provided all people aged 65 or older with healthcare and welfare benefits, but the Adel Reformen shifted the policy to give more welfare benefits to elderly people older than 80 years. The Swedish government introduced this policy because there was a social consensus that most people in their 60s or 70s are still in good health and are active, and so should be given pensions only for their livelihoods. Once they reach 80 years of age, however, health deteriorates and they cannot lead their daily life independently. More than 78% of these elderly live alone after the demise of their spouses, and around 20% appeared to need welfare services desperately due to dementia and stroke. Third, healthcare and welfare services were unified. Generally, in most of the Western world, medical institutions are dedicated to medical care for the elderly, and dedicated social welfare organizations are responsible for welfare programs. Sweden's Adel Reformen significantly reduced elderly welfare costs by integrating healthcare, nursing care, and welfare services for the elderly in late years into a single administrative system.

United Kingdom

In the 1950s and 1960s, the United Kingdom had a fragmented and complex delivery system by which social services were provided by local governments depending on the needs of the elderly, children, healthcare, and education. As a result, services were not properly fit to the diverse needs of the community. To solve this problem, in the 1970s, local governments set up a Social Services Bureau under the Seebohm Reform to establish an integrated support system centered on households, and then, in the 1980s, promoted community care in earnest (Seebohm Report, 1968).[2] Community care in the United Kingdom is a way of providing welfare services based on the National Health Service and Community Care Act of 1990. The legislative intent of this law is still controversial. At the core of the arguments over community care is the main objective of the law: reduction of public costs by adopting market mechanisms. Clearly, the law was intended to cut costs, but, on the other hand, the intent to introduce reasonable and systematic mechanisms for service planning and delivery and increase user influence was as important as cost reduction (Kim Yong-deuk, 2006).

In this context, it would be worthwhile to examine the legislative backgrounds of the National Health Service and Community Care Act. The Act was primarily meant to address the soaring social security expenditures caused by the increase in residential services. Before 1980, local governments were responsible for providing assistance for residential services costs, and whether or not to provide assistance was at the discretion of experts. From 1980, however, recipients had to be qualified legally for social security benefits, and responsibility for the support was transferred to the central government. This change contributed to a dramatic increase in social security expenditures, causing a £500 million increase in social security expenses on residential services in the mid-1980s, from £10 million in 1980 (Kim Yong-deuk, 2006). Second, there was growing criticism that the social security policy led to "perverse effects." Proponents of this view demanded reform measures to eliminate these effects, which alluded to the fact that in reality a growing number of the disabled or elderly were admitted to residential service locations as costs of residential services were charged to social security benefits, although government policies preferred community-based services rather than residential ones. In addition, a care management system was introduced to give care managers the responsibility of budget execution for individual service users, which included assessing individual needs, identifying service providers, and allocating budgets to competing service providers.

People eligible for community care include adults and children living in the community who are in need of physical assistance and mental health services and who have difficulty in performing two or more daily tasks. An assessment is carried out with a focus on individual preferences and needs.

Based on this, a personalized care plan is set up, and the individual and the local government go through a process of consultation. The cost of care is partially or fully subsidized by the government based on income standards.

Japan

Japan became an aging society in 1970, 30 years earlier than Korea, and was declared an aged society in 1994, with a 23-year gap between the two countries. In 2017, the proportion of elderly people in Japan reached 27.7%, making the country a super-aged society. Community care in Japan was initiated in response to its changing population structure, including rapid aging. Japan has a comprehensive system that provides housing, medical and nursing care, preventive healthcare, and life support services so that people can age in place and maintain their existing lifestyles even when they are in serious condition and need nursing care. In Japan, every local community has a community support center where care managers, social workers, and nurses identify the conditions and needs of individuals and provide support, thus enabling seamless services through a care management plan (Lee Geon-sae, 2018).

In 2011, the *2025 Model* initiated full-blown reorganization of the county's social security system as the elderly healthcare system was no longer equipped to cope with a growing demand for healthcare and welfare services for the elderly. Japan reached its final solution after numerous trials and errors and debate: a community care system based on integration of community-based healthcare and welfare. The community care system heralds a shift from the existing hospital-centered system to a community-oriented one. It also means a service combining healthcare and welfare services rather than a healthcare-centered one. This approach ultimately promotes aging in place, which refers to availing care services at the place where the individual lives, to the end of life, via at-home services, not care home services.

Comprehensive community care is defined as a system that can ensure that housing is provided depending on needs, and a wide range of life support services including healthcare and nursing care and welfare services can be delivered appropriately across areas of people's daily lives to ensure safety, security, and health in their lives. Here, the areas for comprehensive community care are communities accessible within 30 minutes from a middle school district. For comprehensive community care, local comprehensive support centers and in-home medical linkage bases are established, and local care meetings are held. Local comprehensive support centers are put in place in every community with a population of 20,000 or so. These community support centers act as an administrative body to coordinate comprehensive care in the community. At every center, nurses, social workers, and care managers are engaged to provide various services such as counseling and provision of information about comprehensive community care services and care planning.

Under the comprehensive community care scheme, uninterrupted continuing services are provided through the process of hospitalization, outpatient visits, and return to home, thus meeting the following five requirements. First, in-home care services are provided 24 hours a day by strengthening the connection with medical care, along with home nursing and rehabilitation services. Second, nursing care is provided through visiting nurse services capable of 24-hour response, along with residential care facilities. Third, self-reliance support and prevention activities are essential. Fourth, rights advocacy and various life support services for nursing care, meals, and shopping has been strengthened. Fifth, housing for the elderly has been improved so that senior citizens can lead their daily lives conveniently.

To promote community care in Japan, numerous systems and laws have been enacted including the Comprehensive Health and Welfare Measures for the Elderly, the Elderly Health Act, the Nursing Care Insurance Act, the Medical Care System for the Elderly, and Community Care Reinforcement Act. The Community Care System was launched in April 2012, under the 2011 amendment to the Nursing Care Insurance Act to strengthen the foundations of the nursing care service. The system began to draw attention with the opening of the comprehensive community support centers, as provided for in the 2006 amendment to the Nursing Care Insurance Act. Related laws include the Law for Promotion of Comprehensive Medical Care and Nursing Care, established in 2014, and the Community Care Reinforcement Act, enacted in 2017. Under the guidelines of the Japanese government, each municipal government is required to formulate a local healthcare plan every 3 years and establish a nursing care plan every second year.

Japan regards the hospitalization of elderly people and their increasing medical expenses as a serious social issue. The community care system operates in the larger context of transferring the delivery system from hospitals to communities. Comprehensive Community Care aims to build a local resources system that supports in-home living, not hospitalization.

Japan's community care takes into account the requirements of an elderly person who needs protection. There are nearly 4,300 local comprehensive support centers across the country per residential area unit with an elderly population of 10,000. The center's care manager sets up a care plan customized to the conditions and needs of individuals. In addition to healthcare, nursing care, and life support services, the center provides senior citizens with services including 24-hour visits and preventive care to help them live in a group home or in their own homes.

Since its launch under the 2014 amendment to the medical fees system, the Comprehensive Community Care Ward system has been covering acute-phase patients to establish an additional safety net that complements the Community Care System. Japan's community care system is basically tuned to providing housing services and is a community-based scheme that ensures effective delivery of diverse life support services including medical and nursing care, preventive healthcare, and welfare services for people's safety and health.

Promoting Community Care to Realize an Inclusive Welfare State

Directions for the Promotion of Community Care

The Moon Jae-in administration has set a "nation that is responsible for my life" as the national goal and announced the concept of an inclusive welfare state for all in order to improve citizen's quality of life. Korean society is facing rapid changes due to sharply dropping fertility rates and rapid aging. To positively accommodate these needs for change and realize a sustainable welfare society, the Korean government pursues an "inclusive welfare state that everyone enjoys." The Ministry of Health and Welfare (MoHW) defines an inclusive welfare state as "a country where every individual can equally enjoy the fruits of economic development and welfare benefits and exert their capabilities and potential to the fullest." Such inclusive welfare is conceived of in philosophical approaches such as humanism, universalism, social integration, mutual benefit, respect for diversity, and realization of the justice of distribution. Ultimately, it will lead to income-led growth by increasing the disposable incomes and expenditures of its people and thereby create a virtuous cycle of welfare, growth, and employment (Kim Yong-deuk, 2006).

The government was driven to consider the adoption of community care because of (1) increasing needs for care services due to rapidly dropping birth rates and accelerating aging, which are expected to drive the country into a super-aged society by 2026; (2) the growing number of mild-case patients admitted to nursing hospitals or residential care facilities due to lack of caring services in the community, resulting in increased medical expenses; and (3) a recognition that current elderly care and healthcare services are based on hospitals and facilities, which lower individuals' quality of life and are not desirable due to concerns over violation of human rights.

The MoHW announced in its January 2018 Annual Report to the President that it was developing plans to promote community-based healthcare and welfare services. In March of the same year, the MoHW made public the promotion of community care and policy directions to realize an inclusive welfare state. The government selected community care as one of the community inclusion policies for all to realize optimal quality of life. Thus, the state will provide comprehensive support depending on the situations and needs of individuals in their homes and communities. In other words, in order to become a people-centered inclusive welfare state, people must be able to live happily where they choose. To this end, the government aims to establish a community care services system that links and supports comprehensive services such as healthcare, housing, and care so that the elderly and the disabled who need care services can settle into and live with their communities.

The MoHW is pushing forward with a comprehensive policy that combines three communities and three care modes through the extension of community and the continuity of care. *Community care* means a system that organizes three dimensions of living in a community—care in the community, care by the community, and decentralization—and three dimensions of care: medical and health service, social care service, and living independently, diversely, and implicitly (Kim Yong-deuk, 2018).

The values that community care espouses are (1) upholding human rights and quality of life for the service user, (2) strengthening of decentralization, (3) ensuring the sustainability of inclusive welfare and job creation, and (4) encouraging community reentry. In upholding these values, community care aims to enhance recipients' welfare experiences by helping them live in their community uninterrupted. It also relates to decentralization and the increasing role of local communities in implementing community care and community reentry. The government also expects that new care services jobs can be added by expanding services such as visiting nurses and 24-hour care services in the process of reducing elderly medical costs and promoting sustainable, inclusive welfare. Finally, to help seniors, persons with disabilities, and children in need of care services lead decent lives in their community, the government is also pursuing the restoration of community networks by raising awareness and boosting the participation of service users and citizens.

Community care has five key objectives: (1) expanding social services, such as care and welfare; (2) strengthening the community-based health management system; (3) supporting the dwelling of people in need of care; (4) inducing rational use of hospitals and facilities; and (5) spreading community care infrastructure among communities and enhancing accountability. Expansion of social services includes strengthening the security of care services, including LTC, and expanding services for safe living. Strengthening the community-based health management system includes reinforcing community-based healthcare services to safeguard the health rights of vulnerable groups and manage chronic diseases. To ensure that people in need of care do not experience any difficulty in settling down in the community, they are provided with support programs to help them return to their community and live in the environment they are used to. The healthcare management system and assessment practices of nursing hospitals and social welfare facilities will be improved to reduce social hospitalization and boost reasonable use of hospitals and facilities. To carry out these tasks, the government has developed strategies to strengthen the local community care infrastructure and enhance accountability, such as building a public–private partnership system and inducing local governments to assume a more active role.

The MoHW provides a basic direction by which community care will be delivered through integrated care desks slated to be installed at various localities (*eups, meyons,* and *dongs*) nationwide. The community organizations providing care and welfare, medical and health care, and housing services will be absorbed as partners or service providers. Thus, community care services will enable medical facilities and those living in residential facilities obtain information from the integrated care desks and help local healthcare institutions, care service providers, welfare institutions, and resettlement support institutions provide the services seamlessly to support individuals to live comfortably in the community. Two persons will be positioned at the integrated care desks. The government is planning to hire 12,000 social welfare officers and 3,500 visiting nurses nationwide. Healthcare facilities such as community health centers (Healthy Lifestyle Support Center, n.d.), local clinics and pharmacies will provide services like visiting healthcare, management of chronic diseases, and visiting health care management and provide community support for people with serious mental illnesses. The services will focus on the management of chronic diseases, centered on primary healthcare and strengthening of the outpatient treatment order system (MoHW, 2018a). Employees of Local Community Health Centers and Mental Health Welfare Centers are required to attend integrated case meetings of the City-Gun Hope Welfare Support Group. A mental health case management system will be established at 243 Mental Health Welfare Centers nationwide, and, if necessary, an Info Link Desk will be opened to handle requests for case management to the Hope Welfare Support Group or customized welfare teams of *eups*, *myeons*, and *dongs* (MoHW, 2018b). Care and welfare services institutions, consisting of case management institutions such as welfare centers, the National Health Insurance Corporation (NHIC), and the National Pension Service (NPS), will provide social services, long-term home care services, elderly care services, and life support services for the disabled. Additionally, assisted living institutions such as public housing and intermediate care facilities will provide residential care services in collaboration with the integrated care desks. Community care meetings will provide support for the promotion of community care services and in-depth case management through the participation of community-related organizations such as city and *gun* public health centers, community security councils, social welfare centers, and local medical organizations.

The Master Plan for Integrated Community Care for Seniors

In November 2018, the MoHW released its Master Plan for Integrated Community Care, particularly for the elderly. The master plan aimed to help seniors lead healthy lives in their homes through dramatic improvements to housing, health, nursing, and care services for them. Since its annual report in 2018, the MoHW formed a Community Care Promotion Bureau consisting of related divisions. The bureau has thus far held four meetings presided over by the Minister of Health and Welfare and 17 working-level meetings presided over by the bureau's head. As part of the process, the Korea National Council on Social Welfare hosted five expert policy forums to collect opinions from all walks of life. In addition, the government carried out research on cases of other advanced countries including Japan, the United Kingdom, and Denmark, and it established the Community Care Expert Committee at the Social Security Committee chaired by the Prime Minster. After many meetings, this group came up with the Master Plan for Community Care for the Elderly.

The Master Plan for Community Care for the Elderly has four key elements: housing, healthcare, nursing care, and service collaboration. The master plan consists largely of two aspects. One is to expand services such as home improvement, visiting healthcare, mobility services, or assistive equipment, and the other is to come up with new service systems like health centers for citizens, comprehensive in-home care centers, and local community care meetings. Under the master plan, first, to expand supported living infrastructure for the elderly, "safe houses for seniors" will be provided on a mass scale so that seniors can avail healthcare and enjoy various care services conveniently in their own homes. To achieve this goal, all public houses for the elderly will be built as safe housing for seniors. In particular, permanent rental houses where many older people live will be improved into safe housing for seniors. In addition, collaborations with social welfare centers will be further encouraged, and a large-scale housing renovation project will be carried out to support the elderly to live independently and prevent falls at home.

Second, the master plan envisions visiting health services by which health professionals like nurses visit seniors with worrisome health conditions at their homes, check blood pressure and blood sugar levels and help them manage lifestyles and chronic diseases. Primarily targeting low-income groups, such as recipients of basic living benefits and seniors in the near poverty group now, the visiting healthcare service will gradually be expanded to a universal service that caters to the elderly in need of well-structured health management, such as seniors moving from a long-stay hospital, those living alone, and elderly couples. Branch offices of the public health centers will be used as "health centers for citizens," providing the basic infrastructure for intensive visiting health service for the time being. There are 66 healthy lifestyle support centers nationwide now, and the number will be progressively increased to 250 by 2022, providing nearly one center for every city, *gun*, and *gu*. Among others, full-swing operation of visiting health services, where medical staff visit homes of the elderly with restricted mobility and provide checkups, will be a high-priority agenda item.

Third, a next-generation LTCI scheme for the elderly fit for community care will be put in place. The number of seniors receiving LTCI benefits will be increased from around 580,000 in 2017 (8% of the entire elderly population), to nearly 1.2 million by 2025 (equivalent to more than 11%). Mobility services taking elderly to the hospital and improvements to the living environment, like the removal of thresholds, may be covered by LTCI. In addition, the number of beneficiaries and items of living assistance devices necessary for seniors to live independently in their homes will be sharply increased. Also, better and more diverse in-home care services than now available will be added with the introduction of integrated in-home care benefits, so that the percentage of seniors using LTC services at home can be raised to 80% of the entire number of LTC recipients. Comprehensive In-home Care Centers will be launched by 2022, so that a single service provider can offer a wide range of in-home care services. The government intends to establish one or more such center per city, *gun*, and *gu* in order to raise the quality of in-home care services for higher satisfaction of service users. Especially, 135 Comprehensive In-home Care Centers directly managed by the (tentatively named) Social Service Center will be established, and existing establishments such as Total Welfare Centers will be designated as Comprehensive In-Home Care Centers. Alternatively, a Total In-home Services Industry will be created as a hub of integrated community care. In-home medical care assistance will be provided to beneficiaries returning home from a long hospitalization. These integrated services will include in-home healthcare, nursing care, and nutrition and mobility support. Furthermore, in conjunction with pilot community care projects, trial programs will be launched from June 2019, and a variety of welfare program guidelines will be reshuffled. Also, the (tentatively named) Framework Act on Community Care will be enacted, and laws including the Welfare for Old Persons Act will be revised to lay the legal and institutional foundation for community care.

Fourth, strategies for public–private service collaboration have been developed to enable the integrated provision of community care. The link between the social security information system and the community health center information system will be advanced to activate information sharing in terms of resources and service beneficiaries. Local community care will be included in local community security planning and community health planning to remove boundaries between health and welfare sectors, a long overdue challenge.

Pilot Community Care Projects

The Community Care Master Plan for the Elderly will be implemented in three phases: (1) undertake pilot projects and develop key infrastructure (2019–2022), (2) pave the way for provision of community care services (2023–2025), and (3) provide community care as a universal service for all (2026–) (see Table 7.1). First, safe houses for seniors, health centers for citizens, and Comprehensive In-Home Care Centers will be expanded by 2022 to develop the key infrastructure of community care. By 2025, before Korea becomes a super-aged society, LTCI for the elderly will be restructured into a next-generation LTCI scheme while providing training and education for personnel, establishing a service quality management system, and coordinating and linking budgets across sectors. The MoHW has a roadmap that shows that Korea will be prepared to launch community care fully from 2026, following infrastructure development.

Over a period of 2 years starting in 2019, the MoHW will undertake pilot projects with the aim of developing a variety of community care models to meet the needs of targeted beneficiaries including seniors, persons with disabilities, the mentally ill, and the homeless. In eight areas selected for pilot projects such as Seo-gu in Gwangju, Bucheon City in Gyeonggi Province, Cheonan City in Chungnam Province, Jeonju City in Jeonbuk Province, Gimha City in Gyeongnam Province, Nam-gu in Daegu City, Jeju City, and Hwaseong City in Gyeonggi Province, citizens' needs will be surveyed. This

Table 7.1 Community care by phase

Classification		Phase 1 (–2022)	Phase 2 (2023–2025)	Phase 3(2026–)
People aged 65 or over (%)		8.13 million (15.6%)	10.51 million (20%)	12.96 million (24.5%)
Eligibility	Region	Areas of pilot projects	Nationwide	Anyone in need of care Wherever available
	Eligibility criteria	Seniors, persons with disabilities, mentally ill persons, and the homeless	Expand to cover persons with chronic diseases, etc.	
Objective		Expand key infrastructure	Lay the foundations for community care	Provide community care for all

Source: MoHW (2018). Promotional directions for community care for community-based welfare.

will be followed by developing and providing necessary services independently. The areas and types of pilot projects by sector are as follows.

First, pilot projects for the elderly will be implemented across five localities. Seo-gu in Gwangju City will divide its 18 *dongs* into five districts, each of which will be provided with arrangements to care for the elderly in its jurisdiction, with each district serving 7,000 seniors. Intensive case management will also be implemented to help the elderly who remain hospitalized because they lack options for appropriate home care return to their communities. Bucheon City in Gyeonggi Province will reorganize its administrative system into ten *dongs*, each of which having a dedicated care service team to provide the elderly with "visiting checkups" in their homes. A Visiting Korean Traditional Medical Care Service will also be launched in collaboration with associations of Korean traditional medicine doctors and pharmacists in the community. Cheonan City in Chungnam Province will designate a Korean medicine doctor for each of the 727 Senior Citizens Centers in the community and provide visiting medication counseling in collaboration with pharmacists as part of a health promotion program centered on Senior Citizens Centers. In addition, Cheonsa (Cheonan City Case Management) Super Vision Group, an expert case management team, will be formed to provide integrated care services. Jeonju City in Jeonbuk Province will provide short-term, temporary in-home care services for the elderly who have no caregivers. Additionally, Jeonju City will dispatch supported living personnel to take the elderly with restricted mobility to hospital and also provide travel expense assistance. Gimhae City in Gyeongnam Province will commence a 24-hour call taxi support system for the transportation of vulnerable people including seniors and check if the Gimhae Community Minimum Requirements are met in the fields of elderly housing (e.g., over 14 square meters of space per person in the household, availability of safe lighting, and hot/cold water) and care services (e.g., visiting care and nursing care service twice a week for over 1 hour).

Second, the pilot projects for the disabled will be performed in two localities: Nam-gu in Daegu City, and Jeju City. Nam-gu in Daegu City will build an Independent Living Experience House where two or three handicapped persons live together to acquire independent living training. Furthermore, Nam-gu will redesign the Daegu City Hope House, a large-scale residential facility for the handicapped, into small-scale units and change its function. In addition, an integrated medical care one-stop system for the handicapped will be established along with improvement to the living environment. Jeju City will operate safe housing for seniors as a public project, provide independent living experience houses to help them gain easy access to health and care services, and open 24-hour emergency care centers. The city government will also position "Happiness Partners" who are responsible for independent living planning for individual handicapped persons and form a care network using social and economic organizations.

Third, Hwaseong City in Gyeonggi Province will undertake pilot projects for the mentally ill. The city government will put in place the "Dudream Team," consisting of mental health professionals, medical care benefit case managers, and public officers responsible for providing support for the discharge of long-term patients at mental health institutions. The number of staff for the Mental Health and Welfare Center will be increased to provide extensive rehabilitation services for the mentally ill.

A common element of these pilot projects is that a dedicated desk (Care Info Desk) is available for those in need of care to seek consultation and information and apply for services in one place. In particular, they are based on a model that makes the most of private service resources, including local hospitals. The MoHW plans to use excellent cases of the pilot projects to disseminate community care nationwide. It will also consider giving financial incentives to those municipalities expanding community care. Furthermore, the ministry has designated eight localities—Busanjin-gu and Buk-gu in Busan, Ansan City in Gyeonggi Province, Namyangju City in Gyeonggi Province, Jincheon-gun in Chungbuk Province, Cheongyang-gun in Chungnam Province, Suncheon City in Jeonnam Province, and Seoguipo City in Jeju—as *areas of pilot projects reserved for the elderly*. Although they cannot receive financial support, like the areas of pilot projects, these localities will be able to develop services customized to the community using various MoHW-led pilot programs.

According to the MoHW, given that community care is not launched across the country in unison and is rather undertaken as a local autonomous policy implemented independently by individual cities, *guns*, and *gus* based on legal and institutional foundations laid by the central government, there might be difficulties in promoting it rapidly. However, considering that advanced countries took three decades to put community care in place, the system will be improved such that the central government will assume responsibility for streamlining laws and institutions, providing financial incentives, and managing the quality of services, and local governments will be responsible for planning and providing services.

Directions for the pilot projects are summed up below. First, the projects will be managed to make the most of the autonomy, creativity, and diversity of the municipalities. The MoHW will provide basic models by subjects and lists (menus) of services (linked projects) that can be used by local governments. On the basis of such models and lists, each local government will set project objectives and subjects and plan and organize diverse services on their own. Second, residents and experts from various fields such as social welfare and healthcare will be brought together to launch and develop the projects. In the process, efforts will be made to identify factors that can lead to substantial connections between various actors in the community and to solve problems. Third, related projects of the MoHW, the Ministry of the Interior and Safety, and the Ministry of Land, Infrastructure, and Transport will be implemented together to make key elements of community care, such as healthcare, nursing care, welfare, community autonomy, and safe housing, available concurrently. Budgets for the pilot projects and various linked projects such as health insurance, LTCI, and in-home medical care assistance benefits; budgets of local governments; and budgets of private institutions will be tapped into as funding sources. The total national budget for 7 months in 2019 is around 6.4 billion Korean won.

Prerequisites for the Establishment of Community Care

To respond effectively to various social issues such as polarization, low birth rate, aging, unemployment, dead zones in welfare, and loss of humanity in Korea, the government's policy efforts and the community-based participation of the private sector are urgently needed. As demonstrated by the example of advanced countries, the welfare state system has failed to successfully overcome structural limitations such as problems of bureaucracy, restrictions on citizens' voluntary participation, and threat to the soundness of national finance.

In the situation where the fourth Industrial Revolution threatens the security of employment and income, it is imperative to establish an ecosystem led by civil society and centered on the local community and community innovation through voluntary participation of citizens (i.e., the establishment of a local welfare community). Community care is a new health-welfare integrated delivery system, and it requires involvement of the local community.

Several steps need to be taken to develop a successful system of community care.

First, the existing care services delivery system in a community should be examined. Community care refers to the purpose and strategy of a comprehensive social services policy, not a specific policy or service. To put community care on firm ground, the overall social services policy, services, and delivery system should be reshaped for community care. A key constituent of the community health and welfare care system is interpreting community care from the intended beneficiaries' point of view. In addition, the government should fully understand the meaning of community care, which is care led by a community, and make policies based on a precise diagnosis of the current local care delivery system. Also, community care should be structured as a regionally integrated care system by sharing roles and encouraging cooperation among service providers.

The core of community care is to solve the problems of recipients in the community through cooperation between health and welfare sectors. This is a common goal of all countries that are undergoing aging, regardless of the kind of system they adopt. To solve this issue, the central government needs to play a role in minimizing the difference between competencies and resources across communities, local governments need to strengthen their responsibility, and health and welfare service providers need to exercise discretionary powers, responsibility, and autonomy. It is especially important to create the most intensively needed social services by national consensus. The types of care services include LTC, care services for the elderly, home care and nursing services, assisted living services for the disabled, and welfare center services, but efforts are needed to provide these services in an integrated manner. In order to build a home-based care service delivery system in a local community, the gap in services between hospitals and facilities and home welfare facilities should be minimized. To this end, the scope of home care service should be expanded to provide a broad range of services to bridge the gap between homes and facilities, and the quantity and quality of services should be improved sufficiently to a subfacility level satisfying care needs.

Infrastructure should be built, considering who will be the provider of the home care services and what kinds of services are offered. When it comes to mental health, in particular, local communities should examine in depth how integrated health and welfare services are provided in the community and find consensus through discussions. In community care, it is important to share public values among service organizations and create public–private partnerships in order to provide services based on consumer needs. Networking methods and active participation should be strengthened to efficiently utilize private resources. No service providers exist in rural areas because there is no institution that can manage a village-level community care service provision unit. Currently, there is a Visiting Welfare Service to serve *eups* and *myeons*. It is time to think about how community care and the (tentatively named) Social Service Bureau can find contact points and what roles and functions the existing social welfare councils, community social security councils, and local welfare foundations should assume.

Second, the authority and cooperative scope of community care operations should be clearly defined. It is necessary to establish a specific schedule for medical fees. "Halfway houses" may be established and operated between the facility and the community to facilitate the process of medical institutions making a discharge plan. Local community care meetings, which manage individual cases at an in-depth level, review regional tasks, and discuss solutions, need to be organized based on formal guidelines for confidentiality and participation obligations.

Stable financing for sustainable community care should be the first priority. Japan adopted community care ahead of Korea partly to reduce facility operation costs and decrease financial burdens due to social admission and entries to residential facilities, but apparently the total health and welfare-related budgets have not decreased (Hwang Kyung-lan et al., 2018). Continued efforts should be made to strengthen the capacity of the local community for community care, link medical care and health services to care and welfare, and secure funding sources for housing services for the community.

Community-based care arrangements require the empowerment of local governments, and it is necessary to establish a delivery system for this purpose. The key function of the Integrated Care Desk, a community care delivery system, is to provide and/or link information, but the decision-making structure and the qualifications of personnel are not clearly defined yet, and any monitoring function after linkage needs to be established. As local community care meetings are responsible for providing support for community care promotion and managing in-depth cases, guidelines on their organization and the operation of community care should be provided (Hwang Kyung-lan et al., 2018).

Rather than depending on any other institution, the central government should ensures the basic living rights of citizens, taking political responsibility and exercising budgetary authority. Because community care is about guaranteeing the quality of lives in the community, local governments as a basic unit, rather than a wider geographic area, should take the lead. In the United Kingdom and Japan, two countries that pioneered community care, local governments are the basic unit that supports the establishment of the system. To minimize the gap between local governments in the process of promoting community care and to improve its effectiveness through continuous capacity building, Korea should evaluate individual local governments based on the policy goal of guaranteeing community life and come up with policies that promote capacity development through various supports (Choi Yeong-joon et al., 2018).

Third, it is necessary to nurture community care professionals. Community care is performed by the people. Professionals from various fields should be encouraged to work together with a sense of duty to organically carry out integrated care, with institutional supports and infrastructure in place. In Korea, welfare and medical care are separated in terms of government ministries and healthcare systems, making the roles of doctors, nurses, social workers, occupational therapists, physical therapists, nursing assistants, and nursing care workers separate from each other. This results in poor communication among them and a very weak basis for trust and cooperation due to conflicting interests. As the government emphasizes community care and discusses financing measures such as budgetary support and adjustment of the medical fees system by participatory community care programs, each functional and institutional group has lodged protests. As practiced in other advanced countries, incentives should be given to various functional and stakeholder organizations as a measure to promote their cooperation for joint provision of care and treatment.

Fourth, it is necessary to build a local welfare community by establishing a contact point between health and welfare. Collaboration between various healthcare and welfare organizations is essential for community care. The essence of such collaboration lies in the formation of a care system led by residents of the community. However, this care system is difficult to form in a short time using policies alone. It is necessary to understand the various welfare needs of the residents naturally through intimate communication and to create a network of collaborative relationships between residents and service providers. In short, intimacy, reciprocity, and civic engagement in society are important factors for care services.

It is important to think about who can play this role well among the various actors in charge of community care. Presently, in developed countries, not only nonprofit organizations in the community but also social and economic organizations such as social cooperatives and social enterprises strongly advocating for public interest and social innovation play this role. Instead of being motivated by policy measures to simply reduce the government's financial burden and responsibility for care, a Korean community care model should be formed based on research to understand the nature of future-oriented community care.

The government should pursue sustainable community care while building a genuine community through earnest dialogue with civil society, including various service providers. In a community care system operated by a local community, it is difficult to provide infrastructure for living such as housing and care, employment, education, culture, and the environment through welfare departments or welfare infrastructure alone. Along with collaborations between related health and medical care ministries and departments, local governments should be given the role of establishing a social protection system for the vulnerable in the community, and the planning and implementation processes should be inspected.

Services to support the needs of those returning to the community, psychological stability, and the restoration of social relationships are also needed. This requires the expertise of specialist personnel. Among others, the two people assigned to the Integrated Care Desk at each *eup*, *myeon*, and *dong* should have expertise in health and welfare. Because it is virtually impossible to recruit medical social workers in rural areas except for some university hospitals and large hospitals with medical social work teams, infrastructure should be built for this.

Community care means expanding the level of care so that it is sufficient for people with severe disability or people living alone and thus reducing the number of cases where people resort to hospitalization or living in a facility because they could not receive sufficient care at home. There is a need for the development and support of a wide range of services, including assisted living homes. In addition, securing quasi-facility services such as 1-day circuit, nighttime, and weekends services as needed is necessary to maintain independence and autonomy.

Fifth, it is necessary to gradually expand and diversify the items and products of welfare equipment by improving the LTCI system for the elderly. Support should be provided to the elderly and the handicapped in need of care so that they can continue to lead their daily lives in their communities conveniently using welfare equipment. There are about 6,100 welfare items covered by nursing care insurance in Japan, but only about 700 are covered by LTCI for the elderly in Korea. As of 2016, Japan's welfare equipment assistance was 247.4 billion yen, whereas it was just 112.5 billion won in Korea. Furthermore, there are 81 permanent showrooms for senior-friendly products nationwide in Japan, and these showrooms are run with the support of central and local governments; Korea has only three permanent showrooms of this kind, in Seongnam, Gwangju, and Daegu. Currently, welfare equipment uses smart technology only in a fragmentary manner. The systematic application of IT, including safety sensors and remote monitoring, can contribute to mitigating the service gap caused by the difference in economies of scale between facility/hospital care and community care. Especially, IT technology related to elderly care should be linked to LTCI. It is also necessary to diversify services to enable customized assistance while standardizing the types of social services provided to local communities, develop professional services to meet specific needs, connect welfare and health services effectively, and develop social care services using the Internet of things (IoT).

Finally, it is important to have an array of services available which can be systematically linked to provide personalized care. This requires expanding the range of services to create a comprehensive system of community care and developing a competent labor force of direct service workers to deliver continuous assistance to those in need. To this end, it is essential to ensure adequate training of care workers and improve their employment conditions.

Notes

1. The number of elderly people benefiting from long-term care insurance was 378,493 in 2013, 424,572 in 2014, 467,752 in 2015 and 519,850 in 2016, showing a rise each year.
2. The Seebohm Report prompted local governments to establish an integrated social service bureau in 1971, contributing to effective coordination of social services. The report showed local communities in a new light, not only as beneficiaries of social services but also as providers of services, with a focus on local community welfare services.

References

Choi Gyun. (2018). Community care and creation of a local welfare community: "Why community care?" Korea National Council on Social Welfare.

Choi Yeong-joon, Kim Bo-yeong, and Kim Tae-Il. (2018). New perspectives on social services in Korea: For a discussion on desirable alternatives. *Korean Society for Social Welfare Policy Spring Conference*. https://kiss.kstudy.com/Detail/Ar?key=3609605

Healthy Lifestyle Support Center, Dementia Center, Mental Health Welfare Center. https://www.korea.kr/special/policyCurationView.do?newsId=148866645

Hwang Do-gyeong, Kim Tae-wan, Pak Geom-ryeong, and Yeo Na-geum. (2016). Survey on the status of long-term hospitalized recipients and appropriate payment of livelihood benefits. *Korea Institute for Health and Social Affairs*.

Hwang Kyung-lan, Hwang Jae-yeong, and Park Hye-seon. (2018). Current situations and issues of community care: Focusing on the case of Japan's local governments. *Gyeonggi Welfare Foundation*.

Kim Yong-deuk. (2006, January). Community care in the UK and user participation mechanisms. Welfare Trends. Serial Report, Global Social Security Today, 1–19.

Kim Yong-deuk. (2018). Welfare service strategy based on deinstitutionalization and local communities: Community care to combine self-reliance and interdependence. Health and Welfare Forum, *Reorganization of Colloquium Community Care and Health and Welfare Services*, 15–38. http://repository.kihasa.re.kr/handle/201002/30365

Korea Institute for Health and Social Affairs. (2018). Report on the survey on the status of the elderly, Statistical Korea (2018). 2018 Social Trends in Korea.

Lee Geon-sae. (2018, August). Challenges of comprehensive local care and community care in Japan. Welfare Trends, 9–26.

Ministry of Health and Welfare (MoHW). (2018a, June 25). Press release. http://www.mohw.go.kr/react/al/sal0301vw.jsp?PAR_MENU_ID=04&MENU_ID=0403&CONT_SEQ=346683&page=1

Ministry of Health and Welfare (MoHW). (2018b, July 23). Press release. http://www.mohw.go.kr/react/al/sal0301vw.jsp?PAR_MENU_ID=04&MENU_ID=0403&CONT_SEQ=346683&page=1

Seebohm Report. (1968). https://navigator.health.org.uk/theme/seebohm-report

8

Filial Piety

Continuity and Change

Kyu Taik Sung

Introduction to the Values of Filial Piety

In recent years, nationwide efforts have been made under joint public and private auspices to preserve the traditional values associated with respect and care for elderly people in South Korea. The Campaign for Respect for Elders, the enactment of Laws for the Welfare of Elders and Filial Responsibility Laws, the provision of various social and health services for elders, and the establishment of Respect for the Elderly Week and the Filial Piety Prize System are all examples of such efforts.

The moral ideal underlying the drive to establish such social institutions is that people who have suffered to raise a generation while contributing to their family and society should be respected and cared for during their old age. It is thus felt that when parents reach the age when they can no longer take care of themselves, it is only right that they should be cared for by those whom they themselves have raised.

Filial piety(孝) is the keystone of such social efforts (Choi, 2001; Sung, 2017). Filial piety consists primarily of the practice of respect and care for the elderly (Sung, 2019). Indeed, East Asian nations—the Chinese, the Japanese, and Koreans—have shared the values of filial piety for many generations. (Filial piety is called *Hyo* in Korean, *Hsiao* in Chinese, and *Oya Kohkohin* in Japanese.)

Societal values guide the perception and treatment of elderly persons (Liu and Kendig, 2000; Streib, 1987). (The term "the elderly" in this volume denotes parents, elderly relatives, teachers, and seniors in the workplace, neighborhood elders, and elders in general.)

Kyu Taik Sung, *Filial Piety* In: *The Korean Welfare State*. Edited by: Kyungbae Chung and Neil Gilbert, Oxford University Press. © Oxford University Press 2024. DOI: 10.1093/oso/9780197644928.003.0009

The values of filial piety have greatly influenced parent care and the parent–child relationship in East Asian nations (Ikels, 2004; Kong, 1995; Lew, 1995; Lang, 1946; Silberman, 1962; Tu, 1995). Indeed, these shared values are reflected in the rituals and propriety practiced in each of the nations. Even minute details governing family systems and the manners of daily living are affected by the same values (de Bary 1995; Park, 1983; Yi, 1983). It appears that the values have strong roots in East Asian culture and that they continue to influence the attitudes and behaviors of young people toward the elderly.

However, as these nations have undergone social changes in the process of industrialization and urbanization, concern over respect and care of the elderly has grown (Koyano, 1989; Yoon and Cha, 1999). Certain social trends have elevated this concern, such as the geographic mobility of young people, the growing number of distant-living parents and children, the expansion of female employment, the movement toward smaller families, and the increasing population of the old (Kim et al., 1996). Along with these trends, the power of the elderly has weakened and some aspects of filial piety are no longer treasured by young people.

Recently, the definition of filial piety has become a public issue in Korea because of these societal shifts and because of the significant impact that the practice of it can have on the welfare of elderly people and on the morality of the young.

Until now, writings about filial piety have invariably dealt with the ideals and precepts of the traditional values in an abstract form. Hence, filial piety has been a concept too general to provide clear guidance for research or to enlighten people regarding its specific implications. However, there has been no empirical analysis of how people in modern times practice these classic values.

What, then, is the de facto interpretation of filial piety today? Specifically, what are the kinds of care and services that filial persons should provide their elderly parents? What motives lie behind filial conduct? How does one carry out filial duties in relation to other family members and neighborhood elders? And, finally, is there an ideal form of filial piety?

This chapter introduces a study conducted to address these critical questions based on data about Koreans who have been awarded the Filial Piety Prize (Sung, 1995, 1998).The prize recipients are adults who exemplified filial conduct and received the prize for such praiseworthy elder care behavior. Findings on this elite group of filial persons may not apply to all caregiving adults. However, their answers are expected to guide us in the development of a descriptive taxonomy of significant forms of filial actions which would lead to respectful and caring attitudes and behaviors toward parents and the elderly in a nation still influenced by traditional elder-caring values. Information from this study is expected to provide some insight into the values which have integrated the elderly with the family and society for generations in this East Asian nation.

Cases of Exemplary Family-Centered Elder Caring Practice

The Filial Piety Prize (孝行賞) (citation and cash), established by the South Korean government, is awarded annually to highly filial persons nominated by town/village offices or by various private organizations. The broad purposes of the prize are to preserve the value of filial piety (a significant part of the cultural heritage of the nation) and to emphasize the importance of the practice of filial piety in order to impede the decline of elder care. The immediate objectives of the prize are to commend the exemplary elder-caring practices of the prize recipients and to influence others to follow such exemplars. Along with this public prize, the two largest corporations in South Korea, Samsung and Hyundai, have also been awarding filial piety prizes annually to individuals, groups, and organizations who have rendered exemplary care and services to parents and the elderly—the former (via the Samsung Welfare Foundation) since 1975 and the latter (via the Asan Social Welfare Foundation) since 1991.

The objectives, recipient selection methods, and the filial performances of prize recipients of these voluntary prizes are similar to those of the public prize established by the government. For both public and private prizes, the nomination of prize recipients takes place nationwide. A committee appointed by the government or by the foundation reviews the nominees.

Altogether, 930 stories of the recipients of the filial piety prize were obtained for this study: 823 stories compiled by the Korean Institute of Gerontology (KIG, 1986), which were selected at random from approximately 3,000 cases filed by the Ministry of Health and Social Welfare from 1973 to 1986, and 107 stories compiled by the author, which were also selected at random from 215 stories of the recipients of the Samsung Filial Piety Prize between 1975 and 1999.

Each story contains a varied amount of empirical data on a filial person (e.g., personal background such as name, address, age, sex, education, occupation, religion), an account of filial attitudes and conducts, a progressive demonstration of caring behaviors, sacrifices made for parents, moving and dramatic episodes deemed highly praiseworthy, and the nature of interaction with parents and other family members. The content of each story is interspersed with comments on the focal subject of filial performance.

Traditional Ideals of Family Care

A discussion of the general meaning of filial piety seems appropriate. Filial piety is a social norm that parents should love and care for their children and that children in turn should respect and care for their parents. It is a moral relationship relevant to both fathers and mothers and sons and daughters. And it is assumed to be a natural and human manifestation.

Respect toward parents is the basic feeling of filial piety. Confucius (also called the Master) said,

> Filial piety today is taken to mean providing nourishment for parents, but even dogs and horses are provided with nourishment. If it is not done with reverence for parents, what is the difference between men and animals? (Analects, bk. 2, ch. 7)

Mere material support without spiritual devotion could not be called filial piety. Therefore, filial piety must be imbued with respect and warmth.

A core ideal of filial piety is the fulfillment of a child's obligations to their parent. The Master said,

> The body with its limbs, hair and skin comes to a person from his father and mother. It is on no account to be spoiled or injured. (Teachings of Filial Piety, ch. I)

This passage reaffirms the greatest debt a child owes to parents.

The Master also said,

While his parents are alive, the son may not go abroad to a distance. If he goes abroad, he must have a fixed place to which he goes. (Analects, bk. 4, ch. 19)

Parents concerned over the child's safety want to keep close contact with their child. Thus, the parent–child relationship starts with the parents' care and concern for the child (de Bary, 1995, p. 62). Indeed, the care and aid that parents provide to their children are great. It is, therefore, an obligation of a child to give his or her parents reassurance by observing these precepts.

Throughout the life of the parents, the child also owes them every comfort and aid. Filial piety essentially directs offspring to repay the comfort and aid received. Therefore, the Book of Rites (bk. 2, ch. 1) admonishes,

Care for parents should not be a tiresome obligation; the filial son and his wife will do it with an appearance of pleasure to make their parents feel at ease.

The Master, therefore, prescribed the affective forms of care for parents.

In caring for parents, filial children should make them feel happy . . . let them see and hear pleasurable things. (Book of Rites, bk. 1, ch. 1; bk. 2, ch. 12).

The Master outlined specific ways of providing instrumental services as well.

In the morning, the couple should pay a call on parents in their room. They should ask the parents if their clothes are warm enough and if they have any pain or discomfort. . . . They should be served foods of their choice. [This shows respect, care.] (Book of Rites, bk. 2, ch. 12).

Thus, filial piety consists in care and service to one's parents (Book of Rites, bk. 2, ch. 1). It reflects an adult child's altruistic concern and compassion expressed in caring for aging parents. Thus, a filial child feels sorrow at the suffering of his or her parents and is disposed toward caring action.

The ethics of parent care is grounded on sacrifice which transcends the child's self-interest. Sacrifice no longer means giving up one's life for the parent, but instead dedicating part of one's energy to parent care.

The sacrifice made for the parent is, however, not one-sided. It would seem a small sacrifice that the children make compared to the many great things parents have done for them.

Filial piety is a value which espouses mutual respect and love between parents and children, husbands and wives, and siblings. Toegye (Yi Hwang), a towering figure in Neo-Confucianism in Korea, taught that the love of parents for children is out of mercy and that the propriety of children for parents is filial piety (Che, 1985, p. 307; Tu, 1985). The aim of his philosophy can be found in his devotion to reverence. *Reverence*, according to Toegye, meant the practice of mutual respect and love (Che, 1985; Park, 1983); the practical meaning of reverence is the ideal of respect for parents. In return, parents must be benevolent toward children. Thus, the prerogatives of age are usually balanced by reciprocal obligations and concepts of fairness (Che, 1985, pp. 307–308). According to Toegye, this precept is rooted in the goodness of human nature. He emphasized the importance of practicing this ideal of reciprocity in daily family living.

Closely connected to filial piety is family orientation (Yi, 1983). A filial adult must be able to uphold his or her obligation to the family. Every person, from an early age, learns to think of his or her family first. Each one does his or her share of obligation to protect and support the whole family. In a family, it is considered essential to harmonize relations between generations. Under the influence of Confucian teachings, Korean society has laid special emphasis on the integrity of household relations, in which the relationship between parents and children assumes top priority.

Ancestor worship and the keeping of the genealogy, still extensively practiced, reinforces family orientation. It is evident in the family where respect for parents and elders is observed and learned. Confucius held that the concept of family is stronger than that of state and society (Yi, 1983, pp. 122–125). To him, strengthening the family meant strengthening the larger society and the state.

An attribute of filial piety is the ability of adult offspring to carry on the wishes of their forefathers, to carry forward their unfinished undertakings, and to pave the way for further development of their family. A filial adult must fulfill his obligation to continue the life and culture of the family. One must, therefore, care for parents while raising children, supporting siblings, providing for the family, and being forever mindful of family continuity.

An adult is also expected to serve dead parents (Book of Rites, bk. 2, ch. 21). This means that in discharging the funeral duties to parents, adults are constrained to do their utmost (Teachings of Filial Piety, ch. 22). Importance is attached to burial and mourning for parents as well. Therefore, Confucius said,

> Parents, when alive, should be served according to propriety; when dead, they should be buried according to propriety; and they should be sacrificed to according to propriety. This may be called filial piety. (Teachings of Filial Piety, ch. 22)

The values of bringing honor to parents and upholding the prestige of family take on great importance to filial children. They invite relatives and friends for parents' birthdays or other important family events. Rebuilding or decorating the family temple or an ancestor's grave is a solemn obligation. Such an endeavor reflects the offspring's ability to bring honor and prestige to their parents, ancestors, and family.

Confucius envisaged harmonious relations between all members of society, and the touchstone of these moral relations was filial piety (Chen, 1986; Lew, 1995). He said,

> Treat with reverence elders in your own family, so that elders in other families shall be similarly treated. (Teachings of Filial Piety, ch. 2).

Thus, a respectful attitude was demanded toward all elderly people, even those who did not belong to one's own family. In this way, the adult's responsibility for elder care extends beyond the boundary of the family.

In chapter 3 of *Teachings of Filial Piety*, Confucius' and his disciples' sayings on filial piety are extensively reviewed as they focus on respect for the elderly.

The ideals of parent care advanced by these precepts are reflected in well-known Chinese folk stories such as "The Twenty-Four Stories of Filial Piety" (二十四孝的故事) (Twenty-Four Stories, 2010) and in documentaries "Dong Yong and Filial Piety Culture" (董永與孝文化) (Li and Dong, 2003). Similar ideals are described by Palmore and Maeda (1985) in their book, *Honorable Elders Revisited: A Cross-Cultural Analysis in Japan.* The ideals are reflected also in the stories of recipients of the Filial Piety Prize compiled in *Dumentaries on Actions of Filial Piety in Korea* (韓國孝行實錄) (KIG, 1986). A few of the Chinese stories carry anecdotal and legendary events, whereas the book about Japan and the stories about Koreans carry empirical examples of filial piety practiced by contemporaries.

Analysis of Exemplary Filial Conducts: Methodological Approach

To identify actions of filial piety, the 961 stories of the prize recipients compiled by the institute and the author were chosen as study subjects.

First, the action content of the stories of the prize recipients was analyzed using the content analysis method, which is appropriate to the analysis of such unstructured stories (Babbie, 2015). Second, the results of this qualitative analysis were cross-checked with findings of quantitative data from a questionnaire survey of the same filial persons. In this way, two different methods were used in a single study design to examine related aspects of a basic concept.

Before undertaking a full-scale analysis, 30 stories were selected at random from the 961 cases and were analyzed in order to develop actions of filial piety as a preliminary step for a subsequent full-scale analysis. This preliminary analysis made it clear that each case was unique and required specific analysis. Therefore, with the exception of socioeconomic characteristics, filial piety performance was viewed without predetermined categories for defining relevancy. Moving reflexively between data collection, analysis, and conceptualization, the analysts increased their understanding of filial piety. The author helped the analysts, who participated in the development of the coding scheme, to familiarize themselves with this procedure of content analysis before the analysis began. Six categories of actions of filial piety were determined systematically: showing respect, fulfilling filial responsibility, repaying debts, expressing affection, harmonizing family, and making sacrifice.

Due to the large number of stories, 10 analysts, all graduate students, were employed and trained to maintain necessary consistency in the process of analysis. They were adults, born and raised in the Korean cultural context, with a basic understanding of the concept and practice of filial piety.

Mutually exclusive meanings of words, phrases, sentences, and paragraphs that fit into the six categories of the actions were located (Babbie, 2015). In order to do this, the content of the story was often reduced by focusing, simplifying, and abstracting and was then summarized in the form of coding (Miles and Huberman, 1984, p. 21). Taking into account the story context, making an inference was done based on the meanings of the words, sentences, and paragraphs. In addition, one word was split or differentiated into two or more categories of the filial actions when appropriate (Miles and Huberman, 1984, p. 222).

Although the six categories obtained in the initial analysis guided the full-scale analysis, other categories were allowed to emerge throughout the process of analysis. Relevant events, situations, styles, and meanings related to filial piety actions were constantly discovered and compared to delineate specific categories of filial actions (Babbie, 2015); one or more such actions were identified for each category. For example, the category of filial sacrifice was assessed by one or more of the following actions: (a) fully devoting to parent care disregarding own personal comfort or convenience; (b) paying for parent's healthcare cost or providing for a large family with the money earned by hard work; or (c) taking care of a bedridden parent while caring for a sick or handicapped family member.

The following are examples of categorization. A statement such as "a son quits his job to provide bedside care to his sick parent" was considered to reflect sacrifice. In contrast, the following sentence depicting "a son who provided emotional care and material services with exceptional courtesy and consideration" was considered to reflect both repayment and respect. Support to a large family while caring for a sick parent was analyzed as either "fulfilling responsibility" and/or "making sacrifice" depending on the context. A situation of "a filial person providing parent care while providing support to siblings" was interpreted as maintaining harmonized family.

Most often, an entire paragraph or even an entire story was dedicated to the description of physical and/or financial sacrifice for parents. In this case, the paragraph or story was translated into the frequency of sacrifice. The following case examples reflect both filial responsibility and sacrifice: "Chi-sun did not marry until 30 years of age but worked as a maid to earn money for the care of her ailing mother." "Kwang-sik, an engineer, reduced his social activity, postponed his marriage, and had an evening job to earn extra income to provide for his hospitalized parent and his brothers in college." "Hyun-ja lived with a physically handicapped husband while taking care of a bedridden parent-in-law." Attention was paid to the intensity of filial behavior. This was accounted for by emphasis placed, repetition of the same statement, the length of the statement, and the placement of the statement in the story. An analyst took 30–40 minutes to code a story depending on its length.

A score was given to each action. The coding scheme applied to this scoring was dichotomous: yes (cited) or no (not cited). The frequency of occurrence of each action (the number of times cited divided by 100) was translated into a summary judgment on that item. Measures of category reliability were undertaken to show that identical judgmental criteria were used in their selection and enumeration. That is, to ensure against selective perception and distortion in memory, the results of the content analysis were cross-checked or triangulated by independent testimonies of the 10 analysts who conducted the same analysis and recorded it (Miles and Huberman, 1984, pp. 62–63). In this way, idiosyncrasies of interpretation and inference were assessed. The reason for this procedure was the belief that reliability produces validity.

A simple test was performed to check the reliability of the results of the analysis. Following the completion of the initial coding of the contents of 961 stories, the 10 analysts were reassigned to recode 96 cases randomly selected from the stories (sampling ratio = 10%) and, for recoding, 15 items (10 categories of filial piety actions and five items of socioeconomic characteristics) were used. The result of the second coding was compared with the initial coding. The differences between the first coding and the second coding were checked by the following method (Miles and Huberman, 1984, pp. 62–63):

(Number of matching categories × 10 analysts) ÷ (15 categories × 10 analysts)

The final score obtained from this computation was 85, which suggests that the initial coding of the various categories was overall reliable as compared with the result of the second coding. Meanwhile, the validity of the idea that the stories represent authentic materials rested on the fact that the stories were based on public papers about the filial people who were reviewed and selected by independent judges through an official screening process regulated by the public agency or recognized nonprofit foundation.

Care and Services Provided by Filial Persons

Of the 961 filial persons, 67% were females, 51% had less than 9 years of schooling, 28% attended high school, and 19% had a college education. The standard of living of 63% was low. In terms of occupation, 46% were housewives (87%, daughters-in-law; 8%, daughters), 22% farmers, 12% laborers, and 20% other. The average length of time of filial practice was 12 years. Of the parents and elders served by them, 65% were female and 80% were 59 years or older. Almost all of them (92%) were members of their families. Parents-in-law numbered more than any other elders served. The number of elders served by the filial persons were 1 (51%) and 2 or more (49%).

The filial persons provided various types of care and services for the elderly. This care and services represent filial conduct practiced in daily living and embody the ideals of filial piety. Most of the elderly relatives, aged and frail, had health and social problems (e.g., paralysis, incontinence, immobility, and widowhood). They required not just devoted but also continuous care. For instance, frequently cited examples were nursing and care for incontinent parents and elders.

The 29 types of care and services provided to the elderly can be grouped into the following:

1. Personal care for the elders (18 types)
2. Support for the family (6 types)
3. Services for elders in the community (5 types)

Personal care might further be classified into three tiers:

Primary services (e.g., housekeeping, laundry work, serving meals, giving
   baths, caring for incontinent elders, nursing care)
Secondary services (e.g., accompanying on outings, carrying
elders, respecting their wishes, providing pocket money)
Tertiary services (e.g., reading books, engaging in conversation, providing
   recreational opportunities)

The filial persons were recognized for providing these types of care and services to their elderly relatives and other elders. The care and services required both "feeling concern" and "performance of services."

In the process of content analysis, which started with six categories, four other categories emerged, bringing the total number to 10. The ranking of the 10 categories were based on the frequency (cases or stories) with which they were cited. According to the ranking, actions showing *respect for parents* stood out among all the action categories. Showing respect was followed by fulfilling filial responsibility. Making repayment emerged as the third most frequently cited, and harmonizing family, fourth. In ranking order, these were followed by making sacrifice, showing affection, expressing sympathy, maintaining family continuity, compensating care, and showing respect for elders at large.

Survey of Prize Recipients

Following the content analysis, a random sample of 162 filial persons was selected from a list of 961 cases (sampling ratio = .17). A 22-item mail questionnaire, consisting of both closed- and open-ended questions, was administered to these persons in order to identify reasons for filial piety. The reason why an adult child cares for his or her parent reflects the child's motivation for parent care, which is central in the determination of filial behavior (Liu and Kendig, 2000, pp. 183–199). This study examines whether their expressed reasons for filial piety are comparable to or match with their actions of filial piety.

The questionnaire included items regarding the socioeconomic status of the respondents and the following 10 reasons for filial piety.

1. Showing respect to parents and other elderly persons
2. Fulfilling responsibility
3. Harmonizing the family
4. Showing affection
5. Making sacrifice
6. Repaying debts
7. Maintaining family continuity
8. Expressing sympathy
9. Compensating care
10. Serving neighborhood elders

Of the 162 filial persons, 143 responded to the questionnaire (response rate = .88). The reliability of the questions about importance based on the 5-point scale was tested and the result was highly positive (alpha = .84, p < .001).

In all, 12 reasons were identified: in addition to the above 10 reasons, 2 others were identified from the survey: complying with religious teachings and maintaining the honor of the family.

Respect and fulfilling responsibility stood out from all other reasons in terms of importance. Other frequently cited reasons of importance were harmonizing family, showing affection, and making repayment. These were followed by making sacrifice, showing sympathy, maintaining family continuity, showing respect for neighborhood elders, and compensating care. Complying with religious teachings and maintaining family face were least important.

The result of an analysis of variance—comparing the reason categories by social characteristics (age, sex, education, and birth order)—did not reveal a statistically significant predictor of the categories. Only income varied by making sacrifice and fulfilling responsibility, respectively (F = 2.24, p < .05; F = 2.41, p < .05), suggesting that the less income, the greater the sacrifice paid for parent and the heavier the responsibility assumed. This seems to suggest also that a sense of respect, responsibility, and sacrifice was present in those filial persons unaffected by characteristic variables.

The rankings of the actions from the content analysis were similar to the rankings of the reasons identified from the questionnaire survey. The two rankings are compared or cross-checked—one based on frequencies of actions (data from the content analysis) and the other based on the ratings of importance of the reasons (data from the survey).

Spearman rank-order correlation between the two rankings (.91, ρ [.001]) for 10 categories (excluding two categories without the ranking of frequency) suggests the high similarity or comparability of both rankings (i.e., the relatedness of the filial conducts and the motivation to care for the elderly).

Discussion

The present study was undertaken to obtain answers to the question "What are the most important action components of filial piety?" Using content analysis and the questionnaire survey, the study developed a descriptive taxonomy of categories of filial piety actions. Throughout the long and arduous process of content analysis, particular attention was paid to encourage the analysts to carry out categorization and quantification validly and reliably. The effective technique most often used in the process of qualitative analysis was cross-checking.

In this exploratory study, a set of 12 categories of filial piety actions emerged in a salient manner. Of these, six stand out: showing respect, fulfilling responsibility, harmonizing family, making repayment, showing affection, and making sacrifice. It is noteworthy that all these categories are virtues which Koreans in East Asia have traditionally cherished. The remaining categories have important cultural and moral meanings as well. These categories may be interrelated in their meanings. However, each of them may reflect moral actions of filial persons which demonstrate particular ways of caring for aged parents, as evidenced by the kinds of care and services they provided to the parents.

Thus, filial piety is explained by multiple action categories. In the description of the holistic meaning of filial piety, all of these categories would have to be considered because they portray it in combination.

Showing respect emerged as the most outstanding category. Clearly, filial persons set the greatest value on respect for parents and other elders. Respect for the elderly remains a social norm and is the foundation of traditional Korean culture (Chi, 1997). Streib (1987), who compared China and the United States in terms of old age in the sociocultural context, identified a major difference between the two cultures as respect for the elderly, which is automatically expressed by people in China. He termed this Chinese cultural trait "automatic respect." Chow's (1995) findings on filial piety in China basically support this view. Similarly, Palmore and Maeda (1985), who studied aging in the Japanese cultural context, discovered that respect for the elderly is rooted in the basic social structure of Japanese society. The authors termed this phenomenon as "residual respect."

Although extreme expressions of elder respect have been modified, there is relatively little decline shown for the weight of this primary attribute of filial piety. As Streib (1987) and Palmore (1989) pertinently indicate, respect for elders remains the key element in maintaining the status and integration of the elderly in our modern societies.

Impressively, fulfilling *filial responsibility* is the second most outstanding category. This is the obligation of a grown child to assume care of parents and meet the needs of aged parents. Throughout the world, the obligation for parent care has emerged as an issue of major concern, one that modern industrial societies must re-illuminate and reassert.

The third salient category is *harmonizing the family*. Centering on parents, a filial child must coordinate his or her family members into an orderly whole, whereby agreement on the actions needed for elder care can be attained. Without such harmony, it would be difficult for an adult to carry out those long-lasting and arduous caring tasks that require the combined effort of all family members.

Making repayment, the fourth category, is also an important moral duty of grown children. However, by the time most adults are prepared to repay the debt, parents are often no longer living. Despite the difficulty of realizing this ideal, filial adults continue their drive toward the goal. For many of them, however, the undone repayment remains a lasting source of guilt.

The fifth category, *showing affection*, is a most stressed virtue along with respect. Children's love and affection for their parents is thought to be an expression of natural instinct. It is the foundation of benevolence and a genuine expression of filial piety (Lew, 1995).

The ethics of parent care is grounded on *sacrifice*, the sixth category, which transcends the grown child's self-interest. A good example is providing care for a parent with a long-term health problem. This seems a small sacrifice for the child to make, compared to the many great things their parent has provided over many years.

The seventh category, *showing sympathy*, is a filial adult's altruistic tendency to share feelings with their aged parents and to have concern and compassion in caring for them. Such an adult, in feeling sorrow at the distress and suffering of frail and sick parents, attends to their well-being.

Maintaining *family continuity*, the eighth category, is the grown children's ability to carry out their parents' wishes and undertakings and pave the way for future development of their offspring while being mindful of the continuity of their family.

Cases of *compensating care*, the ninth category, were found often among the stories. The desire to care for parents often comes from the grown child's regret of his or her unfinished task or role. Thus, the filial conduct of a daughter-in-law, the primary caregiver, is often motivated by her desire to make up for not having cared for her own parents. In addition, the desire to be benevolent to others is characteristic of Korean values infused by Buddhist-Confucian culture.

Regarding *showing respect for neighborhood elders*, filial persons must also assume their obligation to respect and care for elders in the neighborhood and larger society. The practice of filial piety has been overly family-centered. This tenth category is very important to Koreans who need to pay greater attention to the well-being of elders other than their family members. The practice thus extends beyond the boundary of the family.

One practices filial piety in accordance with *religious teachings*, the eleventh category. All religions in Korea—Buddhism, Christianity, and others—teach that children must respect and care for their elders. Buddhism, the oldest religion in Korea, stresses solemn filial obligation and particularly the eternal and fathomless love of the mother, which even the most filial children would not be able to fully pay back. Christianity, the second most influential religion, clearly aims its emphasis on the moral importance of filial obligation, which is rooted in its theological and ethical heritage. The Fifth Commandment in the Decalogue attests it: "Honor thy father and thy mother that your days may be long." Thus, the religions in unison espouse filial duty and obligation.

Maintaining the honor of the family, the twelfth category, takes on great importance to filial children. They invite relatives and friends to parent's birthdays and other important family events. Rebuilding or decorating the family temple or an ancestor's grave is similarly an important obligation. These endeavors reflect the offspring's ability to bring honor and prestige to parents and the family.

These 12 categories of filial actions reflect the ideal of care and services for parents and the elderly possessed by those exemplarily filial persons who have actually performed filial piety. These various categories combined might be seen as the embodiment of filial piety in the East Asian cultural context. The findings on elite filial persons may not apply to all caregiving adults. However, the categories reveal specific meanings of the ideal forms of filial conduct, which concerned Koreans are aspiring to realize today and toward which they are likely to continue to drive.

Identification of the categories leads us to understand that, in practicing filial piety, an adult child might give more emphasis to certain categories while giving less to other categories for tactical and situational reasons. In the case of most filial persons, multiple categories were practiced at the same time. Categories most often practiced include respect, responsibility, harmony, repayment, sacrifice, and affection. Ideally, all of the 12 categories should be practiced concurrently. For many adults, though, it would be a great challenge to do so because of constraints associated with their family, work situation, and social environment.

Impressively, the filial persons who practiced filial piety in terms of these categories did actually provide various types of care and services for their elderly relatives and others. Most of the elderly, aged and frail, had health and social problems. They required not just devoted but also continuous care. The care and services included personal care for the elders, support for the family, and services for elders in the community. The filial persons were recognized for providing these types of care and services—affective as well as instrumental—for their elderly. These care and services—filial conduct—embody the ideals of filial piety.

The present study evidenced the important association between the inner process or values of the filial adults and their moral action of elder caring. That is, there was a positive relationship between the filial persons' professed value placed on filial piety and their actual filial conduct (i.e., care and services). So, although the relationship between attitude and action is complex (Andrews and Kandel, 1979), it appears that the higher the level of filial attitude, the more filial the conduct to be expected.

Although its function and structure are changing, the family is still the context in which most prize recipients performed filial conducts. Thus, the stories of the prize recipients invariably stress that the filial person supported the family in an exemplary manner. In fact, 3 of the 12 categories—family harmony, family continuity, and family honor—point to their family orientation. These categories, combined with Korean orientation toward family cohesiveness and dedication of self for family well-being, would indicate traditional cultural patterns (Streib, 1987) that enhance filial piety, the ideal of family-centered parent care. In such a family context, Koreans still teach that children must revere their parents, teachers, and elders, although in a less intensive manner than in the past. Educational influence comes also from outside the family. For instance, the performance of filial conduct exemplified by the prize recipients and other filial persons is widely publicized in the forms of news, documentaries, field reports, plays, and literary works via mass media and educational channels.

As the data revealed, women—mostly daughters-in-law—were still the major source of filial care. Sons provide emotional and financial support and resources outside the family, but they are less likely to help with instrumental, hands-on services, as do women or daughters-in-law. However, conflicts between daughters-in-law and mothers-in-law generally diminish the gratification the former feels in assisting the in-law. Moreover, the declining availability of women to serve as primary caregivers to old parents has emerged as a major social issue in this nation with an increasingly aging population.

A modification of certain phases of this traditional value seems to be necessary. For instance, it is becoming crucial to move away from authoritarian and patriarchal relationships to egalitarian and reciprocal patterns of mutual help and respect between generations and between genders. In fact, the ways in which filial piety is expressed are being modified and modernized to adapt to changing times.

Traditionally, the son and his wife have been obliged to care for his parents by living with them. Today, adult children of both genders fulfill their filial duties to a growing number of parents who live in separate households for their privacy and convenience. These distant-living adults very often practice filial piety by telephone call, mail, and visitation. Lately, a growing number of young people express respect and affection toward parents and elders in a more frank, open, and friendly manner than their parents did. For so long, the practice of filial piety has been overly family-centered, but filial piety is now conceptualized and practiced more expansively to cover care and services for an increasing number of disadvantaged elders in the community. Indicative of this trend, some of the study subjects were elderly persons who were not members of the filial persons' family. (Lately, the number of filial piety prize recipients who have served neighborhood elders and elders at large is growing.)

The actions of filial piety identified in this study provide us with insights into an ideal of parent care which resulted in the integration of the elderly with the family and society. The action categories will be useful in constructing a measure of filial performance which can be used to assess the quality of parent care and the moral aspect of parent–child relationships.

The resurgence of social concern over the traditional values of respect and care for the elderly and the increased social effort to exhort these values (Choi, 2001; Pak, 1989; Sung, 2017) reflect the resilience and adaptability of Korean people with which they respond to the challenges of social change. This obvious social phenomenon largely approximates the continuing influence of the traditional values in the East Asian nation.

In summary, it should be noted that, in the empirical studies presented in this chapter, *respect for parents* emerged as the form of prime importance. Respect for parents is also the most stressed point in traditional teachings (*Teaching of Filial Piety*, ch. 10). Being filial to parents meant treating them with propriety, and the nexus of propriety is caring for parents with respect (*Analects*, bk. 2, ch. 7; de Bary, 1995). The teachings furthermore envisioned respectful relationships between the young and the elderly of the larger society. "One should treat with respect elderly members in one's own family, so that elders of other families shall be similarly treated (*Teaching of Filial Piety*, ch. 2; *Analects*, bk. 1, ch. 2). Thus, propriety extends beyond the boundary of the family. It is noteworthy that the analyses presented in this chapter entailed these essential and extensive implications of respect for the elderly.

Implications for Social Welfare Policy

As noted in this chapter, filial piety—the humanistic values of affectionate and respectful care and services for the elderly rooted in the teachings and beliefs of Confucianism and Buddhism—is still being upheld and practiced by ordinary Korean families. The importance of such care and services to the informal family group has been addressed in the development of social welfare policies in Korea.

In recent years of rapid social changes, the grave concern arising among social welfare policymakers is the surge of unprecedented nationwide issues. These issues include a large number of families who are becoming less able to provide home care, an increasing number of the elderly in need of services of professional caregivers outside the family, and public demand that the government intervene to promote at-home care for the aged and impaired elderly.

Some social changes appear to hinder or weaken home care: families have fewer children (actual or potential caregivers); the majority of adult children live physically separate from their aged parents; many elderly prefer independent lives and not to be a burden on their relatives; as elderly persons become older, they become more frail and impaired; and there often exists interpersonal tensions and conflict with caregiving family members.

Several policy initiatives directed to support needy families would be effective in resolving these issues and promoting home care (e.g., providing services to cope better with the health problems of elderly relatives, respite services for caregivers, financial support, subsidized paid care, counseling, and referral services among others).

Looking ahead, public policies need to be aimed at extending these public supports for families in order to strengthen their traditional function of caring for the elderly with the humanistic values of filial piety, particularly in terms of upholding the dignity of the elderly.

Social welfare policies can be designed to reinforce the values represented in Confucianism and Buddhism, which have been dominant cultural and religious values for generations.

References

Analects of Confucius (Lun Yu). (1996). [English translation, 2nd ed.] Sinolingua.

Andrews, K. H., and Kandel, D. B. (1979). Attitude and behavior: A specification of the contingent consistency hypothesis, American Sociological Review, 32, 298–310.

Babbie, E. (2015). The practice of social research. Cengage Learning.

Book of Rites (Li Chi). (1993). [Collection of Confucian teachings of rites.] O. S. Kwon (trans.). HongshinMoonwha-Sa.

Che, M. S. (l985). Comparative study on philosophies of Toegye and Yulgok [Toegye-Yulgok Chulhak-ui Bikyo Yunku]. Sungkyunkwan University Press.

Chi, K. H. (1997). The foundation of spiritual history of Korean people [Hanminjok-ui Jungshinsa-ju Kicho]. Academy of Korean Studies.

Choi, S. J. (2001). Changing attitudes to filial piety in Asian countries. *Paper presented at The 17th World Congress of International Association of Gerontology.* Vancouver, Canada, July 1–6.

Chow, N. (1995). Filial piety in Asian Chinese communities. *Paper presented at 5th Asia/Oceania Regional Congress of Gerontology,* Hong Kong, November 20.

de Bary, W. T. (1995). Personal reflections on Confucian filial piety. In *Filial piety and future society* (pp. 55–76). Academy of Korean Studies.

Ikels, C. (Ed.). (2004). Filial piety. Stanford University Press.

KIG. (1986). Dumentaries on Actions of Filial Piety in Korea (韓國孝行實錄). KIG.

Kim, I. K., Liang, J., Rhee, K. O., and Kim, C. H. (1996). Population aging in Korea: Changes since the 1960s. Journal of Cross-Cultural Gerontology, 2, 131–137.

Koyano, W. (1996). Filial piety and intergenerational solidarity in Japan. Australian Journal of Ageing, 15, 51–56.

Lang, O. (1946). Chinese family and society. Yale University Press.

Lew, S. K. (1995). Filial piety and human society. In *Filial piety and future society* (pp. 1–19). Academy of Korean Studies.

Li and Dong. (2003). *Documentaries on Dong Yong and filial piety culture.* (董永與孝文化).

Liu, W. T., & Kendig, H. (2000). Who should care for the elderly? An East-West value divide. Singapore University Press.

Miles, M. B., & Huberman, A. M. (1984). Qualitative data analysis: A sourcebook of new methods. Macmillan.

Moroney, E. F. (1976). The family and the state: Consideration for social policy. Longman.

Nakasone, R. Y. (1990). Ethics of enlightenment: Essays & sermons in search for a Buddhist ethic. Dharma Cloud.

Pak, J. K. (1989). Traditional ideal of filial piety and its modern meanings. In *Modern illumination of traditional ethics* [Juntongyunli-uihyundai-jukjomyung] (pp. 89–117). Academy of Korean Studies.

Palmore, E. B. (1989). Ageism: Negative and positive. Springer.

Palmore, E. B., & Maeda, D. (1985). The honorable elders revisited. Duke University Press.

Park, C. H. (1983). Historical review of Korean Confucianism. In Main currents of Korean thoughts. *Korean National Commission for UNESCO* (pp. 80–88). Si-sa-yong-o-sa.

Silberman, B. (1962). Japanese character and culture. University of Arizona Press.

Streib, G. F. (1987). Old age in sociocultural context: China and the United States. Journal of Aging Studies, 7, 95–112.

Sung, K. T. (1995). Measures and dimensions of filial piety in Korea. Gerontologist, 35, 240–247.

Sung, K. T. (1998). An exploration of actions of filial piety. Journal of Aging Studies, 12, 369–386.

Sung, K. T. (2011). Respect for the elderly in China, Japan, and Korea [노인을존중하는중국인, 일본인, 한국인]. Korea Studies Information Company.

Sung, K. T. (2017). Social research on Koreans' filial piety [한국인의효애대한사회조사]. Jimoondang.

Sung, K. T. (2019). Care for parents with respect and affection [부모님을위한돌봄]. Korean Studies Information Company.

Teachings of filial piety [Hsiao Ching]. (1989). Sacred books of the East, vol. III. J. Legge (Trans). Oxford University Press. Originally published 1879–1885.

Tu, W. M. (1995). Yi-toegye's perception of human nature. In W. T. de bury (Ed.) (pp. 767–782). Columbia University Press.

Twenty-Four Stories of Filial Piety. (2010). (Bilingual edition). Chen Ta Press

Yi, S. E. (1983). On the criticism of Confucianism in Korea. In Main currents of Korean thoughts. Korean National Commission for UNESCO (pp. 89–101). Si-sa-yong-o-sa.

Yoon, H. S., & Cha, H. B. (1999). Future issues for family care of the elderly in Korea. Hallym International Journal of Aging, 1, 78–86.

9

Confident Aging

A Solution for Longevity with Dignity

Sang Chul Park

Introduction

Longevity is no longer a dream but a reality. Within a mere hundred years, the human life span in developed countries has skyrocketed by 30 years, just in the 20th century. This increasing pattern of population aging is expected to continue in coming decades as well. This unprecedented rapid population aging has forced communities worldwide to reconsider the traditional image of seniors, one developed from the experiences of a handful of venerable persons. Moreover, the presumed concomitant expansion of disability and dysfunction brought about by aging has alarmed many communities considering the imminent social and economic burden. As a consequence, many hold a tarnished image of the elderly, and this damages the dignity of the aged population. Restoring the dignity of senior citizens is an essential step for a society in which successful aging is the norm. Most importantly, concepts on aging should be reassessed on the basis of biological research and lessons from human aging and centenarian studies, all of which provide irrefutable evidence that aging can be reversed or slowed down based on strengthening cellular health. This new understanding can then be used to develop a realistic and humane approach toward a coming society of longevity.

Recent biological discoveries raise questions about traditional deterministic views on aging. Based on reassessment of old beliefs on aging and new discoveries regarding biological aging, science presents a new concept, on of "confident aging." This concept provides a justification for the continuing active participation of seniors in their own lives as well as in the lives of their communities, uninhibited by any preconceived notion of inexorable loss of function by aging and its unalterable decline to death.

Sang Chul Park, *Confident Aging* In: *The Korean Welfare State*. Edited by: Kyungbae Chung and Neil Gilbert, Oxford University Press. © Oxford University Press 2024. DOI: 10.1093/oso/9780197644928.003.0010

To add additional scope, the longevity consequences of the recent out-break of COVID-19 could be examined using the consolidated study to discover some of the pandemic's long-term impacts on health and well-ness, especially among the elderly population. It is likely that countries hard-hit by the coronavirus will see declines in life expectancy as a re-sult of the pandemic, while other countries may not see any appreci-able impacts. The pandemic highlights the urgent need for all countries, worldwide, to invest in strong health systems and primary healthcare in order to confront the human crisis, particularly concerning the high mortality of senior citizens.

Evolving Views on Aging Based on the Biology of Aging

The traditional, simplistic concept of aging is based on the phenotypic se-nescent features of aged organisms, culminating in death. Thus aging is summarized as a universal, progressive, intrinsic biological process leading to functional deterioration and death. This definition implies the irreversi-bility and inevitability of the aging process and presents a deterministic view on aging. Thereby, the strategy of "discard and replace" has been embraced as a priority for the management of aging in either biological or social aspects. However, recent biological discoveries give rise to questions about this tra-ditional, deterministic view on aging. Lessons from the major fronts of re-search are discussed below.

Lessons from Cellular Aging

The first issue related to biological aging is the disputed idea that aged cells or organisms are more susceptible to death. When the susceptibility to death of a young or old cell in response to increments of toxic stress is tested and compared, the young cell is found to be more vulnerable to stress-induced death than the old cell. In other words, old cells are more resistant to death-inducing stress compared to young cells. This in vitro finding has been con-firmed in vivo by a comparative study of young and old rats subjected to toxic stress. This study revealed that the apoptotic index in the tissue of young rats is higher than that of old rats, as summarized in Table 9.1. These unexpected findings clearly contradict the conventional concept of death-proneness of

Table 9.1 Difference in responsiveness between young and old cells and organisms

Response	Growth factor response	Apoptotic stress response
Young	Sensitive	Sensitive
Old	Resistant	Resistant
References	Park (2002, 2011, 2017)	

the aged and call for a new adaptive view on aging that can appropriately replace the deterministic view (Park, 2011).

The second issue presented by biological aging is the conventional understanding of aging as an irreversible and inevitable process. When the growth factor responses of young and old organisms are compared, it is seen that young cells and tissues exhibit a very active response in contrast to delayed or absent responses in old cells and organisms. The underlying mechanism for age-related hyporesponsiveness to growth factors is related to defects in the signal transmitting system at the membrane level, especially in the receptor-mediated endocytosis system (Park, 2002). Simple adjustments to the endocytosis system recover the growth factor response concomitantly with a remarkable morphological restoration of senescent cells. In addition, activation of the lysosome-mitochondrial axis can restore the senescent cells back to a younger state in terms of shape and function (Park et al., 2018). This restoration can be induced not only in normal senescent cells but also in the prematurely senescent cells of those with progeria as well. These findings show that the concept of aging can be revised from an irreversible and inevitable process to a reversible and controllable one (Park, 2006a).

The third debate on biological aging is whether the core concept of cellular aging needs to be modified in terms of "secondary aging" versus "primary aging." Hayflick's limit of cellular replication theory conforms to the limit of telomere length by number of replication, which has raised the assumption that aging is an intrinsic phenomenon caused by primary cellular aging. However, advances in molecular and cellular studies of cell-to-cell interaction or cell-to-matrix interaction introduce the possibility of regeneration of tissues and restoration of cellular growth potential in aged cells, contrary to Hayflick's theory of a limited life span. Furthermore, recent successes in the development of normal organisms by somatic cell nuclear transfer (SCNT) as well as the induction of intact stem cells by induced pluripotent stem (iPS) cells even from aged cells and organisms demonstrate the potentiality of aged cells or organisms to recover a young state. These recent fundamental discoveries in the aging phenomenon necessitate a revised and adaptive view of potentiality on aging instead of the traditional deterministic view of aging as a state of progressive deterioration.

These considerations led us to propose a new hypothesis on aging, the *gate theory of aging*, in which the new possibility of aging control has been suggested. This study suggested that adjusting signal transmission into cells may modulate the cellular aging phenomenon. Subsequently, this hypothesis was further extended to the *nuclear barrier hypothesis of aging*, which illustrates that the core barrier to cellular signals is the nuclear membrane rather than the cellular membrane (Park, 2011, 2017). This revolution in the concept of aging has made it imperative to abandon the old "replace" principle on aging and seek a new "restore" principle, implying that aging is a continuing process rather than the dead-end consequence of life.

Lessons from Human Aging

The recent issue of population aging has so far heralded a worrisome future from the perspective of the financial and medical burden caused by a rapid increase in the number of aged and dependent people. But when the actual statistics are reviewed, the reality does not appear so gloomy. A global analysis of modal length of life span shows a continuing increase in the actual life span in general. Furthermore, the pattern of its standard deviation reveals a continued narrowing down with time. These data illustrate the possibility that, with time, most people can live longer, achieving an overall equality of life span and implying a universal public longevity in the future as distinguished from the specific, private longevity of the past. This trend of population aging is not limited to advanced countries but rather extends to developing countries as well, thus underlining the correlation of public longevity with improved socioenvironmental conditions. In addition, the ratio of elderly people who have difficulties with activities of daily living (ADLs) and instrumental ADLs (IADLs) is dropping, accompanied by a parallel increase in healthy life expectancy (life expectancy without disability). These data indicate that, with population aging, the portion of healthy older people is increasing faster than that of unhealthy older people. Moreover, emerging social movements for the development of an "ageless society" are encouraging seniors to participate more actively in social programs than before. Currently, the trend of seniors is to pursue active lives rather than a passive lifestyle of retirement and retreat, as the past. Since active labor by senior citizens can efficiently reduce the costs of health insurance and social care, the formulation of new policies that mobilize the aged community will not only benefit aged individuals but also the public as a whole. These data strongly support bright prospects for an aged society with better health and greater social participation.

Lessons from Longevity Studies: The Korean Experience

A large number of studies have been carried out on human longevity, not only at genetic and medical levels but also at social and psychological levels. Among them, the Korean Centenarian Study is unique in that a multidisciplinary team approach has been adopted successfully that includes medical, genetic, psychological, nutritional, ecological, economic, family, social, and even anthropologic experts. The study presented the tight interaction among many variables impacting longevity (Park, 2012). The listed variables for longevity are genes, gender, habitat, nutrition, physical activity, social care, lifestyle, etc. To explain the integration of these variables, a new model of human longevity, *Park's temple model for human longevity*, was proposed. The longevity-associated variables are classified in three different layers as if they were the foundation, pillars, and rooftop of the temple. The bottom components are basically fixed or not readily changeable variables such as genes, gender, personality, ecology, and social cultures, over which individuals have no choice. The pillar components are related to personal lifestyles and those changeable or readily modifiable variables that depend on personal decision and choice, such as exercise, nutrition, relationships, and participation. The rooftop components are socially or politically determined variables such as security, economic stability, social care, and medical support system, which are again not readily modifiable. These different layers of the components interact and compensate one another, building up the temple of longevity in the process. Therefore, lengthening of human longevity requires reinforcement of each component in a balanced manner.

In the aforementioned Korean longevity study, two remarkable features of gender and geographic localization have attracted some special attention. Gender difference in Korean centenarians is conspicuous, with female-dominant longevity at a greater than 10 to 1 ratio (Park, 2012). Another eye-catching feature pertaining to higher longevity is a geographical difference: greater longevity for those in mountainous areas. When the gender difference and localization effects are considered together, it is seen that female longevity is higher in southwestern Korea, which has medium-altitude mountains, while male longevity is higher in northeastern Korean, with its high-altitude mountains. Thus it is apparent that eco-environmental factors affect gender difference in Korean longevity. Most of male centenarians in the mountainous area work continuously until the final stage of life, in contrast to male centenarians in low-lying areas who follow sedentary lifestyles. These differences are rooted in the local diversity in the senior care tradition of the Yang Ban culture (traditional Korean aristocratic system). A passive life attitude causes a reduction of physical mobility and social activities, leading to an increased prevalence of age-related degenerative diseases, reduced quality of life, and shortened longevity. These data again emphasize the importance of active strengthening of longevity variables, with special emphasis on an improved lifestyle.

Why Confident Aging?

Limitations of the Concept of Successful Aging or Productive Aging
The theme of "successful aging" or "productive aging" has gained much attention among aging societies in recent times. Although outwardly attractive, most senior citizens discount this concept because it mostly reflects the degree of his or her past economic or social achievement. Since the present situation of most seniors might not be satisfactory enough to warrant the label "successful" or "productive," this past-oriented concept might only frustrate them. However, this symbolic norm remains persuasive and effective for the soon-to-be-old generation as they prepare for their later lives.

Senior Koreans who have experienced significant cultural turmoil but are unprepared for later lives are in peril of losing traditional family and community support. Therefore, they might be dismayed by the concept of successful aging. In order to encourage these presently unprepared seniors, it is urgent to reconsider the key issues of aging and redirect management of seniors from the past-dependent passive concept to a present-centered, activeness-oriented concept.

Biological Basis of Confident Aging

The concept of confident aging points in this new direction. The main principle of confident aging is the active participation of an individual in their personal life and community life without any restriction or fear of being weak and frail, but with confidence. Since aged cells or organisms are found to be resistant to apoptotic or toxic stress, it is time to discard the conventional concept of aging as a proneness toward death. Recent biological data on aging strongly emphasize that the prime mission of a biological organism is the maintenance of integrity and adaptability until the last moment of life. Therefore, the first axiom for confident aging based on biological studies of aging is *survivability*.

The concept of primary cellular aging itself is questioned, and secondary aging by environmental influence has been emphasized, pointing to the importance of the interrelationship between the cell and matrix, cell and cell, and between host and environment, as well as human interaction. This new observation places great emphasis on the priority of human relationships. Therefore, the second axiom for confident aging is *relationships*.

Studies in recent years have established beyond doubt that the senescent phenotype of the aged cell could be restored not only for growth potential but also for shape formation, thus disputing the validity of the deterministic view on aging. This restorative pattern of life can be readily observed in the lives of active seniors as well. This fact calls for a new restorative principle of plasticity and refutes the conventional "replace" principle of irreversibility. Thus, the third axiom of confident aging is *restorability*.

The attitude of seniors, especially centenarians, has evolved into one of activeness and mobility. Since health status is affected strongly by lifelong exercise and work, the level of longevity and quality of life might be altered. When centenarian health status has been monitored, it is remarkable that the incidence of diabetes in centenarians is significantly lower than those of 60+ seniors in most countries (Table 9.2). Since diabetes is one of the "typical" (representative) lifestyle-related diseases, its reduced incidence in centenarians strongly indicates their high mobility with exercise or labor until extreme age. Therefore, the mobility factor is one of the utmost important conditions for well-being and quality of life in later life. Accordingly, the fourth axiom of confident aging is *mobility*.

Based on these prime axioms of survivability, relationships, restorability, and mobility, the concept of confident aging connotes a growing number of

Table 9.2 Incidence of diabetes in centenarians

Age cohort	65+	100+	References
Korea	30%	2–5.6%	Park, 2011
Japan	15%	6.0%	Takayama et al., 2007
Italy	20%	4.9%	Davey et al., 2012
USA	17%	2–4.0%	Martin et al., 2019

active and interactive seniors with the confidence to adapt and restore their active lives. This concept requires the principle of ageless action in practical lives. This new concept will mark a turning point in mankind's understanding of aging, from a devastating consumptive viewpoint to a promising productive perspective. This conceptual change on aging will have profound effects on both science and society as they concern the problems of the aged.

Confident Aging and the Community

It is now necessary for seniors to design and form societies of seniors, by seniors, and for seniors. The elderly should boldly face others in the community with confidence. Although aged people usually face several challenges in terms of health, income/savings, knowledge, and ready access to modern technology, they should strive to participate in and contribute to the family and community, independently and with confidence. The Korean centenarian study has revealed a very eye-catching change in residence (housing) patterns of centenarians during last two decades of the study period. For the super-aged, residence has shown a significant influence on longevity depending on whether the elderly can live alone or need social care. In general, it would be naturally assumed that super-aged people require care. However, when the centenarians living in Gu Gok Sun Dam zone of Korea were analyzed in 2001, 12% of them lived alone and 80% of them lived with family; in 2018 centenarian study, the number living alone increased to 25%, and the number living with family decreased to 52% while the number living in a nursing home increased from 2% to 20% (Table 9.3). These figures strongly illustrate the possibility of confident living by centenarians. Those 100 years and older can live alone; the fact that their numbers of those living alone are increasing implicates their independent living and the acquisition

Table 9.3 Changing in residence
pattern of Korean centenarians

Residence pattern	2001	2018
Living alone	12%	25%
With spouse only	6%	3%
With family	80%	52%
Nursing home	2%	20%

of better health with the improvement in social welfare system in the community. It is considered that these data support the concept of confident aging.

For seniors to develop confidence, it would be useful to follow the "Three It Action Rule": "Do it, Give it, and Prepare it." This rule encourages seniors to do something actively and voluntarily, give and share something with neighbors and the community, and prepare for the future regardless of age (Park, 2005). Furthermore, following the "Three Do Principles" may help seniors. The first is the "I *will do* it principle," which encourages active volunteer activity. The second one is the "I *can do* it principle," which recommends appropriate age-optimized activity. The third one is the "*Let's do* it principle," which suggests collaborative activity for aged people. These "Three Do Principles" will help seniors to independently pursue their new lives with dignity and confidence (Park, 2005).

In order to achieve the goals of "Three Do Principles" for confident aging, several action plans for actual service have been designed and distributed all over Korea, initiated by the Seoul National University Institute on Aging. To facilitate nutritional support for seniors, cooking classes for male seniors have been developed under the Gold Cook program. To address senior fitness, the Woori Chum Chejo program has been designed to encourage physical and mental activities based on traditional dance and music (Park, 2004).

For senior medical security, the Mini-Med School program that provides integrative medical knowledge for health has been developed. Furthermore, the University of Third Age program has been established to relieve retirement stress for seniors. These action programs have been running successfully for more than two decades in several spots of the municipal zone and local areas, mainly through university and governmental support. In addition, the community is required to do its best to optimize the living conditions and ensure confident aging of their seniors, such that the paradigm of *security, culture, productivity* (SCP) flourishes in the community with active participation of seniors, thus enabling them to live long and with dignity (Park, 2005).

Multidisciplinary Approach to Confident Aging

Given the complexity of the aging process and the influence of environment on health and disease, ongoing advances in science and technology will play major and as yet unknown roles in understanding the aging phenomenon and ensuring quality of life for the elderly. Based on our current understanding of the biology of aging, the prime requirement for longevity is to maximize mobility and strengthen relationships. Therefore, science and technology should contribute significantly to such endeavors by supporting seniors to move efficiently and live comfortably without physical difficulties and in good relations with family and neighbors. Therefore, the key roles of science and technology for confident aging might be categorized.

The primary contributions science and technology can make toward confident aging through mobility include rehabilitation, surgical approaches, wearable mobility aids, robotic mobility aids, and housing and automatic driving or supported moving facilities.

Second, science and technology can do much to improve quality of life by devising tools for maximizing the capacity of the aged individual for sensing and thinking. To enjoy life, a fundamental requirement is the ability to eat well without ill effects; smell, hear, and see well; feel well; think well; and be free from pain.

For the purpose, a variety of apparatus can be developed in forms of assisiting, enhancing, substituting, replacint or restoring functional equipments. This can be summarized as the science and technology for quality of life.

Third, science and technology can improve connectivity. Seniors may face problems not only in interpersonal relationships but also in their relationship to the environment. Human interactions could be enhanced by supporting devices that connect people. Since the socioecological variables of aging include geographic and ecological locations and cultural conditions, it is essential to optimize interactions between aged individuals and their families, neighbors, and community, and encourage and strengthen relationships with environments. Clearly, these approaches will be effective only if the individual and the community strongly believe in the adaptability and restorability of the body regardless of age based on the recent biological breakthroughs on the aging process. For the better relationship, the principle of *"give and take"* should be applied, for which the seniors need to be independent in their own living. Therefore, this can be termed the science and technology of relations.

These multidisciplinary approaches of science and technology for mobility, quality of life, and relations together will ensure longevity with dignity for both the individual and their community.

Revitalizing Support for Healthcare Delivery to Vulnerable Medical Service Communities: A Community Development Perspective

Many isolated towns with large populations of elderly (aged 65 and older) face unmet healthcare needs due to lack of transportation and the strains of caring for the aged senile. Many in these isolated towns neglect obtaining early, preventive care.

It is therefore imperative to adopt measures that can improve healthcare outcomes for vulnerable, chronic patients. This may require structural changes to the primary care, ambulatory delivery system in those localities identified as having shortages. Unmet healthcare needs necessitate a new measurement of access to healthcare services which provides information about the problems and barriers that individuals may have encountered during the process of accessing care.

In an aged society, the majority of the population will be seniors who are traditionally retired or, in other words, "out of service" for the community. This phenomenon may have a negative influence on the national and global economy and damage the social system as well. However, the majority of older people are healthy enough to work at whatever mission they can afford to take up. Therefore, it is essential to develop a strategy to encourage and enhance the role of older persons as vital social resources and active contributors to their families and communities.

The Longevity Consequences of COVID-19

This section on the longevity consequences of COVID-19 discusses how my research might be able to mitigate and prevent some of these long-term impacts on health and wellness and also future infections, especially among the elderly population. Life expectancy is one of the factors that determine the demand for healthcare and social services. It is likely that countries hard-hit by the coronavirus will see declines in life expectancy as a result of the pandemic, while other countries may not see any appreciable impacts.

Largely Abandoned by the Staff: Elderly Care Homes

Authorities of several countries confirmed that 57% of deaths from the coronavirus in Italy, Spain, France, Ireland, and Belgium were linked to care homes for the elderly. In New York, in the United States, where 40% of coronavirus deaths were linked to homes for the elderly, the state's governor ordered a probe into nursing home deaths. In the Canadian city of Montreal, officials are investigating the status of elderly care homes after health authorities were called to the Residence Herron elderly home, which had been largely abandoned by its staff. In England and Wales, the number of people dying of COVID-19 in care homes more than quadrupled in the space of a week (Grabowsky and Mor, 2020; Suñer et al., 2021).

In Italy, the country's National Institute of Health estimated that 40% of the deceased were residents in elderly care facilities, and that number is only a fraction of the country's total nursing home deaths. Spanish soldiers helping to fight the coronavirus pandemic have found elderly patients in retirement homes abandoned and, in some cases, dead in their beds. Sweden was forced to face runaway care home deaths, and Swedish state prosecutors have launched an investigation into the high death rates at care homes.

The pandemic highlights the urgent need for all countries to invest in strong health systems and primary healthcare as the best defense against outbreaks like COVID-19 and against the many other health issues that threaten people around the world.

Urgent Necessity to Build a Post-Pandemic Social Security Network

The outbreak of COVID-19 has exposed beyond doubt the weak points in the conventional social security system for older people that resulted in unprecedented high mortality of seniors and social dilemmas related to medical care.

In order to address the chaos, it is urgent to design some social strategy that ensures international partnership to confront upcoming issues of a similar nature. This pandemic of unprecedented dimensions muddled the whole world in a short period, blocking all global exchanges on account of the quarantine policy adopted by many nations. Furthermore, the seriousness of the gaps in aging security was obvious even in developed countries. Therefore, priority should be given to the issue of aging security worldwide. For this purpose, the following actions are recommended, based on the new concept of confident aging.

Working Group on Aging Security

The Post-Pandemic Social Security Network (PP-SSN) is a nongovernmental organization devoted to promoting social welfare and social justice worldwide.

The PP-SSN supports establishment of the Working Group on Aging Security, aimed at strengthening the human rights of older persons. In many cases, the elderly group remains one of the most vulnerable, often facing multiple deprivations and widespread age discrimination. Current measures remain inadequate for the effective protection of older persons. Furthermore, every effort should be designed and activated worldwide to uphold the principle of dignity, leading eventually to higher care standards—a goal of great significance to older persons everywhere.

In this light, it is urgent to support the elaboration of the existing Convention on the Rights of Older Persons. This goal remains of paramount importance. The PP-SSN initiative recognizes the rights of everyone to social security and to a standard of living adequate for the health and well-being of all persons and families. Basic income security along with universal access to essential health services should be guaranteed as national priorities.

The Working Group recommends that human rights principles and standards should be integrated throughout the design, implementation, and evaluation of all social securities. It includes, inter alia, the adoption of specific measures to ensure transparency, access to information, participation, and coordination among healthcare policies.

Conclusion

Recent advances in research on the biology of aging are revolutionizing the conventional views on aging. A key development is a revision of the classic traditional deterministic view on aging into a more adaptive concept. This conceptual change demands that the "replace" principle be itself replaced with the "restore" principle as the major strategy for controlling the aging process. This new concept on the biology of aging calls for new approaches to dealing with the medical and sociocultural needs of the aging populations. Here we propose a novel approach called confident aging: designed for the aged individual as well as for their community, this approach presents guidelines for addressing the social and health problems confronting the elderly. This approach encourages seniors to participate actively, voluntarily, and confidently in social activities. Furthermore, it calls for the community to facilitate such participation for seniors, ensuring their safety and productivity in the cultural context and aided by efforts of governments and appropriate agencies to promote new scientific and technological advances for confident aging. Through these integrative endeavors toward confident aging, the seniors would live long with dignity.

References

Davey, A., Lele, U., Elias, M. F., Dore, G. A., Siegler, I. C., Johnson, M. A., Hausman, M., Tenover, J. L., Poon, L. W., and the Georgia Centenarian Study. (2012). Diabetes mellitus among centenarians. *Journal of the American Geriatric Society, 60*(3), 468–473.

Grabowski, D. C., and Mor, V. (2020). Nursing home care in crisis in the wake of COVID-19. *JAMA, 324*(1), 23–24.

Martin, P., Gondo, Y., Arai, Y., Ishioka, Y., Johnson, M. A., Miller, L. S., Woodard, J., Poon, L. W., and Hirose, N. (2019). Cardiovascular health and cognitive functioning among centenarians: A comparison between the Tokyo and Georgia centenarian studies. *International Psychogeriatrics, 31*(4), 455–465.

Park, J. T., Lee, Y. S., Cho, K. A., and Park, S. C. (2018). Adjustment of the lysosomal-mitochondrial axis for control of cellular senescence. *Ageing Research Review, 47*, 176–182.

Park, S. C. (2002). Functional recovery of senescent cells through restoration of receptor-mediated endocytosis. *Mechanisms of Aging and Development, 123*(8), 917–925.

Park, S. C. (2004). Korean experience: New elderly exercise program based on traditional culture. *IAG Newsletter, 17*(4), 5.

Park, S. C. (2005). SCP Community and 3 Do Principle: A new paradigm for the aged community. *Korean Journal of Gerontology, 15*(3), 1–9.

Park, S. C. (2006). New molecular target for modulation of aging process. *Antioxidant & Redox Signaling, 8*(3–4), 620–627.

Park, S. C. (2011). Nuclear barrier hypothesis of aging as mechanism for tradeoff growth to survival. *Advances in Experimental Medicine and Biology, 720,* 3–13.

Park, S. C. (2012). Comprehensive approach for studying longevity in Korean centenarians. *Asian Journal of Gerontology and Geriatrics, 7,* 33–38.

Park, S. C. (2017). Survive or thrive: Tradeoff strategy of cellular senescence. *Experimental Molecular Medicine, 49*(6), e342.

Suñer, C., Ouchi, D., Mas, M. A., Alarcon, R. L., Mesquida, M. M., Prat, N., Bonet-Simó, J. M., Izquierdo, M. E., Sánchez, I. G., Noguerola, S. R., Colet, M. T., Puigvendrelló, J. V., Henríquez, N., Miralles, R., Negredo, E., Noguera-Julian, M., Marks, M., Estrada, O., Ara, J., and Mitjà, O. (2021). A retrospective cohort study of risk factors for mortality among nursing homes exposed to COVID-19 in Spain. *Nature Aging, 1,* 579–584.

Takayama, M., Hirose, N., Arai, Y., Gondo, Y., Shimizu, K., Ebihara, Y., Yamamura, K., Nakazawa, S., Inagaki, H., Masui, Y., and Kitagawa, K. (2007) Morbidity of Tokyo-area centenarians and its relationship to functional status. *Journal of Gerontology: Medical Sciences, 62A*(7), 774–782.

Postscript

Korea's Response to COVID and Universal Basic Income

Responding to the tremendous disruption of economic life wrought by COVID-19, many wealthy industrialized welfare states implemented an unprecedented increase in universal cash transfers directly into the hands of their citizens (Investopedia, n.d.). In the United States, for example, between April 2020 and September 2021, three programs—stimulus payments, augmented unemployment benefits, and the child tax credit—implemented in response to COVID-19 provided a massive cash transfer to many unemployed families (Watson, 2021). The Korean government also implemented a number of fiscal emergency relief measures in response to the economic crisis triggered by COVID-19. These measures initially included a significant infusion of cash to households which provided up to 1 million won (US$840) to a household of four, received in the form of credit/debit card points and local gift certificates.

The substantial fiscal measures implemented to provide relief to citizens suffering the effects of the pandemic's economic disruption primed the pump of public opinion for a general expansion of income maintenance programs. In the United States, for example, the Biden administration sought to establish the temporary US$3,600 Child Tax Credit as a permanent universal benefit without any work requirement, which can be seen as a precursor to a Universal Basic Income (UBI). Although initial efforts to extend this benefit have stalled, it remains a politically contested measure that may yet gain acceptance.

In Korea, the COVID-19–related emergency basic income measures generated a lively campaign for the establishment of a UBI championed by Lee Jea-myung, the ruling Democratic party's leading progressive candidate in the 2022 presidential election. Serving as the governor of Gyeonggi Province, Lee promised that, if elected, he would make Korea the first industrialized Asian country with a UBI. As governor of Gyeonggi Province, he had already introduced a basic income for youth in the province, funded through debit cards that could only be used to purchase goods from local

Postscript In: *The Korean Welfare State*. Edited by: Kyungbae Chung and Neil Gilbert,
Oxford University Press. © Oxford University Press 2024. DOI: 10.1093/oso/9780197644928.003.0011

businesses and traditional markets. Later this was expanded to cover all the citizens under the COVID-19–related emergency basic income measures.

As part of his presidential campaign, Lee proposed to establish a UBI for all Korean citizens. He claimed that "basic income is an inevitable economic and welfare policy in the era of the Fourth Industrial Revolution after COVID-19" ("Dongwoo Kim," 2020). Lee's plan for a UBI was to start with an annual basic income payment of 250,000 won per person; this payment would then increase to an annual payment of 1,000,000 won (US$840) over the 5-year presidential term. Lee's ultimate goal was to provide a monthly income of 500,000 won (US$420) to the entire population, which would amount to almost 14% of the average salary (US$34,000) (Yonhap News Agency, 2021). In contrast to the neoliberal view that the Digital Revolution would create as many new jobs as it destroyed, Lee believed that a UBI was necessary to mitigate the displacement of jobs in the digital economy. He proclaimed that "Without a universal basic income, capitalism will break down" (Rocca, 2020). His concerns were not without reason. A considerable amount of work in Korea is already automated. According to the International Federation of Robotics 2021 report, Korea "has by far the highest robot density in the manufacturing industry—a position the country has held since 2010" (International Federation of Robotics, n.d.).

The UBI is an idea that has been around for a long time, advanced by both progressives and conservatives, despite their ideological differences. In *Road to Serfdom*, the 1944 landmark defense of classical liberal doctrine, Friedrich Hayek agreed that the state should provide a guaranteed minimum income for sufficient food, shelter, and clothing to maintain one's health and capacity to work. His main concern was that this basic measure of income should not obstruct the functioning of market competition or endanger general freedom (Hayek, 1944).[1]

In 1962, the Nobel prize–winning conservative economist Milton Friedman came out in support of a negative income tax scheme that would provide a guaranteed annual income of, for example, US$1,200 to a family of four, close to the average payment to public assistance recipients at that time (Friedman, 1962). In 2006, Charles Murray (2006) crafted a more generous proposal for a guaranteed income of US$10,000 per year for every US citizen 21 and older, of which US$3,000 would have to be used to purchase health insurance. Both Friedman's and Murray's proposals came with the proviso that they would replace all the other government social welfare benefits, essentially eliminating much of the welfare state's public bureaucracy. Most recently, in the 2020 United States presidential election, a UBI proposal formed the cornerstone of Andrew Yang's platform. Yang's plan was to give US$1,000 a month to every US citizen older than 18 years of age. His argument for this benefit is similar to Lee Jea-myung's. Both are concerned about the likelihood of automation shrinking future employment opportunities, which would increase many citizens' needs for economic security. However, whether robotics, artificial intelligence, and digital technology, sometimes referred to as the Fourth Industrial Revolution, will destroy more jobs than it creates is a highly contested issue.

The arguments of those who back a UBI go beyond what some perceive as a need to compensate for a future decline in work. Those who support the UBI see many immediate benefits related to the decommodification of labor; a guaranteed income, would give workers the financial security to withhold their labor while searching for desirable jobs, returning to school to gain additional skills, or remaining home to care for dependents. The income transfer would alleviate poverty and inequality. And, as an automatic transfer to everyone, there would be less need for bureaucracy and lower administrative costs than typically associated with conventional means-tested social welfare programs and welfare programs that have work requirements.

Those who oppose the UBI fear that it could create a formidable disincentive to work, a particular concern in Korea with its huge aging population. Moreover, one of the central criticisms of the basic income is that the economic costs for significant benefits would be unsustainable and could spark inflation. A UBI that provided everyone in the United States with US$10,000 a year would cost more than US$3 trillion a year. This cost equals more than three-fourths of the entire yearly federal budget and about 14% of the country's gross domestic product (GDP) in 2020 (Greenstein, 2019). For Korea, it is estimated that Lee's ultimate goal of a 500,000 won (US$420) a month stipend to everyone would cost about 31.3 trillion won per year for 51.71 million population, or about 16.7% of the 2021 GDP. In both cases, the overall costs of these benefits to government could be reduced if the UBI served as a substitute for existing social welfare income maintenance programs, as proposed by conservative supporters such as Milton Friedman and Charles Murray. But this approach was not advanced by Lee Jea-myung's proposal.

In the run-up to the Korean presidential election, the idea of a UBI was sharply debated. The Korean electorate appeared to have been divided over support for this program. The left-of-center daily *Hankyoreh* reported on a poll taken in 2020, which revealed that 48.6% of respondents favored the idea of a basic income while 42.8% were opposed and 8.6% were undecided. (The difference between supporters and the opposition was not statistically significant; see Noh Hyun-woong Poll, 2020). A different perspective was offered by the right-of-center Nikkei reporting on a poll conducted 2021, which found that 65.1% of respondents opposed the program, with 34.9% supporting it. Those opposed to the basic income were concerned that it might create a formidable disincentive to work and upset the country's financial stability ("Kim Jaewon cash for all," 2021).

According to a survey of policymakers by the Hankyoreh and the Korean Association of Party Studies, the UBI appears to have had more support in the 21st National Assembly than among the general public. On a scale of 0 to 10 (where 0 represents strong support and 10 strong opposition), the Democratic Party politicians scored 2.08 and those in the United Future Party (UFP) scored 5.35. Preparing for the 2022 presidential election, the UFP was renamed the People's Power Party (Noh Hyun-Woong Poll, 2020).

Although public opinion was divided, as the Korean presidential election of 2022 approached, the prospects for a UBI looked promising. With politicians in the Democratic Party firmly approving of the idea and those in the People Power Party at least lukewarm to it, Korea seemed to be on the verge of creating a UBI program for all its citizens. As it turned out, the progressive candidate Lee Jea-myung of the ruling Democratic Party faced conservative Yoon Suk-yeol of the People Power Party in tight race that Yoon won with a razor thin margin. For the time being, Yoon's victory has put a brake on the political momentum for a guaranteed income.

Had Lee won and introduced a UBI, it would have had a consequential impact on modifying the social investment model of the Korean welfare state. The provision of cash benefits to able-bodied citizens with no requirements to engage in work or skills training undermines the social investment philosophy that welfare policies should promote human capital activation and mobilization. Some people receiving a basic income would no doubt continue working, others might go to school to improve their skills, while others might just seek more leisure time and withdraw their labor from the market.

Yet, as a member of the Basic Income European Network (BIEN) observes, the election outcome may not spell the end to basic income in Korea (Truston Yu, 2022). The Democratic Party may rebound at the next election. And, in January 2020, the Basic Income Party was founded in Korea, Oh Jun-ho, presidential candidate for the Basic Income Party, ran on a platform that pledged a basic income of 650,000 won (US$545) per month (Basic Income Party, 2022).

Although the Democratic Party lost and the Basic Income Party had a very weak showing in the 2022 presidential election, the Korean political tides ebb and flow. Policymakers have not heard the last of the Korean debate on a UBI.

Note

1. Hayek shared his Nobel Prize with Gunnar Myrdal, whose competing views about the relationship between the market and the state fostered the 20th-century development of the Swedish social democratic welfare state.

References

Basic Income Party Manifesto. (2022). https://basicincome.org/wp-content/uploads/2022/01/Oh-Basic-Income-party-manifesto.pdf

Dongwoo Kim (2020). South Korea mulls universal basic income post-COVID. The Diplomat. https://thediplomat.com/2020/06/south-korea-mulls-universal-basic-income-post-covid/

Friedman, M. (1926). Capitalism and freedom. University of Chicago Press.

Greenstein, R. (2019, June 13). Commentary: Universal basic income may sound attractive but, if it occurred, would likelier increase poverty than reduce it. Center on Budget and Policy Priorities. https://www.cbpp.org/research/poverty-and-opportunity/commentary-universal-basic-income-may-sound-attractive-but-if-it

Hayek, F. (1944). The road to serfdom. University of Chicago Press, p. 120.

International Federation of Robotics. (n.d.). https://ifr.org/news/robot-density-rises-globally/

Investopedia (n.d.) https://www.investopedia.com/government-stimulus-and-relief-efforts-to-fight-the-covid-19-crisis-51

Kim Jaewon (2021, November 16). Cash for all: Lee Jae-myung's radical plan to reshape South Korea. Nikkei Asia. https://asia.nikkei.com/Spotlight/Asia-Insight/Cash-for-all-Lee-Jae-myung-s-radical-plan-to-reshape-South-Korea

Murray, C. (2006). In our hands: A plan to replace the welfare state. AEI Press.

Noh Hyun-woong (2020, June 9). Poll reveals S. Korean public is split on universal basic income. Hankyoreh. https://www.hani.co.kr/arti/english_edition/e_national/948589.html

Rocca, N. (2020, February). Do South Koreans want a universal basic income? Le Monde diplomatique. https://mondediplo.com/2022/02/05korea-box

Truston Yu. (2022, March 15). Basic income takes a hit in Korea. BIEN. https://basicincome.org/news/2022/03/basic-income-takes-a-hit-in-korea/

Watson, G. (2021, March 17). U.S. COVID-19 relief provided more than $60,000 in benefits to many unemployed families. https://taxfoundation.org/total-covid-relief-unemployment-insurance/

Yonhap News Agency. (2021, July 22). Gyeonggi governor pledges to distribute universal basic income if elected president. https://en.yna.co.kr/view/AEN20210722005200315

Index

For the benefit of digital users, indexed terms that span two pages (e.g., 52–53) may, on occasion, appear on only one of those pages.

Occupational Safety Agency, 100–1
Old-Age Income Security system, 73–80

parent–child relationship, 183–87
Park Chung-hee, 31–32, 39, 104
Park Chung-hee paradigm, 50, 52–53
Park Geun-hye, 3, 22–24, 41, 65–66
Parkinson's disease, 121
Park's temple model for human longevity,
    205
Peng, Ito, 2
pension system
    Basic Pension, 80–82, 83t, 84t, 86–87
    beneficiaries, 76, 78t
    benefit types/amounts, 34, 71–72, 76,
        86–87
    childbirth credit, 85–86
    contribution rate, 74
    credit support policies, 85–86
    described, 71–72, 75
    development of, 4–5, 13–14, 17, 19, 21,
        23–24, 25, 34
    Durunuri subsidy, 22, 26, 85
    eligibility, 34, 71–72, 76, 84, 85t, 86
    farmers/fishermen premium support,
        84–86
    fund financial condition, 78–80, 79t,
        80f, 81t
    household income calculation, 88
    income replacement rate, 74–75
    insured persons, 75–76, 77t
    military service credit, 86
    reforms, 75, 82–84
    replacement rate optimality, 78–80, 82t
    status of, 74–75
    structure of, 73–80
    subsidiarity principle/Basic Pension, 87
    unemployment service credit, 86
pharmacists, 123
Porter, M., 52, 62
postmodern welfare state, 1–2
Post-Pandemic Social Security Network
    (PP-SSN), 213
pregnancy benefits, 87–89
"President's Welfare Initiative for Bringing
    Quality of Life Up to the World
    Standard," 14–15
Private Teachers Pension system, 73–74

productive welfare approach described,
    2–3, 25
prosperity sharing policies, 43
prosthetic equipment, 120–21
Public Assistance, 103–4
Public Long-Term Care Committee, 136
Public Long-Term Care Insurance
    Steering Group, 21
Public Senior Care Insurance Executive
    Committee, 21
Public Works Program, 90–91

Republic of Korea. See Korea
Residence Herron elderly home, 212
Respect for the Elderly Week, 180
Restriction of Special Taxation Act (2007),
    19
Rhee Syngman, 31–32, 65
Roh Moo-hyun, 3, 5, 18–22, 25, 39–41, 135
Roh Tae-woo, 13, 34, 107–8
Rural Pension Act (1993), 14–15

safe houses for seniors, 168
Samsung, 182
Schumpeterian workfare state, 1–2
Second Integration Debate, 107–8
Seebohm Reform, 160–61, 178n.2
self-employed benefits
    health insurance, 104, 111–13
    income security, 25–26, 28–29
Senior Citizen Pension, 80
Seo-gu project, 171
separatism-integrationism debate, 106–8
shareholder capitalism, 62, 66
Singapore, 100
small businesses, 22, 25–26, 28–29, 35,
    45, 63
Smith, Adam, 53–54, 57
social entrepreneurs, 60
social impact bond (SIB) system, 60
Social Insurance, 103–4
social investment state
    cash benefits, 19, 45, 217–21
    challenges of, 45–47
    clientelism in, 26–27
    defined, 65
    development of, 2–5, 11–15, 24–27
    family-friendly policies, 1–2